PELICAN BOOKS
A1100

McLUHAN: PRO AND CON

Raymond Rosenthal, the editor, was born in 1914 in Brooklyn. He has taught at Long Island University and the City College of New York. Well known for his translations of Italian Literature, Mr. Rosenthal has contributed a regular column of literary criticism to the New Leader.

McLuhan: Pro and Con

Edited and with an
Introduction by
Raymond Rosenthal

Penguin Books

Penguin Books Inc., 7110 Ambassador Road, Baltimore, Maryland 21207
Published first by Funk & Wagnalls, *A Division of* Reader's Digest Books,
Inc., 1968
First published in Pelican Books 1969
Reprinted 1969, 1972
Copyright © 1968 by Raymond Rosenthal
Printed in the United States of America

Arthur A. Cohen, "Doomsday in Dogpatch: The McLuhan Thesis Examined." Reprinted by permission from the *Journal of the American Institute of Graphic Arts.*

John Culkin, S.J., "A Schoolman's Guide to Marshall McLuhan." Reprinted by permission from *Saturday Review*, March 18, 1967.

Theodore Roszak, "The Summa Popologica of Marshall McLuhan." Reprinted by permission from *New Politics*, Vol. V, No. 4.

James W. Carey, "Harold Adams Innis and Marshall McLuhan." Reprinted by permission from *Antioch Review*, Vol. XXVII, No. 1, in which the article was originally published.

Hannah Arendt, from *The Human Condition.* Reprinted by permission of The University of Chicago Press.

W. H. Auden, "After Reading a Child's Guide to Modern Physics." Reprinted from *About the House* by W. H. Auden by permission of Random House, Inc.

The articles by Irving J. Weiss, Nathan Halper, Milton Klonsky, and Elémire Zolla were written especially for this book.

contents

McLuhan: Pro and Con

raymond rosenthal
introduction

The reader of this book will find a detailed, lively, often stimulating and revelatory discussion of Marshall McLuhan's ideas
in the pages that follow this preface. Until now, that is, until
the time when the all-engulfing, instantaneous electronic communications system that McLuhan has envisaged completely
takes over our world, the ideas in books have bred other books.
If you write a book, the "last word" is given to others—parti-
sans or opponents, critics or eulogists. This is the law of life in
the particular network of society that the subject of this anthology of opinion, a professor of literature turned communications analyst and prophet, inhabits. On the whole it is a
beneficent law and can, if rightly adhered to, lead to enlightenment and clarification of the ideas discussed.

Now, compared to the major networks, this intellectual network is a rather hemmed-in, restricted affair. Even if one includes in it all of the schools and universities, all of the magazines, publishing houses, and newspapers, and all of the scholars and critics who still find books interesting enough to get
excited about them and discuss them, the actual size and power

of this network in the frame of the larger society, with its great networks of industry, business, politics, and communications, are pretty paltry and unimposing. Yet the truth is that this network is the only one that discusses ideas for their own sake—for its sake, as a matter of fact, since a world that regarded ideas from a purely functional, practical standpoint would be a world in which that already small, beleaguered network no longer existed in any viable and significant form.

Marshall McLuhan has predicted the end of this book-oriented world and therefore the end of the special network to which he happens to belong. This, I believe, accounts for much of the passionate controversy he has caused—nobody likes to hear that he's on the way to the historical junkheap, not even a professor, a scholar, or an artist, from whom one would expect a greater than average degree of objectivity. What's more, the end of this network would bring to a close a whole human adventure, the adventure that started with Homer, Socrates, and Plato, created rational discourse, science, poetry, and religion, and many other things, including that very electronic world which, if McLuhan is right, will be doing them all in.

McLuhan, of course, is not the first thinker and analyst to foresee an apocalyptic demise for our civilization. He is the first, however, to base his prediction on the blind functioning of the mass media. And he is also the first to claim (a claim that is not entirely true) that he has invented what might be called a grammar of the emotional, sensuous, and sensational "language" used by the mass media. The momentousness of his prediction has all the weight, the dead weight, of everyday life to give it substance. When it comes to the mass media, all of us are in a sense "experts," and so we can see how fast and furiously things are tending in the McLuhanite direction. The "barbarism of sensation," which the cultural historian Vico identified as one of the unmistakable signs of social and cultural collapse and which McLuhan praises as a return to forthright primitivity and tribal consciousness, has, after stultifying the masses, also won many adherents in the intellectual sphere. This, too, has intensified the vehemence of the debate.

Marshall McLuhan has also made it plain that the merging,

swirling, fusing world of electronic communications will have no place for the old-fashioned man with the fixed point of view. McLuhan's attitude on this score is somewhat hazy: sometimes he seems to be saying that one can maintain a point of view only by getting into the act of electronic disintegration (which would seem to be a contradictory way of behaving, to say the least), and at other times he seems to be saying that the deliquescent and crumbling effect of the mass media will leave the individual no firm ground to stand on (which, after all, is what one means when talking of a "point of view" and a distinct personality). But the deliquescent apocalypse is not here as yet, and the editor of this book considers himself blessedly old-fashioned, utterly out of step with the latest scientific theories, and cantankerously skeptical of all merging, ecstatic systems that would destroy the humanness we know and supplant it with a future inhumanness based on only dimly apprehended categories. He has therefore edited this book with the firm intention of presenting all sides of the McLuhan question, pro and con, together with all nuances in between, and with the equally firm belief that only this method can help readers to make up their minds—if they still have minds to make up. He believes that they have, that the stunning environment of babble and glare and blare produced by the predominant means of communication has not yet led to complete somnambulism or complete mental inertia.

Indeed, McLuhan's very success, the cult that has sprung up around him, points to just the opposite conclusion. People are disoriented, troubled, dismayed by this environment, and not only the people who read books. I have seen customers of an entirely unbookish aspect, typical mass-media folk, enter bookstores as though treading on foreign territory and ask the clerk, in the hesitant tones one uses with strange, semimagical beings, for the "latest book by McLuhan." They too want to know what's happening to them and they think, or at least they've heard, that McLuhan can tell them.

So the intellectual network I mentioned before has repercussions that range far beyond its narrow limits. It is listened to. The makers of opinion and fashion in the big-circulation magazines and on the television and radio networks keep their ears cocked for unusual noises from that quarter. These programmers are busy feeding the great cultural consumption machine —that omniverous maw that gulps down and somehow eventually evacuates all the frantic fashions in art, clothes, furnishings, and ideas. McLuhan has had the fortune or misfortune, depending on your point of view, to have been fed through this hopper; in this collection, however, you will encounter only the serious, analytical and personal reasoning of the hemmed-in intellectual network; an iron selectivity has excluded anything that smacked of flack-talk.

The inner intentions and interests of the large public conjured up by McLuhan's books can only be guessed at. Yet it may be worthwhile to examine the factors that have certainly worked in his favor and have surrounded him with an attractive aura. At stake here are a number of modern myths, gross or subtle myths that existed in the culture-buying public's mind long before McLuhan appeared on the scene.

The first and most important myth is, of course, the myth of science. McLuhan's books are not scientific in any respect; they are wrapped, however, in the dark, mysterious folds of the scientific ideology, which expresses itself chiefly in the jargon that graces, with a kind of incantatory effect, the pages of his last books, notably *Understanding Media* and *The Medium Is the Massage*. True science rests on the experiment, and McLuhan, unlike such European investigators of the mass media as Gilbert Cohen-Séat and Henri Walloon, cannot point to a series of controlled experiments on which he has based his conclusions. His relations to science are in the main ideological, that is to say, mythical. Let me explain. The enormous advances of science, particularly in physics, have led to a distressing split between common-sense knowledge with its direct, sensuous apprehension of the world and scientific knowledge, which is formulated on the basis of algebraic hypotheses that no scientist has yet been able to present in a model that can be perceived by the human senses. Hannah Arendt has put it very well in her remarkable book *The Human Condition:*

. . . the mathematization of physics, by which the absolute renunciation of the senses for the purposes of knowing was carried through, had in its last stages the unexpected and yet plausible consequence that every question man puts to nature is answered in terms of mathematical patterns to which no model is ever adequate, since one would have to be shaped after our sense experiences. At this point, the connection between thought and sense experience, inherent in the human condition, seems to take its revenge: while technology demonstrates the "truth" of modern science's most abstract concepts, it demonstrates no more than that man can always apply the results of his mind, that no matter what system he uses for the explanation of natural phenomena he will always be able to adopt it as a guiding principle for making and acting. . . . In other words, the world of experiment seem always capable of becoming a man-made reality. and this, while it may increase man's power of making and acting, even of creating a world, far beyond what any previous age dared to imagine in dreams and phantasy, unfortunately puts man back once more—and now even more forcefully—into the prison of his mind, into the limitations of the patterns he has created.

Hannah Arendt has here outlined the philosophical preconditions for the myth of science as it exists in most laymen's minds. The scientist has become the magician, the black or white magician, of our technological world, and people frightened and harassed by his incomprehensible successes, stifle their anxieties by filling him with the "magic" of his deeds. But there is a hard-headed, demythologizing response to science, and it has been wittily expressed by W. H. Auden in his poem "After Reading a Child's Guide to Modern Physics":

> If all a top physicist knows
> About the Truth be true,
> Then, for all the so-and-so's
> Futility and grime,
> Our Common world contains,
> We have a better time
> Than the Greater Nebulae do,
> Or the atoms in our brain. . . .
>
> Though the face at which I stare
> While shaving it be cruel

> For, year after year, it repels
> An aging suitor, it has,
> Thank God, sufficient mass
> To be altogether there,
> Not an indeterminate gruel
> Which is partly somewhere else.

The point Auden is making in the entire poem, which I haven't the space to quote, is that the scientist is a poor, limited human being like all the rest of us and that he should behave accordingly, with more modesty, more concern with human values, more awareness of the human scope and predicament. Auden is trying to deflate the myth of science, which he rightly regards as pernicious and obfuscating. McLuhan, on the contrary, rides along on the wave of the scientific myth, exploiting its wonder-working aura without asking himself any of the questions that should occur to someone interested in either culture or science. For although many of these questions are abstruse and difficult, science, as it works, has glaringly evident and uncomfortable practical consequences. As Paul Valéry said, ". . . *everything we know,* which is to say, *everything we can do,* has finally been turned against *what we are.*" McLuhan would agree with that statement, he would even admit that many of the changes are not entirely for the better, yet he does not take into sufficient account the fact that these changes, brought about by science, run against the biological grain of something unchangeable and precious in man. What many historians, anthropologists, and philosophers consider the fatal stumbling block of our technical civilization— namely, that it has no place for man in its future, or only a place that makes the human a tool of science's inhumanity— has been blithely incorporated into the very tone and color of McLuhan's vision. It is his special cachet, his announcement that "he's with it." He seems utterly unconcerned to discover, as Rousseau said, "what in the present nature of Man is original, and what is artificial." Or even to entertain the problem with the seriousness it so obviously deserves.

The second great myth that has operated in McLuhan's favor is the myth of modern art. His pages are sprinkled with references to such famous modern artists as Picasso, Proust, Joyce, Mallarmé, and to such modern artistic movements as Cubism, Surrealism, and Dadaism. But what one soon notices about all these references is that they play a purely prestigious, ideological part in McLuhan's system. A mere literary critic, like R. P. Blackmur, T. S. Eliot, or William Empson, also has a didactic purpose in interpreting a work of art, though it is not a purpose that distorts the work of art in order to fit it into a predetermined schema. McLuhan, however, is a one-idea man, and he drives through modern art like a tendentious bulldozer. After he gets through with, say, Mallarmé or Proust, there is little that casts light on their works and a great deal that supports, often on only the slimmest pretexts, McLuhan's special idea. McLuhan is using, even abusing modern art to gain credit with an audience that feels about it much the way they feel about science: they respect it, are in awe of it, but at a safe distance. If they were to read Joyce or Proust or Mallarmé, they will discover a gulf between what these artists said and felt about technology and what McLuhan interprets them as saying and feeling.

It is not at all true, for example, that Mallarmé and Proust changed their ideas about art and the reality that surrounded them because of the advent of the newspaper, the photograph, and the cinema. If anything, they became even more convinced that the area of authentic personal experience, which is what they were concerned with, had been vastly constricted by these mechanical developments. If they got suggestions from the new devices for their prose or poetry, it was entirely without the emotional identification with, or approval of, such devices that McLuhan is trying to foist on them. A perfect instance of McLuhan's bulldozing approach is his interpretation of Mallarmé's highly suggestive prose causerie on the relation between books and newspapers. If one reads Mallarmé, one gets the distinct impression of an ironic distaste for newspapers; if one reads McLuhan on Mallarmé, the irony has been expunged for the purposes of a thesis, the expectable thesis.

But there is another aspect of the modern art myth with which McLuhan has enveloped himself that is harder to un-

9

derstand and to disentangle. Modern art is prestigious, and not always for the best reasons. It is often a cult word, an idol, and the horde of interpreters that swarm over it seem to approach it in a wholly superstitious fashion, so unlike the iconoclastic attitudes of the great modern artists themselves. McLuhan, from his practice, is a member in good standing of this idolatrous horde. He would like one to believe that modern art is not a series of works done by discrete and separate individuals but a close-ranked, unified movement that marched side by side with another progressive movement—technology. This is a pure distortion. Modern art is not a term of praise or blame, or an ideological catchword, but rather a description of the art produced during a period that stretches roughly from 1867 to the years just before the Second World War; and there are aspects of modern art that must be considered ambiguous and retrograde, above all because they exhibit a blind, irrational subservience to the going concern of technology.

In general, the modern artist did not support technology; he reacted to it, or appropriated it for his own ends. With the Dadaists and Futurists, however, the nihilist currents in modern art rose to the surface. Today it is clear that both these groups succumbed to the environment of technical power and tried desperately to convert political and social experiences into esthetic ones. This was in essence the Fascist contribution to modern art—when, as Walter Benjamin, the German critic, said, "Mankind, which in Homeric times had been a spectacle for the gods, became a spectacle for itself." The horror of mechanized warfare, with its starlike explosions and its titanic clashes of armored tanks and enormous projectiles, was seen solely as an esthetic spectacle by the Fascist artists and became the occasion for the artistic enjoyment of the new forms of sensory perception created by technique. These artists' self-estrangement had gone so deep that they could experience their own annihilation as a first-class "show." Both Dadaism and Futurism were arts founded on the esthetic of calculated shocks—art used as a projectile against the audience—and soon after, as Benjamin pointed out, they found their popular apotheosis in that incessant series of pictorial shocks known as the cinema.

Which brings us to a third important ingredient in McLuhan's mythical appeal: his exaltation of sensation for its own sake. In contemporary life sensation has become a myth precisely because so much of contemporary life blunts and impoverishes sensation, or transforms it into an abstract, bloodless "program." Wyndham Lewis put his finger on the nub of the question when he said:

Sensation is drilled to masquerade as intelligence. Animal lives of plain, unvarnished sensation are now compelled to adopt a hundred pretentious disguises. Each little sensation has to be decked out as though it were a "big idea." Again, simple sensation has become ashamed of itself. It is persuaded to complicate itself, invert itself with a movement of mechanical paradox. So, in reality, sensation pure and simple is disappearing, and a sort of spurious idea is everywhere taking its place. But side by side with this disintegration of sensation, a very learned, intricate, and ingenious philosophy of sensation is built up. The result is that the more sensation borrows from the intellect, the more it abuses itself and points to sensation (which it no longer is in the purest sense) as the aim and end of life. Similarly, the more self-conscious it becomes, the more it repudiates consciousness and also (for another reason) "self." The more "conscious" it grows, in a limited and ineffective way, the more it talks about the "unconscious." It is as though it were breaking into a dithyramb about what it just no longer was.

That was written more than thirty years ago, yet it perfectly describes the sensation myth that underlies everything McLuhan says about the movies and television as they affect our senses, our consciousness. Or is it our consciousness? McLuhan never makes it clear exactly how the sensations that he claims exposure to a television show produce in us are registered in our minds. The way he describes the process, the people watching television seem inert bundles of sensational, perhaps even of emotional receptivity, but with no direct consciousness, for consciousness would spoil the picture of sheer sensation by introducing extraneous elements, such as thought, interpretation, rational response. Yet he knows, being a Thomist, that sensations that are not elaborated by the consciousness cannot be considered imaginative experiences; sensations of this kind are just raw materials, grounded stimuli that have never been redeemed by the psyche and that flow away into oblivion, like so many of our experiences on the sensory level. But if television is supposed to have the revolutionary effect on us that McLuhan claims, he will have to build a bridge between sensation and consciousness. He hasn't until now because he was too anxious to prove that the sensations evoked by the new electronic environment were effecting a revolution in consciousness, *without the intervention of consciousness*. But his description of the esthetic experience, even on its lowest, television level, is incomplete and lopsided, unsupported by any system of esthetic or emotional perception that he can advance in its behalf. The only creatures who can have sensations without an attendant charge of emotion and consciousness, are the lobotomized or robots: and perhaps that is what we will become under the massive pressure of the televisional environment. But it hasn't happened yet.

The fourth and final myth that powerfully pervades and enhances McLuhan's books is the myth of mystical participation. Confronted by the complexity and disorder of contemporary existence, by its increasing materialism and regimentation, and also by their own feeling of impotence, many people want to find a quick, easy way out of the blaring, befuddling labyrinth and back to the uncomplicated life of faith and emotion. They have tried drugs, they have tried eroticism, and more recently they have tried what could be called instant mysticism, since it is a mysticism shorn of all religious and ritual meaning. McLuhan's work is imbued with the hues of instant mysticism, if not its actual content, for he intimates strongly that electric circuitry will reattach us willy-nilly, without any effort on our part, to the natural cosmos from which technology has separated us. It is an alluring prospect; yet it is neither good mysticism nor good history nor even a good way to get back to the nature we have lost. Simone Weil, a true mystic and therefore a rigorous rationalist who knew the boundaries of rationalism, that is, knew what thought could express and what thought couldn't fully express, regarded the collectivity as the greatest and most insidious of man's oppressions, the most constant enemy of his spiritual aspirations. She insisted that a good society was one in which the collectivity gave man not only a way of defending himself from it but of escaping from its pressure. Collectivities cannot think; only the individual can do that. And, she explained, "since collective thought cannot exist as thought, it passes into things (signs, machines). It is the thing that thinks, and the man who is reduced to the state of a thing." Now this is an excellent description of the collective, oppressive mass media—and also an excellent lesson to all would-be mystics: you can become a mystic only by thinking in solitude, all by yourself, not as a swooning part of some resonating whole.

All these matters have been brushed aside by McLuhan in his haste to announce the new millennium, or is it the new cataclysm—again it is hard to decide on the basis of all the contradictory things he has said. But one thing is certain: the means of communication are indeed changing our world, and at a furious rate, though they are making this change with old, often ancient, perhaps ultimately intractable human materials. Man still remains a thinking, physical creature tied to nature, essentially the same creature he has been for about five hundred and fifty thousand years of a long history. On the other hand, radical humanism does not see him as finished or complete, but as a project. The civilization man inhabits is opposed to this project in both its most ordinary and its most idealistic aims. So it is the civilization that must be changed. In some small way, I hope, this book may help toward that goal and offer its illumination to the central problem of our civilization, as Simone Weil has so brilliantly and accurately defined it:

Capitalism has brought about the emancipation of collective humanity with respect to nature. But this collective humanity has itself taken on with respect to the individual the oppressive function formerly exercised by nature.

This is true even with material things: fire, water, etc. The community has taken possession of all these natural forces. Question: Can the emancipation, won by society, be transferred to the individual?

To make an inventory or criticism of our civilization, what does this mean? To try to expose in precise terms the trap which has made man the slave of his own invention. How has unconsciousness infiltrated itself into mechanical thought and action? To return to a primitive state is a lazy solution. We have to rediscover the original pact between the spirit and the world in this very civilization of which we form a part.

current biography*
mcluhan, (herbert) marshall

July 21, 1911– Communications specialist; university professor; writer

ADDRESS: b. c/o *Centre for Culture and Technology, University of Toronto, Toronto 5, Ontario, Canada;* h. *29 Wells Hill Ave., Toronto 4, Ontario, Canada*

Hurdling the disciplinary borders of literature, art, education, philosophy, physiology, and sociology, Marshall McLuhan proposes that many of the radical social changes of the technological twentieth century can be attributed to the effects of electronic communications. "The medium is the message," he asserts; it is the nature itself of television, computers, and other media, far more than their content, that is reshaping civilization. An intellectual explorer, McLuhan intends to probe, expose, and provoke, rather than to explain or prove, and even the more skeptical of his critics recognize the heuristic importance of his controversial *Understanding Media* (1964) and other books. Since the mid 1940s he has been teaching at the University of Toronto and since 1963 has been di-

* *June 1967, pp. 20–22.*

recting its Centre for Culture and Technology. On a leave of absence from Toronto, in the fall of 1967 he will assume the $100,000-a-year post of Albert Schweitzer Chair in the Humanities at Fordham University in New York City.

A native of the Canadian West, which he regards as an uncluttered and unconfused world compared to the East, Herbert Marshall McLuhan was born in Edmonton, Alberta, on July 21, 1911, to Herbert Ernest and Elsie Naomi (Hall) McLuhan. His Scotch-Irish parents were of Methodist and Baptist faiths, but they sometimes attended services of other churches, and his brother became an Episcopal minister. An outgoing man who enjoyed talking with people, his father made his living as a salesman of real estate and insurance. His mother was an actress and monologist who, in his opinion, surpassed Ruth Draper.

The family moved eastward, to Winnipeg, in McLuhan's boyhood. At the age of ten, he recalls, he made crystal sets for himself and his friends and was thrilled by picking up broadcasts from a radio station in the United States Midwest. When he enrolled at the University of Manitoba, his intention was to become an engineer. But, as he put it, during a long summer vacation, "I read my way out of engineering and into English literature." He was awarded his B.A. degree at Manitoba in 1933 and his M.A. degree in 1934.

During one vacation McLuhan took a trip to Europe on a cattle boat with a fellow student, W. T. Easterbrook, now Professor of Political Economy at the University of Toronto. Shortly afterward McLuhan went abroad again, to study at Trinity Hall in Cambridge University, where he displayed considerable skill as an oarsman. He also attended the lectures of such brilliant scholars of English literature as I. A. Richards and F. R. Leavis. Although he left the campus after taking his B.A. degree in 1936, he continued his academic study of medieval education and Renaissance literature, obtaining his M.A. degree from Cambridge in 1940 and his Ph.D. degree in 1942. Fascinated by Elizabethan rhetoric, he submitted as his doctoral dissertation "The Place of Thomas Nashe in the Learning of his Time."

Meanwhile, in 1936, McLuhan had begun his career as a teacher in the United States, at the University of Wisconsin. *Newsweek* (March 6, 1967) quotes his comment on his first practical encounter with popular culture: "I was confronted with young Americans I was incapable of understanding. I felt an urgent need to study their popular culture in order to get through." It was, apparently, about a year or so after his move to the United States that he entered the Roman Catholic Church. The seeds of his conversion are said to have been nourished by a collection of G. K. Chesterton's essays, *What's Wrong with the World.* McLuhan's early critical literary articles for professional journals show a range of appreciation that covers such diverse writers as Coleridge and John Dos Passos, and he is the author of the introduction to a textbook of the selected poetry of Tennyson (Rinehart, 1956). His explorations in literature and in the study of communication also include the work of Gerard Manley Hopkins, T. S. Eliot, James Joyce, and many other writers who quite likely reflected or strengthened his interest in Catholicism.

McLuhan's religious persuasion may also account for his preference for teaching in Catholic institutions. He joined the faculty of St. Louis University in 1937 and then returned to Canada in 1944 to teach at Assumption University in Windsor, Ontario, a Basilian school, where he served for two years. Not long after going back to Canada he became associated with St. Michael's College, the Roman Catholic unit of the University of Toronto, at which he was named a full professor in 1952. Just a year before his promotion he had published *The Mechanical Bride; Folklore of Industrial Man* (Vanguard). Attacking the "pressures set up around us today by the mechanical agencies of the press, radio, movies, and advertising," he hit among other targets the Luce Magazines, *Reader's Digest,* momism, the Great Books Program, and the professional mortician. Somewhat sparsely reviewed, his first book attracted widespread attention only after his later work had made him popular in intellectual circles.

From 1953 to 1955 McLuhan, as chairman, directed a seminar on culture and communications sponsored by the Ford

17

Foundation. With part of the $40,000 grant and in collaboration with the anthropologist Edmund Carpenter, he founded a periodical called *Explorations* to give seminar members a creative outlet. Together with Carpenter he also edited an anthology of selected material from the nine issues of the magazine, *Explorations in Communications* (Beacon, 1960). By the late 1950s his reputation as a specialist in communications had extended below the Canadian border, bringing him an appointment for 1959–60 as director of a media project for the United States Office of Education and the National Association of Educational Broadcasters.

At the University of Toronto, McLuhan had come to know the political economist Harold A. Innis, the author of *The Bias of Communication* (1951) and other books, who was one of several scholars that influenced him in formulating his theories about the effect of media on human development. Drawing liberally on his own impressive erudition, in 1962 McLuhan published *The Gutenberg Galaxy: The Making of Typographic Man* (University of Toronto Press), which won the 1963 Governor-General's Award for critical prose, Canada's top literary award. In his study of the impact of the invention of movable type in the fifteenth century on the culture of Western Europe, he maintained that the linear forms of print account for linear development in music, for example, and for serial thinking in mathematics and the sciences. When print superseded oral communication, the eye, rather than the ear, became the principal sensory organ, and, according to McLuhan, this revolution produced self-centeredness in man and a fragmentation in society that in turn led to chauvinism.

With the dawn of the electronic age, and the development of electronic "circuitry," in the twentieth century, however, McLuhan argues, man has been restored to certain of his tribal ways and the world has become a "global village." Electronic media, particularly television, he explains, have brought a redistribution and a heightening of sensory awareness, along with an immediacy in communication that reduces the separation between thought and action and diminishes isolation in human behavior. McLuhan's purpose in writing *Understand-*

ing Media: The Extensions of Man (McGraw-Hill, 1964) was to call attention to how and why radio, telephone, TV, motion pictures, computers, and all other electronic forms of communication are restructuring civilization.

Any medium, McLuhan asserts, in a borrowing from Buckminster Fuller, is an extension of man, and because of electricity man's central nervous system has become extended outside his body. The content itself of television, for example, is therefore less important than its effect, in making man a screen, or in intensifying his tactile and kinetic powers. TV, which McLuhan finds to be low in definition and to require audience "involvement," is what he calls a "cool" medium, whereas the informative book is a "hot" medium. The participation conditioning of a "cool" medium has implications on many fronts. In education, for instance, children of the TV generation are inclined more toward discovery than toward instruction; they want roles rather than goals.

It would seem that having expressed his disgust with the vulgarity and shabbiness of values of contemporary society in *The Mechanical Bride*, McLuhan refuses to judge whether the influences of electronic media on patterns of living are good or bad. Rather, he seems to say that in the interests of man's own destiny, according to whatever sort of future he prefers, man should inform himself of what is happening to him and should be equipped with awareness to fight back if he so desires. As he told Richard Kostelanetz in an interview for the *New York Times Magazine* (January 29, 1967), "My entire concern is to overcome the determinism that results from the determination of people to ignore what is going on. Far from regarding technological change as inevitable, I insist that if we understand its components we can turn if off any time we choose. Short of turning it off, there are lots of moderate controls conceivable."

Several of McLuhan's critics think that he takes too submissive an attitude toward the fate of the book, which he describes as "obsolescent," if not "obsolete." His own acclaim testifies, ironically, to the continued power of the printed page, although some reviewers of his books complain that his writing is repetitious and disorganized, lacking the sequential thinking of linear man. In his segmented treatment of his subject he imitates the structure of electronic media.

One of his more severe critics, Dwight Macdonald, described *Understanding Media* in *Book Week* (June 7, 1964) as "impure nonsense, nonsense adulterated by sense." A few reviewers went to the other extreme in adulation. Perhaps the most general and considered reservation regarding his work arose from his insistence upon pushing his insights and his arguments too far, to include every phenomenon of contemporary society—from the hybrid forms of pop art to the outcome of the 1960 Presidential election in the United States. Overstatement, McLuhan has replied, is a means of stimulating discussion.

MacLuhan's obscurity, which someone once said he uses "like a blackjack," has generated a spate of articles in mass-circulation magazines on understanding McLuhan. Acknowledging that his own "stuff" is so difficult that he has trouble understanding himself, he attempted a clearer explanation of his theories in *The Medium Is the Massage: An Inventory of Effects* (Bantam, 1967), The title, adapted from his best-known proposal "the medium is the message," is an example of his fondness for aphorisms and puns and characterizes his sense of humor. The co-author of this often entertaining and witty book, Quentin Fiore, presented more than a hundred illustrations to show how media are transforming every aspect of man's life.

In an hour-long program about McLuhanism on NBC-TV in March 1967 McLuhan explained that the title of his book "is intended to draw attention to the fact that a medium is not something neutral—it does something to people. It takes hold of them. It rubs them off, it massages them, it bumps them around." People are unaware of the new media, he pointed out in the telecast, as he had in his books, because its content is the old media. Since it is emotionally more secure to live in the old media, people look at the present through a rear-view mirror.

Much in demand as a speaker at educational and other professional conventions, during 1966 McLuhan addressed the

P.E.N. Congress, the National Bureau of Standards symposium on technology and world trade, the Public Relations Society of America, the Modern Language Association, and perhaps a score of other gatherings. He also worked on several books scheduled for publication in 1967, including "Culture Is Our Business," and his articles for periodicals ranged from "What TV Is Really Doing to Your Children" for *Family Circle* (March 1967) to "The Memory Theatre," a learned book review for *Encounter* (March 1967). [In 1967 CBS produced a recording of *The Medium Is the Massage*. Two new McLuhan books were scheduled to appear in 1968: *Through the Vanishing Point: Space in Poetry and Painting* (Harper & Row) and *War and Peace in the Global Village* (Bantam).—Ed.]

Meanwhile, at the University of Toronto, McLuhan continued to teach courses in modern drama and poetry, modern literary criticism, and media and society. Since 1963, he has also been the director of the university's Centre for Culture and Technology, which is engaged in research on questions of sensory perception and other matters relating to communications. In December 1966 McLuhan was appointed to the Albert Schweitzer Chair in Humanities at Fordham University in New York City. Supported by the New York State Board of Regents, the award pays $100,000 a year for the salaries of McLuhan and his anxiliary staff and for research expenses. He planned to take a leave of absence from his positions at the University of Toronto to begin work at Fordham University in the fall of 1967.

During the late 1930s, while visiting California to do research at the Huntington Library, Marshall McLuhan met Texas-born Corinne Keller Lewis, who was studying drama at the Pasadena Playhouse. They were married on August 4, 1939, and are the parents of six children: Eric, Mary (Mrs. Thomas James Colton), Theresa, Stephanie, Elizabeth, and Michael. The family home is an unpretentious house in Toronto, and according to Kostelanetz's *New York Times* article, "The professor is a conscientious family man. . . . Every Sunday he leads his brood to Mass."

McLuhan is tall and slim and has graying hair. His "hot"

21

and "cool" classification, which he says applies to persons as well as media, seems to bog down when his somewhat nondescript appearance is contrasted with his dynamic, stunning, and offhand outpouring of brand-new ideas on the lecture platform or in conversation. He is a fellow of the Royal Society of Canada and holds an honorary D. Litt. degree from the University of Windsor. In an interview with James R. Dickenson for the *National Observer* (May 30, 1966) he spoke about the pride he takes in understanding media and quoted Coleridge's Ancient Mariner, "We were the first that ever burst/Into that silent sea."

REFERENCES

Life 60:91+ F 25 '66 pors
Nat. Observer p20 My 30 '66 por
N.Y. *Herald Tribune* mag p23+ N 21 '65 por
N.Y. *Post* p26 Ja 7 '67 por
N.Y. Times Mag p18+ Ja 29 '67 por
New Yorker 41:43+ F 27 '65
Newsweek 67:56+ F 28 '66 pors; 69:53+ Mr 6 '67 pors
Toronto Globe and Mail Globe Mag p8+ Ja 4 '64 pors
Canadian Who's Who (1964–66)
Who's Who in American Education, 1963–64

hugh kenner*
understanding mcluhan

Marshall McLuhan's name flies about these days the way
"Technocracy" did in the Thirties: a picture story in *Life;*
status as resident sage in the files from which they confect the
Time Essay; random allusions in the columns of every journal
one picks up, from *National Review* to the *National Catholic
Reporter,* not to mention *Encounter, Popular Photography,*
and the *Times Lit. Sup.* A season ago one of the better-heeled
monthlies was phoning about offering a grand or so to the lean
hungry free-lancer who'd tool a few thousand words to go
under the title, "Against McLuhan." And I've forgotten which
magazine writer, reaching for a handy simile, said that to
broach a simple topic with so-and-so was "like talking to Marshall McLuhan about the weather": he's achieved eponymous
status, like Dr. Fell and Dr. Pangloss and Dr. Einstein. I've

* HUGH KENNER *is the well-known literary critic whose books include
studies of Ezra Pound, T. S. Eliot, Wyndham Lewis, Samuel Beckett, and
James Joyce. His recent work* The Stoic Comedians, *a series of essays on
Flaubert, Joyce, and Beckett, has been followed by* The Counterfeiters, *a
study of new developments in modern art.*

23

even come across his name, misspelled, in a popular novel.

In all of which he resembles the fly that has gotten into the movie projector and overlays, in silhouette, random scenes. For it's understood (1) that no one has, *really,* dug him; (2) that he's nonetheless "in"; (3) that "the medium is the message," and if you don't understand that, you are to keep quiet until you'll say that you do.

As one of his oldest—ah—fans (we met in 1946, when I was about to take over the teaching job he'd taken over from Wyndham Lewis) I'm willing to claim (1) that I dig him; (2) that he's perhaps the best commentator on his own in-ness; (3) that the medium ain't the message, and if you don't understand that, keep quiet till you've been led through Basic McLuhan as follows:

The initial principle is that there are three McLuhans. The first is a genius. The second is a gear-stripper, who tends to believe that what the first tells him is an adequate ersatz reality. The third is what you imagine the Delphic Oracle must have been like, when you survey the ruins of Greece: a dealer in *appoggiaturas* and *tremolos* that would give the first fits were he not insulated by the machinations of the second.

With these three there cohabits a goblin who unnerves criticism by the paradigmatic force of his routine exercises (performed on every other page) to show that X, the acknowledged expert on Y, has in the larger analysis Missed the Point. It will soon be quite clear that I have Missed the Point, the Whole Point. But I hope to fix a point or two of my own.

To begin with the Genius, whom *The New Yorker* some years back sought to locate by calling him the first Pop Philosopher. He is. Like Andy Warhol, whose works we don't need to see to appreciate their point, McLuhan is the writer his public doesn't need to read. (The same was true of Newton.) He's carved out a topic (he says, The Topic) virtually by naming it—Media. (One secret of genius is timing; Media were ready to be discovered, just as gravitation was.) Once we'd heard that he'd pointed it out, we could understand at once, without reading him, that TV wasn't just a different way of seeing movies, but a different experience, shaping the movie it shows:

gregarious, tight, low-definition, casual: as against tranced, alone-in-a-crowd immersion.

Nor are film and book optional ways of giving us *David Copperfield,* film's discrepancies attributable merely to Hollywood tastelessness. Attempts to translate from print to a mass medium tend to ignore the fact that print is itself a medium, and a mass medium (the printed book was the first mass-produced artifact). Print, encountered in silence and solitude, isn't speech; nor, perfectly uniform in its thousands of identical copies, is it writing. It's a freezer and standardizer of language. (McLuhan's former pupil, Walter J. Ong, S.J., has given these insights two decades of patient attention.)

Thus (and much more) McLuhan No. 1, the genius who tells us things we were just ripe to hear, as we know from the fact that we understand them as soon as told. To him enters McLuhan No. 2, whose material is not the substantial intricate world but the insights of McL. No. 1. McL. 2 extrapolates from "this book is the content of this film" to things like "The content of any medium is always another medium. The content of writing is speech, just as the written word is the content of print, and print is the content of the telegraph." (All references are to the McGraw-Hill editions of *Understanding Media.* That one's on page 9.)

Forget about content then, which is an infinite regress, and look at the medium before you. What is the message of movies? The fact that there are movies, with all that *that* entails. And of books? The fact that there are books. And *this* book, called *The Dialogues of Plato,* whose content is writing whose content is speech whose content is thought whose content is the central nervous system, places before our hypnotized eyes yet one more sequence of uniform pages stamped with uniform lines made out of permuted uniform symbols; and all copies of this book are alike, so that an entire freshman class can turn to page 29, line 3, third word; and this fact, which is the message of the medium, is more important than any thought of Plato's.

And before we have a chance to protest that surely Plato

counts for something, McLuhan 2 plunges on to enumerate more media than we had thought possible. Railway is a medium, creating new environments, new kinds of cities, in ways "quite independent of the freight or content of the railway medium." (Ignore the content, remember?) "The airplane, on the other hand, by accelerating the rate of transportation, tends to dissolve the railway form of cities, politics and association, quite independently of what the airplane is used for."

If you think it matters whether airplanes carry people or goldfish keep it to yourself and don't bug No. 2, he's away, away. The wheel is obsolescent (this is the electric age). The electric light is a medium, its content whatever is done in its glow—baseball or brain surgery (forget the content). Its message is the human interactions it makes possible. And money is a medium and games are media and clocks are media and—. . . And their message is just the difference they make by existing.

And everything, alas, is something else; and if content is negligible, so are facts. Though there's much show of factuality: "One of the most advanced and complicated uses of the wheel occurs in the movie camera. . . . It is significant that this most subtle and complex grouping of wheels should have been invented in order to win a bet that all four feet of a running horse were sometimes off the ground simultaneously. The bet was made between the pioneer photographer Edward Muybridge and the horseowner Leland Stanford, in 1889. At first, a series of cameras were set up side by side, each to snap an arrested movement of the horse's hooves in action. The movie camera and the projector were evolved from the idea of reconstructing mechanically the movement of feet. The wheel, that began as extended feet, took a great evolutionary step into the movie theater."

Now. Muybridge was an agreeable eccentric who spelled his first name Eadweard. He made no bet with Stanford (do photographers make bets with multimillionaires?). He settled the horses' hooves question working on his own, in 1872. What Stanford did was offer facilities for further research, which was finished by 1879. The wheels, with which Muybridge had nothing to do, were means of holding and moving the strip of film, which Muybridge didn't invent, and they never moved Muybridge's pictures of horses' feet. We have here quasi-facts, grouped around the word "feet," an earlier postulation that wheels were extensions of feet having made it seem a bright idea for feet to have inspired further wheels. That's No. 2's problem, he likes a bright idea, and insight breeds on insight in a void through which quasi-facts drift like dust motes.

The point is not to be picky about the facts; no one is going to *Understanding Media* for information anyhow. The point is that McLuhan 2 cares very little for facts' gristly specificity; their function is not to feed the mind but, like dust, to make insight visible. *Understanding Media* is mostly filled with bright ideas, which is why readers wonder if they're digging it or not; it's undiggable.

And the void where the insights cross is agitated by the pneuma of McLuhan 3, not the genius nor the gear-stripper but the Oracle. The Oracle keeps conscripting artists into his chorus, telling us for instance that Shakespeare "understood the Forest of Arden as an advance model of the age of automation, when all things are translatable into anything else that is desired." Any especially plangent vaticination turns out to be what Shakespeare or Joyce or somebody "really" meant, artist being a handy label for the frogman among media (we hear little of works of art).

McLuhan 3 envisages "the golden age as one of complete metamorphoses or translations of nature into human art, that stands ready of access to our electric age." For "The poet Stéphane Mallarmé thought 'the world exists to end in a book.' We are now in a position to go beyond that and transfer the entire show to the memory of a computer." And "if the work of the city is the remaking or translating of man into a more suitable form than his nomadic ancestors achieved, then might not our current translation of our entire lives into the spiritual form of information seem to make of the entire globe, and of the human family, a single consciousness?"

Watch that Teilhardian "spiritual." For explicitly, "We are certainly coming within conceivable range of a world automatically controlled to the point where we could say, 'Six hours less radio in Indonesia next week or there will be a great falling off in literary attention.' Or, 'We can program twenty more hours of TV in South Africa next week to cool down the tribal temperature raised by radio last week.' Whole cultures could now be programmed to keep their emotional climate stable. . . ." This will presumably happen when "the artists move from the ivory tower to the control tower of society," and "the Executive Suites are taken over by the Ph.D.s." Lawsy, now. *Et quis custodiet?* McLuhan 3?

Understanding Media, a book that immanentizes every eschaton in sight, has moved from McGraw-Hill hard-cover ($8.50) to McGraw-Hill paperback ($1.95) to drugstore paperback (95¢), becoming each time a different book though with the same words in it: since format is medium, not packaging. And the medium is the message? Then the message has become that of paperbackery, which is pop eschatology.

And a pity. A brilliant man, a man to whom friends and students owe incalculable debts, a man who has accurately perceived things the implications of which we shall be following up for decades—this man has not only taught us to say, but keeps putting us in the position where we must say, disregard the content, the medium is being spoken through by bad spirits.

dwight macdonald*
running it up the totem pole

Understanding Media: The Extensions of Man is one of those ambitious, far-ranging idea-books that is almost certain to be a *succes d'estime* and may well edge its way onto the best-seller lists. It has all the essentials: a big new theory about an important aspect of modern life—in this case what is called Mass Media, or Communications—that is massively buttressed by data and adorned with a special terminology. An early example was James Burnham's *The Managerial Revolution*, which wasted a great deal of print, talk, and time two decades ago. Later, and more respectable, examples are *The Lonely Crowd* ("other-directed"), Norman O. Brown's *Life Against Death* ("polymorphous perverse"), and C. Wright Mills's *The Power Elite*.

Mr. McLuhan's book outdoes its predecessors in the scope and novelty of its theory, the variety of its data (he has looted

* DWIGHT MACDONALD *is a trail blazer in the field of popular culture. His book of essays,* Against the American Grain, *is appropriately subtitled* Essays on the "Effect of Mass Culture." *At present Mr. Macdonald is writing a column on politics for* Esquire *and is on the staff of* The New Yorker.

all culture, from cave paintings to *Mad* magazine, for fragments to shore up against the ruin of his System), and the *pa-
nache* of its terminology. My only fear is he may have overesti-
mated the absorptive capacities of our intelligentsia and have
given them a richer feast of Big New ideas than even their
ostrich stomachs can digest. I have a sneaking sympathy for
"the consternation of one of the editors of this book," who, we
are told on page 4, "noted in dismay that 'seventy-five per cent
of your material is new. A successful book cannot venture to be
more than ten per cent new.'" Not that this fazes our author.
"Such a risk seems quite worth taking at the present time when
the stakes are very high and the need to understand the effects
of the extensions of man becomes more urgent by the hour." If
the worse comes to the worst, as the hours tick by, no one can
say that Marshall McLuhan, director of the Centre for Culture
and Technology at the University of Toronto and a former
chairman (1953–55) of the Ford Foundation Seminar on Culture and Communication, didn't do his best to wise us up.

Compared to Mr. McLuhan, Spengler is cautious and Toynbee positively pedantic. His thesis is that mankind has gone
through three cultural stages: a Golden Age of illiterate
tribalism that was oral, homogeneous, collective, non-rational,
and undifferentiated; a Silver Age (the terms are Ovid's, not
his) that set in after the invention of the alphabet during
which the spoken word began to be superseded by the written
word, a decay into literacy that was facilitated by the fact that
alphabetic writing is easier to learn and use than Egyptian
hieroglyphs or Chinese ideograms, whose desuetude he de-
plores; and the present Iron Age that was inaugurated by
movable-type printing, an even more unfortunate invention,
and that is visual, fragmented, individualistic, rational, and
specialized. McLuhan's *The Gutenberg Galaxy* is really Vol. 1
of the present work, describing the sociocultural changes,
mostly bad, brought about by the post-Gutenberg multiplication of printed matter, with its attendant stimulation of literacy. A gloomy work.

Understanding Media is more cheerful. It is about a fourth

RUNNING IT UP THE TOTEM POLE

Age into which for over a century we have been moving more and more rapidly, with nobody realizing it except Mr. McLuhan: the Electronic Age of telegraph, telephone, photograph, phonograph, radio, movie, television, and automation. This is a return to the Golden Age but on a higher level, as in the Hegelian synthesis of thesis and antithesis; or a spiral staircase. These new media are, in his view, making written language obsolete, or, in his (written) language, the Electronic Age "now brings oral and tribal ear-culture to the literate West [whose] electric technology now begins to translate the visual or eye man back into the tribal and oral pattern with its seamless web of kinship and interdependence."

This preference for speech over writing, for the primitive over the civilized—to be fair, McLuhan's Noble Savage is a more advanced model than Rousseau's, one equipped with computers and other electronic devices that make writing, indeed even speech, unnecessary for communication—this is grounded on a reversal of the traditional hierarchy of the senses. Sight, Hearing, Touch was Plato's ranking, and I imagine even in the Electronic Age few would choose blindness over deafness or touch over either of the other two. But McLuhan's 75 per cent of new material includes a rearrangement to Touch, Hearing, Sight, which fits his tropism toward the primitive. He seems to have overlooked the even more primitive Taste and Smell, which is a pity, since a historical-cultural view based on them would have yielded at least 90 per cent new material.

If I have inadvertently suggested that *Understanding Media* is pure nonsense, let me correct that impression. It is impure nonsense, nonsense adulterated by sense. Mr. McLuhan is an ingenious, imaginative and (above all) fertile thinker. He has accumulated a great deal of fresh and interesting information (and a great deal of dull or dubious information). There is even much to be said for his basic thesis, if one doesn't push it too far (he does). I sympathize with McLuhan's poetic wisecrack about "the typographical trance of the West"—he is good at such phrases, maybe he should have written his book in verse, some brief and elliptical form like the Japanese *haiku*. It is when he develops his ideas, or rather when he fails to, that I become antipathetic.

One defect of *Understanding Media* is that the parts are greater than the whole. A single page is impressive, two are "stimulating," five raise serious doubts, ten confirm them, and long before the hardy reader has staggered to page 359 the accumulation of contradictions, non-sequiturs, facts that are distorted and facts that are not facts, exaggerations, and chronic rhetorical vagueness has numbed him to the insights (as the chapter on Clocks, especially the pages on Donne and Marvell which almost make one forget the preceding page, which tries to conscript three Shakespeare quotations which simply won't be bullied) and the many bits of new and fascinating information: the non-English speaking African who tunes in to the BBC news broadcast every evening, listening to it as pure music, with an overtone of magic; the literate African villager, who, when he reads aloud the letters his illiterate friends bring him, feels he should stop up his ears so as not to violate their privacy.

If he had written, instead of a long book, a long article for some scholarly journal, setting forth his ideas clearly—and once —Mr. McLuhan might have produced an important little work, as Frederick Jackson Turner did in 1893 with his famous essay on the frontier in American history. At the worst, it would have been Provocative, Stimulating, maybe even Seminal. And Readable. But of course he wrote the book because he couldn't write the article. Like those tribesmen of the Golden Age, his mind-set doesn't make for either precision or brevity.

"Mr. McLuhan has an insoluble problem of method," Frank Kermode observed in his admirable review of *The Gutenberg Galaxy* in the February 1963 *Encounter*. "Typography has made us incapable of knowing and discoursing otherwise than by 'a metamorphosis of situations into a fixed point of view'; that is, we reduce everything to the linear and the successive, as computers reduce everything to a series of either-ors. And since he himself is unable to proceed by any other method, he cannot avoid falsifying the facts his book sets out to establish." He goes on to paraphrase a letter he received from McLuhan: "he says the ideal form of his book would be an ideogram. Or perhaps it could be a film; but otherwise he can find no way 'of creating an inconclusive image that is lineal and sequential.' " Alas. A writer who believes that truth can be expressed only by a mosaic, a montage, a *Gestalt* in which the parts are apprehended simultaneously rather than successively, is forced by the logic of the typographical medium into "a fixed point of view" and into much too definite conclusions. And if he rejects that logic, as McLuhan tries to, the alternative is even worse: a book that lacks the virtues of its medium, being vague, repetitious, formless, and, after a while, boring.

One way of judging a polymath work like this, or an omniscient magazine like *Time,* is to see what it says about a subject you know about. On movies *Understanding Media* is not very understanding, or accurate. McLuhan is a fast man with a fact. Not that he is careless or untruthful, simply that he's a system-builder and so interested in data only as building stones; if a corner has to be lopped off, a roughness smoothed to fit, he won't hesitate to do it. This is one of the reasons his book is dull reading—it's just those quirky corners, those roughnesses that make actuality interesting.

• Page 18: "The content of a movie is a novel or a play or an opera." This suits a McLuhan thesis: "the medium is the message," the content of a medium is always another medium, so the only *real* content is the technology peculiar to each medium, and its effects. Many movies, especially Hollywood ones, are made from novels and plays. But many are not, and those usually the best. "Even the film industry regards all of its greatest achievements as derived from novels, nor is this unreasonable." (By "not unreasonable" McLuhan means It Fits.) "All" is the kind of needlessly large claim McLuhan often makes: common sense would suggest there might be a few films not derived from novels that are well-regarded by the industry. In fact, there are many; I imagine that even Hollywood—which has given Oscars to Bergman and Fellini, after all—would include among the cinema's "greatest achievements" *Potemkin, Caligari, Ten Days That Shook the World, Citizen Kane, Intolerance, 8 1/2, La Dolce Vita, L'Avventura, La Grande Illusion, Wild Strawberries,* and the comedies of Keaton and Chaplin.

• Page 287: Pudovkin and Eisenstein did not "denounce" the sound film. Quite the contrary: their famous 1928 Manifesto begins, "The dream of a sound film has come true" and concludes that, if sound is treated non-realistically as a montage element, "it will introduce new means of enormous power . . . for the circulation . . . of a filmic idea." Again McLuhan knew this, for he refers to the Manifesto, but he suppressed this knowledge for Systematic reasons.

• Page 293: "This kind of casual, cool realism has given the new British films easy ascendancy." On the contrary, British films of the last decade—as the chief British film journal, *Sight & Sound,* constantly laments—now stand low on the international scale. McLuhan makes this misjudgment because one of his theories is that "cool" media suit the Electronic Age better than "hot" ones—I'll explain shortly—so since British films are indeed on the casual-cool side, either they must be ascendant or the theory must be wrong.

An occupational disease of system-building that is perhaps even worse than the distortion of reality is a compulsion to push the logic of the system to extremes. The climactic, and much the longest, chapter in *Understanding Media* is the one on television. A happy ending: TV is reforming culture by bringing us the real stuff, tribal, communal, and analphabetic —none of that divisive book larnin'—and restoring the brotherhood of man. It is the finest flower of mankind's finest Age, the present or Electronic one.

In *The Gutenberg Galaxy,* McLuhan with his usual originality denounces the "open" society of individual freedom we have kept alive, with varying success, since the Greeks invented it. He prefers a "closed" society on the primitive model ("the product of speech, drum and ear technologies") and he looks forward, as the Electronic Age progresses, to "the sealing of the entire human family into a single global tribe." TV is the demiurge that is creating this transformation. Already it has changed things in many ways, most of them beneficial—I predict a brisk sale for the book on Madison Avenue. Among them are: the end of bloc voting in politics; the rise of the quality paperback (had thought Jason Epstein was the demiurge there, but maybe he got the idea from Jack Paar); the recent improvement in our criticism ("Depth probing of words and language is a normal feature of oral and manuscript cultures, rather than of print. Europeans have always felt that the English and Americans lacked depth in their culture. Since radio, and especially since TV, English and American literary critics have exceeded the performances of any European in depth and subtlety." Well, an *original* judgment anyway); "the abrupt decline of baseball" and the removal of the Dodgers to Los Angeles; "the beatnik reaching out for Zen" and also their public poetry readings ("TV, with its deep participation mode, caused young poets suddenly to present their poems in cafés, in public parks, anywhere. After TV, they suddenly felt the need for personal contact with their public." Agreed, but in opposite sense: the tripe manufactured all day and night by TV may well have made poets feel the need for personal contacts in their work); the picture window; the vogue for the small car; the vogue for skiing ("So avid is the TV viewer for rich tactile effects that he could be counted on to revert to skis. The wheel, so far as he is concerned, lacks the requisite abrasiveness." Skis seem to me *less* abrasive than wheels, but let it pass, let it pass); the Twist; and the "demand for crash-programming in education."

TV has been able to accomplish all this because it is not only Electronic but also very Cool. Hot media (radio, cinema, photography) are characterized by "high definition" or "the state of being well filled with data." Thus, comic strips are Cool because "very little visual information is provided." He rates speech Cool ("because so little is given and so much has to be filled in by the listener"). McLuhan's own style, incidentally, is one of the hottest since Carlyle: *cf.* the chapter headings: "The Gadget Lover: Narcissus as Narcosis"; "The Photograph: the Brothel-without-Walls"; "The Telephone: Sounding Brass or Tinkling Symbol?"; "Movies: the Reel World" (now reelly).

TV is the Coolest of medias because the engineers haven't yet been able to give us a clear picture. Or, in McLuhanese: "The TV image is of low intensity or definition and therefore, unlike film, it does not afford detailed information about objects." (He can say that again.) So the viewer is forced to participate, to eke out imaginatively the poverty of what he sees, like the readers of those Cool comic books—all very stimulating and educational. In the McLuhanorama, Picasso is inferior to Milton Caniff because he goes in for "high definition." Another virtue of TV is that it "is, above all, an extension of the sense of touch, which involves maximal interplay of all the senses." Touch would seem to me to involve *less* interplay than, say, sight, and I have always thought of TV as oral and visual. But touch is No. 1 in the McLuhan hierarchy of the senses and TV is No. 1 in the McLuhan hierarchy of media and so . . . .

Watching TV is also gregarious—"the TV mosaic image demands social completion and dialogue"—with the spectators chatting while *Gunsmoke* flickers by, and this is also Good. (It doesn't seem to have occurred to McLuhan that TV may Demand Social Completion simply because there isn't much of interest on the screen.) How different are the passive, isolated, mute moviegoers, who must put up with clear, complete and sometimes even beautiful images that give them nothing to fill in (Cinema is Hot) and no chance for creative or social activity. They might as well be looking at a Mantegna or a Cezanne or some other high-definition, non-participatory image. "Since TV nobody is happy with a mere book knowledge of French or English poetry," McLuhan writes or rather proclaims. "The unanimous cry now is 'Let's *talk* French' and 'Let the bard be heard.'" Unanimous cries I doubt ever got unanimously cried. But I do like that "mere."

I found two statements I could agree with: TV is "an endless adventure amidst blurred images and mysterious contours"; and "TV makes for myopia." For the rest, the chapter reveals with special clarity two severe personal limitations on his use-fulness as a thinker about media: his total lack of interest in cultural standards (he praises Jack Paar because his low-keyed, personal manner is well suited to a Cool medium like TV—as it is—but has nothing to say about the quality of the material Paar puts across so Coolly); and his habit—it seems almost a compulsion as if he wanted to be found out, like a sick klepto-maniac—of pushing his ideas to extremes of absurdity.

The most extreme extreme I noticed was the millennial vi-sion that concludes the chapter on "The Spoken Word: Flower of Evil?":

Our new electric technology that extends our senses and nerves in a global embrace has large implications for the future of language. Electric technology does not need words any more than the digital computer needs numbers. Electricity points the way to an extension of the process of consciousness itself, on a world scale, and without any verbalization whatever. Such a state of collective awareness may have been the preverbal condition of men. . . . The computer promises by technology a Pentecostal condition of universal under-standing and unity. The next logical step would seem to be . . . to bypass languages in favor of a general cosmic consciousness which might be very like the collective unconscious dreamt of by Bergson. [Only McLuhan would see the conscious as "very like" the uncon-scious—D. M.] The condition of weightlessness that biologists say promises a physical immortality may be paralleled by the condition of a speechlessness that could confer a perpetuity of collective har-mony and peace.

I think Madame Blavatsky would have envied the writer ca-pable of that paragraph.

irving j. weiss*
sensual reality
in the mass media

When Narcissus made a postage stamp of his reflection in the water, TV was born. / MALCOLM DE CHAZAL

An offhand way of identifying an intellectual might be by how little a man uses his TV. If he doesn't even own one, you could almost swear he was an intellectual. It's not that he's poor and certainly not that he's indifferent but that he cares. He takes mass culture much more seriously than do those who do own TV sets. He tends to look on TV the way most people regard disease, as something to deplore at a safe distance.

If this picture isn't entirely accurate, it's because the mass media in disseminating information widely have turned all men into intellectuals of a sort. But most people don't recognize themselves as mental leaders, which is what they mean by intellectuals, or as book-learned. Most people, if they read anything at all, rely on newspapers and magazines. The intellectuals are the ones who read the books.

At one extreme the intellectual is a special kind of bookman,

* IRVING J. WEISS is a Professor of Communications in the State University College at New Paltz, New York.

the writer rather than the reader of opinions; at the other extreme he is the artist, who need not, if his art is non-verbal (and then often cannot easily), express himself in writing but is mentally bold and decisive because he is always originating things. These two extreme types often take a noncommittal attitude toward the mass media as they project through the gross modernism of their environment a fine modernism of their own or make their unpredictable constructions partly out of recent trash and other barbaric yawps. The most radical of such writers and artists often share with midcult bosses and performers an indifference to any standards of truth or beauty that prevent them from transforming the energy of the historical moment into a form of their own choosing; whereas the general run of writers and artists share with bookmen—professionals, holders of degrees, and the well read—a respect for the traditions that have shaped our culture, traditions found mostly in the print stored in our libraries.

Bookmen don't like mass culture because they think it has coarsened the quality of modern life. Although they are likely to recognize that the superiority of their own class derives from the printing press, they don't tend to think of the book as part of the media revolution of the nineteenth century, when technology and democracy combined to produce cheap periodicals and journalism. Nor do they think of the book review as an elegant type of kitsch, an instant version that saves the reader the trouble of making his mind up about the original.

The intellectual knows by his wide and deep book experience what great thoughts, profound myths, and enjoyable stories are available in books, alongside much else less worth reading; but he hardly finds anything of comparable importance in the sight and sound information forms that have come about since photography entered journalism. He looks with dismay therefore on the apparently insatiable demands of the masses for the prettified and preformed material that the newer media feed out, and he is shocked by the disparity between the steadiness of the diet and the lack of lasting nourishment. He extends his disapproval to all other areas of modern life affected by the same shoddiness, hypocrisy, commercial cynicism, vanity, deliberate confusions of feeling, and moral callousness, whether in the arts and sciences, religion, or practical affairs.

While denouncing horrendous examples or trends, the intellectual as social philosopher and literary critic, and more recently as sociologist, has hoped for education to improve taste. As early as the French Encyclopedists and the political philosophers of the American Revolution, the greater availability of printed matter made it even seem likely that men who could read might aspire to the highest intellectual attainments. The university without walls was opened in the eighteenth century with works like Chambers' *Cyclopædia* and *The Works of the British Poets* that subsumed much of the then acknowledged cultural past. Eric Hoffer is only one of the most remarkable in a long line of autodidacts that cheap print made possible. But the flood of material became too powerful, and the tabloid press and, later, radio and television deflected the stream of information from didacticism, workbench self-sufficiency, and literary learning to sensationalism, pornography, sentimentality, and brainwash. Later intellectuals saw radical change in the means of originating information and distributing it, or in the political system itself, as the only possible way of improving the quality of life.

Some critics, like Gilbert Seldes, Dwight Macdonald, and James Agee, have sorted the good from the bad according to the most cultivated standards of the literary and fine arts traditions, implying as they surveyed the cultural horizon that fraud and bad taste would probably increase unless some change occurred in social or economic organization. Others, like Reuel Denney, Parker Tyler, and Martha Wolfenstein, concerned themselves with tracing the underlying psychosocial patterns in both the form and content of media products, since as marketable commodities they reflect the deepest defensive and aggressive impulses of masses of people rather than the fully intended thoughts of a few imaginative minds. And in the last forty years hundreds of other critics of various abilities have worked up a sweat analyzing social and cultural groups

40

and the manifest content of the media material they consumed.

With few exceptions highbrow and scholarly analyses have taken for granted the qualitative differences between media products and works of art. Rarely have the best critics dwelt with any attention on similarities in esthetic mode between the avant-garde tradition in the arts and the rampant modernism of the media, or on the disappearance of art into technology, or the merging of art and reality. Hence a good deal of the outcry against Marshall McLuhan's *Understanding Media.* The old soldiers used to fighting classical popular culture battles see McLuhan applying Leslie Fiedler's hot glosses on events with Wyndham Lewis' rudeness and Spengler's polyhistor recklessness to all popular culture discussions and giving aid and comfort to the popeyed Middle by blurring distinctions between art and dreck, labeling all modern culture forms "extensions of man," damning 1984 and 1894 as rear-view mirrorism, hailing mass cult thrill-seeking as avant-garde adventurousness, and expanding historical-wave predictions into anthropological-tide prophecies.

The Mechanical Bride was acceptable to critics of popular culture because it was imbued with the déclassé intellectual's scorn for middlebrow vulgarity that had been *Partisan Review*'s response to its environment for decades. McLuhan's attention to detail, inventiveness, and aggressive high spirits were startling, but the viewpoint was recognizable. Nevertheless, he was beginning to look at advertising journalism almost completely as lurid graphic and verbal combinations and not as examples of commercial art in settings of debased language. In later articles and books, especially the journal *Explorations in Communication,* which included contributions from poets, artists, and scholars, McLuhan developed his scanning view of modern culture, changing his emphasis from media content to technological environment as he gradually came to see media horizons more clearly. When he stuck discreetly to scholarly interpretations, his resourcefulness and learning were acknowledged; meanwhile his neo-Dadaist cheering for the historical drift began to pick up a following among the intellectual populists in teachers' colleges and communications departments.

Understanding Media lay dormant for about a year after its publication in 1964 before the big-media organs—having already spewed up Pop Art and getting ready to disgorge pop drugs, happenings, and camp—found in the Canadian professor their justification for continuing to do without blushing what McLuhan said they were already doing beautifully out of blind force.

It is probably the print and book bias of the BBC and CBS that renders them so awkward and inhibited in radio and TV presentation. Commercial urgency, rather than artistic insight, fostered by contrast a hectic vivacity in the corresponding American operation.*

This kind of thing from a scholar, teacher, and contributor to literary reviews was really rocking the highbrow boat. McLuhan's insistence that he's just a frontier scout who tells it like it is looks bad in a time of renewed political and social commitment, when Vietnam and the Negro Revolution demand "point of view"—an idea excoriated in *Understanding Media* as philosophically backward in the electronic age.

It's a pity that McLuhan shoots from the hip so much at anything stirring on the cultural horizon because he has indeed developed a sensitive system for interpreting signals.† He has made it possible as the aboveground spokesman for many burrowing scholars and philosophers, and as a direction-finder for willing explorers trained in arts and letters, to use their keenness of observation on, as well as their powers of invention in, the mass media. Mainly by concentrating on the "creative process of human cognition," by hammering out distinctions between the old world of visual logic and the new one of

* *Understanding Media,* p. 307.

† Critics are so quick to attribute polemical intent to the observations McLuhan makes about the transforming powers of technology that they ignore him when he also writes, for example: "Once we have surrendered our senses and nervous systems to the private manipulations of those who would try to benefit from taking a lease on our eyes and ears and nerves, we don't really have any rights left" (*ibid.,* p. 68).

acoustic space, McLuhan has pointed out in detail how the extensions of our selves have brought about the anesthesia and "passivity" that critics of popular culture have been remarking for decades without understanding clearly.

The complex change in culture that has been gradually taking place since the invention of movable type, and more rapidly since the increasing use of electric communications after the middle of the last century, comes from our having exchanged primary sensuality for technological sensuality through the mass media, which, in turn, hastened the disintegration of public life into mass life.

The Latin plural *media* (popular practice is turning it into a singular) still bears too much of its trade sense to suit critical discussion comfortably. Yet its upstart fanciness is right for the job. The mass media are technological means for getting, storing, and giving sensory information. In their instrumental departure from the human mode they differ radically from those media hitherto used in the arts: spoken or written language, graphics, solid constructions, bodily movement, etc. The organizing principles in the arts depend as much on formal clarity and cohesion as on monumentality, making what we call works of art independent things in themselves because they are products of thought and work. Their message lies in being self-standing representations of the human imagination. Once we use the term "media," however, we are dealing with channels or extensions of our sensory, involuntary activities rather than the results of our esthetic activities. Some movies are thought of as works of art in the old sense—though nobody talks of radio or television programs in the same way. But we tend to think of all three media indistinguishably as a combination of (1) the apparatus, (2) the performance produced by it, and (3) the process of its operation. The movie we go to, the radio we listen to, the TV we watch all mean the transmitter, its mechanical operations or electrical flow, and its program segments.

The medium is the message because the instrument is so technically smug, extended so far beyond the activity of primary sense perception—each man's private use of his unaided sense organs—that much, if not most, of what it perceives, records, and transmits requires as little human intervention as tooling along in an automobile on a freeway. It operates as any and every man's multiple-eyed and/or multiple-eared roving sense bank. Unstop camera or microphone, spring it into action, and you feed into it that documentation that constitutes the substantial poetry of its function. One's esthetic delight derives from the medium's smooth stupidity, so much of which easily turns trite or arty when affected by human decisions.

The actuality of time seen or heard, consequential only according to its own passage, corresponds to what we often refer to as the surreality of unconscious thinking. What our primary senses take in before we begin to shape the information linguistically or symbolically is the animal world in which there is no distinction between chance and necessity. As soon as the mind pays attention to the flow of information, our least act of observation interprets it, giving the information a franchise to enter the moral world. And this is what we do on an elementary level to the shots, takes, cuts, and sequences edited from mike and camera: we make them artifacts each time we interrupt the process to attach one time segment to another. These segments of actuality broken off from the animal activity of the apparatus are equivalent to the sections we break off from our own day dreaming or night dreaming whenever we can recover the pieces. The reason we tend to consider mass media productions as dreams and fantasies is not primarily that they are controlled by commercial interests appealing to the pre-adult or appetite level in all consumers, but that like our subconscious minds the media sense rather than think. In dreaming and daydreaming we use our minds as if they were our senses; in the operations of the mass media the senses are used as if they were minds. Every time we put a caption to a photograph we make it mean relatively what it has already seen and reported absolutely. The vogue for crazy captions is a catchy nihilistic refusal to accept conventions in meaning and a tribute to the camera's sensory self-sufficiency.

Ortega said in *The Revolt of the Masses* that in mass man,

unlike man in multitudes, quantity has become converted into a "qualitative determination . . . the common social quality, man as undifferentiated from other men, but as repeating in himself a generic type. . . . Strictly speaking, the mass as a psychological fact can be defined without waiting for individuals to appear in mass formation."* What was not quite evident from radio over thirty years ago but is clear from television today is that mass man no longer *needs* to appear in mass formation. Indeed, the notorious loneliness of modern post-industrial man comes from his having so easily domesticated numberless sensual images of his fellows as substitutes for the communities and crowds he was once part of.

Gatherings, crowds, and mobs are groupings defined by physical location or physical cohesion. Each member of the assemblage becomes part of the total organism. Men in public space are like ants or wolves. In the mass, however, each member is not part of some physical whole but the embodiment of an abstract content, of an invisible wholeness. Men in the mass are like printed books. The original of the book is the words, whose written form is a recording of the sound-meaning and whose printed form standardizes the written recording with no loss of fidelity to the meaning. Once the cliché is set any number of typographic images may be thrown off, indistinguishable from each other. Mass communications no longer need to convene men: each message recipient can get his information at will through print or recording, or separately and simultaneously at any time of broadcasting.

One need not struggle to witness the performance, hear the word, see the leader, share the experience. It is easier than talking to one's neighbor—as easy as going to sleep with the pillowspeaker plugged in, or the Sony on the tummy. The bite in the phrasing reflects the ad world's influence on our thinking about the latest media devices: it still seems ridiculous for us to be able so effortlessly to know so much of what there is to know . . . yet reading in bed is taken for granted.

The mass idea is revolutionary in human history, not because mass culture has quantified man but because it makes

* 25th edition (New York, 1957), pp. 13, 14.

consideration of quantity pointless: man has not been reduced to the level of the social animals or of objects but refined to the limit of his latest symbol systems: the mass media.

As long as human ingenuity can only fashion a second object *like* the first, a third like the other two, and so one, the addition of each new example satisfies in us the primitive desire for making correspondences; and the collection of a heap of such objects will satisfy what Elias Canetti in *Crowds and Power* calls "the lust for counting, of seeing numbers mount up, which "derives largely from treasure. . . ."* Counting is an attempt to change likeness into sameness, correspondence into identity, multiplicity into unity—although the tension between the extremes never disappears. But the exactly repeatable image of mass production is the result of embodying hand and eye operations in a machine that eliminates any distinction between likeness and sameness, converting the massiveness of the product seen or collected into a distributive massness. This is the historical stage Ortega describes, at which individuality becomes appreciated by the masses and even revered just as it begins to become invisible.

The delusion of mass man, and of the intellectual as well, is that his "identity" is precious to him and ought to matter, by which he means his name-face importance. But name and face can't resist conversion into number and fingerprint in a society in which the ego, capable of heroism, has become the self, capable of pathos only. Montaigne was still a casual Hamlet writing for publication in the sixteenth century. The pathetic self began to reveal itself nakedly in the boasts and complaints of diaries only in the next century.† When the twentieth-century semiliterate imagemakers and the consumers of their messages harp on the word "individuality," they hope they are talking about any man's irreducible singular prominence, whereas they themselves probably suspect that their meaning amounts to "the lowest degree of any man's accountability," or that which he shares with all others—his selfness. They are

* Trans. Carol Stewart (New York, 1966), p. 89.

† See *A Review of English Diaries from the 16th to the 20th Centuries*, ed. Arthur Ponsonby (London, n.d.).

looking at themselves with anxiety according to the conventions of a literate culture that has begun to disintegrate.

The first mass revolution was that of the printing press, which made reading a silent practice, so that in any public library several hundred people could gather not for communion but separation. The second mass revolution took place after the newspaper (1670) became journalism (1833), no longer defined by the newness of information but by the time of its issuance; journalism becomes the literary appearance of time. By the end of the nineteenth century advertisements, news, and features have become equally time announcements crowding the page space to hound the eye for attention; the telegraph has compressed news into headlines, or telegrams; the halftone photograph suddenly punches real holes into newspaper's linear sign system; and the comic strip, returning print to the block lettering of sounds—without upper- and lower-case distinctions—staggers movement into graphic sequences.

The exact repeatability of images no longer corresponds to a recording of any content model. Although newsprint may still be considered the conceptual rendering of an event, the photograph is no less than the event itself. As we know from tourism, the aim of the photographer is to photograph what will look good: he saves his looking for the photoprint version of the subject rather than waste it on the original.

From the twentieth century on any movie, or radio or TV recording, justifies its own authenticity. It does not have the uniqueness of the painting before the work is reduced to print. Media uniqueness is the moment of time recorded, not any collector's original. It is even purer in its perfection because it has refined the fluctuating sensory reality of the live moment into sound and sight signals only.

If we ever achieve multisensory recording, there will of course be only a quaint distinction between reality and appearance or image, original and copy, thing-in-itself and simulacrum, even if it falls short of the superb interchange between modes of being in Ray Bradbury's story "The Nursery" in which real people are eaten by imagined lions. Hi-fi stereo has been gently accustoming us to the acoustic future. The Beatles in Shea Stadium are for the tin-eared teenies; the engineered sound of their LPs constitutes the sensual reality. And although sports annals may have something to say about last Sunday's football game in the arena which most fans saw on the screen, and social and political history about JFK's funeral, one's desperate or sentimental on-the-spot attendance at such events begins, in a sense, to belong to personal scholarship.

That involvement with the TV image, in McLuhan's view, increases our tactile abilities, Europeanizes us Americans more than ever, doesn't mean TV, as well as the other media influenced by it, is having a "good" effect on us, is returning us to nature and bringing us closer to our neighbors in its own despite. It means that TV has become the vital source from which we drink, it has become our water though we thought it was beer or soda. Those people who now take their transistor radios along to the gathering or the event to check their own participation are refusing to be limited to a mere crowd-members' view, the private soldier's version of the war, any longer. The hippies in California have gone even further: they have given up TV watching to wire their whole environment for sound and sight and live inside their rock and lightings.

It is the shocked but obscure awareness of this second mass revolution that impels Daniel Boorstin to coin the term "pseudo-event," because he thinks images are denaturing and driving out originals. But the 1967 riots in Newark and Detroit did not turn into pseudo-events just because some Negroes may have decided to join in or start new commotions elsewhere after seeing the news reports on TV, as the ponderous newspaper commentators opined. And asking the networks to avoid playing up the visual violence in riots or to keep from giving free advertising to quotable performers like H. Rap Brown won't prevent the media from sullying the waters of reality. The medium, not the master self-interests behind it, is the real threat. Ultimacy in images is what modern society aspires to, for the image is the film-derived equivalent in the mid-twentieth century of the virtue, honor, and reputation that used to serve as our moral stand-ins in the minds of others. Negores won't stop rioting until they can afford to sit back and watch the East Indians riot. The purpose of TV is to get everyone to stop rioting so that all violence can be converted to ritual entertainment.

People rely on the world of events being recognizable and dependable, so that to the extent that the mass media betray our trust in "reality" we tend to call their offerings entertainment, escapism, and fun. Any TV comedy or gun series mixes credible façades of people and things with self-indulgent plots in a technologically sensual swim of surrealism and *symbolisme*—a concoction so strong it might have choked Rimbaud. This power of the TV image is so great that we have to dismiss it lightly or despise it whenever we measure it reasonably against the world we think we ought to live in. McLuhan is the first media observer to point this out.

All drawing or painting—all representational art—makes its statements metaphorically, the real always seen as the ideal. Try to extricate a literal meaning, the illustration from the representation, and all you do is satisfy your rationalistic curiosity with the comfort of a sequence or a snapshot. According to Collingwood in *The Principles of Art,** even primitive abstract designs represent essentially some ceremonial action with the actors and scene reported only in terms of the ritual pattern. The invention of the photograph made it apparent that painting had never been illustration, for the photograph took the illustrative characteristics *en bloc* out of our viewing frame. The photograph exchanged the sensibility of the artist for the mechanism of light, the expressiveness of hand and eye for the imprimatur of the eye alone. The photograph captures the literal world as an intact fantasm.

The camera-extended eye, contemporary with Naturalism in the arts, seemed to superficial observers to bring us closer to truth than any medium previously used by man. But it was not until the movie camera began to crank its thoughts that natu-

* 5th edition (New York, 1964), p. 55.

ralistic truth could be seen as the point at which the literal and the fantastic became inseparable. Film montage cut us into the body of time itself.

It was the photograph interrupting the placid regularity of the newspaper page—with the other developments that led toward journalism—that broke the connection between cause and effect, view and viewpoint, event and interpretation, which literacy had accustomed us to accept.

"The step from the Age of Typographic Man to the Age of Graphic Man was taken with the invention of photography," as McLuhan announces it. By making "visual reports without syntax" * photo, movie, and later TV accustomed us to see into pictorial imagery instead of reading it in the fading light of the print tradition. After the seed of the photograph bloomed as closeup, microview, aerial shot, angular distortion, montage, sight and sound juxtapositions, and, much later, the visual anecdote of the TV commercial, the oppressive silence in the photograph's lights and shadows could be felt stirring with sound. The visual world became auditory again—as it had always been for the child, the naturalist, the primitive, and the poet; as it is for all of us whenever we catch ourselves startled by the appalling hold our senses have over our wills.

What distinguishes sight and seeing from the other senses is that the frontal location of our eyes gives us a measure of control over what we tend to see, *i.e.*, we cannot take in anything visually unless we are somewhat ready to approach it intentionally—it cannot clamor for our attention and hope to get noticed immediately as can so much of the information directed to the other senses. Furthermore, the visual world is the only sensory domain in which the data are sufficiently distant from our bodies and stay still long enough to be engaged unemotionally. We have therefore been able to construct systems that perpetuate this temporal and spatial separation for our own reconsideration and the notice of our descendants: those of our print culture. Setting up the eyes in the business of recording concepts led us to develop a derivative visuality that froze out all the other sensory signals, including direct visuality:

* *Understanding Media*, p. 190.

when we read words, for example, we substitute "imagining" for the fuller sensual participation of hearing them as we would in the theater.

Derivative visuality lost force when visual technology returned us to a new form of direct seeing, or that mixed use and interplay of our senses that characterizes every living moment. As Malcolm de Chazal, the most exhaustive investigator of sensory plasticity, says in *Sens-Plastique*:

There is no such thing as absolute flatness because all color is an impasto of form. Touching is inseparable from seeing. Shut your eyes and color will be there like the head of the Cheshire Cat. The eye's sense of touch and the finger's sense of sight combine to "deform" everything man touches. He experiences the sensation of absolute flatness only in death, when color lies stretched out in the eye and the human sense of touch becomes coextensive with the absolute itself. . . .

We ordinarily rely to some extent on our eyes to tell where a sound is coming from. In a colorless world we would be partly deaf. In a soundless world perspective would flatten out. While we are asleep we hide in the corridors between the senses until a sudden awakening makes us reach for our ears to see where we are and our eyes to hearken with. . . .

Speech is broadcast not only from the lips and nostrils but from the whole face in superfine waves that are heard not only by the ears and eyes but the whole face. The voice of the person you love sets up station-to-station broadcasting between your two faces.*

The new electric technology heralded by the photograph enabled us to put on the visible world, drink it in, absorb its vibrations, hold it close instead of trying to decode its signs. The photograph is the point at which this new technology begins to absorb machine technology, reassuring us with the familiarity of chiaroscuro, disturbing us when it shows what no eye ever saw, frightening us with the humor of the subconscious. The animated cartoon is the point at which electric

* 5th edition (Paris, 1948), pp. 194, 32, 12. This and all other quotations from Chazal's writings are my own translations, not yet published in book form.

technology takes over completely, rubbing off some of its characteristics on all photography. The animated cartoon is the viewfinder in which one can recognize what McLuhan calls tribal man, for it shows everything id-side outside. From Mickey Mouse to Astro Boy it exemplifies frank demonism: beasts, anthropomorphs, and other projections of ourselves doing juggling acts with human conflicts at the speed of the nervous system and in a slapstick performance that zaps the opposition too awesomely for laughter. The animated cartoon is the only media type that intersects color and form perfectly because its visual scale is infrahuman; a coarse psychomyth whose violence represents an electromechanical amplification of the trills we play on the sensory keyboard; a physics that makes no distinction between impact and absorption; two thousand years of fable and epos, animism and magic, mummery and peasant iconography, jousting and *commedia dell'arte* and nursery tales sprung tight. Even the media prime movers are afraid of the animated cartoon. Said an executive in charge of Saturday morning cartoon scheduling, as reported in a recent *New York Times Magazine* article: "I can't defend Saturday morning at all. I'm scared to death about what all those cartoons are going to do to kids who don't have the stability and background to resist violence." * One of the cartoon-show producers even admits he's "ashamed that the American public allows its children to view them." †

One cartoon is as good as another for the immediate needs of those in charge who knew the medium was the message before McLuhan tumbled to the idea. The reason children are addicted is that the cartoon's ritual story is an anagram of their own psychic drives; but the likely explanation for the entrepreneurs' discomfort lies in the thinly disguised malice toward kids that most juvenile funfare, not excluding books, contains. And the malice is understandable: for two centuries we've practiced cultural Apartheid on children, as Philip Ariès

* Sam Blum, "Who Decides What Gets on TV—And Why," September 3, 1967, p. 23.
  † *Ibid.*

explains in *Centuries of Childhood,* * providing them with their own proper art and literature at considerable strain to our sensibilities. Now with TV in the home we have constant proof that the kids want to stay up late to watch our "cartoons" also if not more so.

Television offers the most expressive sensory syntax for the kind of statements animated drawings make because, as Mc-Luhan points out, TV cartoons everything. Whereas movies glamorize, TV undresses. TV is a "cool" medium offering intricate, barely conscious satisfactions. It surpasses the achievements of the newspaper mosaic, making a rough, continuous art form of reality, an art form whose crude siftings are as problematical and demanding of interpretation as those of any Mesopotamian archeological site.

The refractory, wobbly, granular TV image, always threatening to dissolve or disintegrate, presents the form of things as a hard-edged container of bloblike energy, which in black-and-white TV is like quicksilver. Color television injects the images with skin dye. The thick cartoon outlines hold the mythos together; but it's the elusive mineral in the membrane, the compound of face and body gestures orchestrating human speech that mold the viewer's senses into rapt involvement. From the schematic art of the animated cartoon, through the buffoonery of quiz shows, the ballet of football games, and the opera of news violence, to the epiphanies of certain faces and figures in action as different as those of J. Robert Oppenheimer, Charlie Mingus, and Lyndon Johnson, television trains its bathyscope on our culture unremittingly. What it does better than any previous mass medium is capture the naked lip-and-eye truth in our jargon, the promiscuity of our relations with possessions and opinions, the voluptuousness in our mayhem, and the squeamishness in our pornographies—the loose fit of our bodies over our living selves. As Chazal puts it:

> "I've taken a trip
> around the world,"
> the man said.

* Trans. Robert Baldick (London, 1962).

—"Don't fool yourself,
you haven't even moved
one inch forward
in your own body." *

Unlike the movies, which until recently were regarded almost exclusively as units or features, the TV process is a Protean show that won't stay still long enough to be programmed convincingly, its packaging being as arbitrary in comparative value as the products whose sales support the medium. One can just as easily regard the programs as interrupting the commercials as the other way round.

What is ridiculous about any hope of increasing "good" programming on TV is that turning the screw of its art tighter nearly always results in the embolism of hallowed triteness. Where vast sums are involved as in television, art means Lincoln Center. Alas, TV gets better all the time anyway because it thrives on the panic of executives whose judgment curries favor with their fear and greed.

Magazines used to have cartoons of the wife furious at her husband's ignoring her at the breakfast table for the newspaper. Now, as in a recent *New Yorker,* the husband sits over his coffee, his eyes transfixed by the curlered head he sees enshrined in a twenty-one-inch screen opposite yattering out the 8 A.M. wife report. What horrifies the educated, literate observer is that the newspaper Bible of man's religion of leisure which at least pretended to give him more information than entertainment has been supplanted by a medium that reverses the proportions. But the TV truth is that there is no difference any longer between information and entertainment. The newspaper's prose page still seemed to intervene between the observer and reality. TV, the art form of reality, has made the world over in its own image. Television is what is left after they take you away.

In the hands of any teacher capable of reading and explaining sensory shorthand the deliberately indiscriminate use of commercial TV programming one or two hours a day in the classroom would be the most powerful magic slate imaginable.

* *Sens-Magique* (Tananarive, Île Maurice, 1957), p. 4.

For its inadvertent banalities, piquancies, and absurdities brought into focus to fill out the irrepressible central image amount to the total reality of our culture. As McLuhan says, the intellectual's disgust at TV comes from trying to read it like a book or go to it like a movie. The only way to watch TV is to use it as a thick window and let your senses judge.

Turn the set on during the late morning or early afternoon hours on weekdays while its rate of respiration is low and even —although almost any time will do. Switch to any channel and ungrudgingly accept whatever is on—feature or commercial, it makes no difference—in that ideal way in which you would look at paintings in a museum, without caring who painted or is supposed to have painted what; or in that easy-eyed forgiving state in which you sit at a sidewalk café or on a balcony in some Mediterranean country, letting the human, animal, and mechanical traffic argue its own progress. Unlike the occasion of a movie in a theater—which amounts to scrutinizing the animals under laboratory conditions—attending to any old sequence of TV images with relaxed magnanimity should be like occupying a tree crotch in the bush at the pleasure of forest's comings and goings. The natural speed of TV is the viewer's insouciance, not *TV Guide*'s injunctions.

For what gradually rises to the surface, as the disinterested viewer can observe in soap operas, true-life re-enactments, children's programs, game shows, interviews, *Our Guiding Light, Divorce Court, Alan Burke,* or *Dating Game* is the sub-drama of the human face, voice, and gesture—the source and estuary of all sensuality short of the act of love itself—mixing self-betrayals and revelations more intricately and rapidly than one ever finds them in real life. We could not possibly observe the process of human interaction fully if we were dramatically concerned ourselves. This is TV as McLuhan's "posture of forms," which enables us to become "more deeply involved in the actuality of the human condition."

Is his statement a ponderous piece of claptrap? The starving African or Asian on television is more gripping than he ever was in newsphotos but no less sentimental. The agonies and ecstasies of the game-show winner of a Hawaiian vacation com-

IRVING J. WEISS

plete with freezer, dryer, and two Arabian stallions never obliterate completely the truth of the sufferings of others, as critics shocked by hideous parallelisms on facing pages of *Life* or adjacent columns in *The New Yorker* have insisted. There is still a sense in which television, and the other media to a lesser degree, accustom us to recognizing that all media messages are multiple in meaning. Media "reality" doesn't formulate a situation, it only presents or poses it. What TV offers are eyes, lips, hands, voices, motions—tones of meaning and other sensuous arguments.

Marshall McLuhan's thesis about the imploding future in which human interdependence may survive as tribalism rather than the social individualism of mass culture can in the end be tested only by the kind of direct observation of media fare that sociologists have been boring us with dutifully and exhaustingly but that too few artists and literary men have thought to consider. These hidden dimensions of the human psyche have been revealingly discussed for a number of years now in other contexts, however, by such students of human behavior and conventions as Edward Hall, Konrad Lorenz, Jurgen Ruesch, Ernest Gombrich, and Gyorgy Kepes. Again, Malcolm de Chazal's epical grammar of our faces, bodies, and gestures, and his ultrasonic insights into our sensual destinies, point out the grounds for believing so much of what we glimpse fleetingly in our electronic mirrors:

We can see two objects at the same time but not two faces at the same time, because the human face is a whole, whereas any and every object is never more than a particle of some entirety. Only the human face can milk our glance dry. . . .

Any object's opening is its eye. The sphere, being smooth all over —all back and no front like God-Himself, whose eye we never see— is pure narcissism, all the parts of its body drawn up out of sight fronting its inward stare. . . .

The mouth repeats all the eyes' messages reduced in form and at a lower rate of speed: lips and eyes speak intelligently enough without saying a word. But to read the mouth's meaning one's eye must, as it were, fix its telescopic sights inside its microscopic lenses, must refine

56

its perspicuity to a hypermetropic probe for the infinitesimal, poised on the threshold of an invisible world. . . .

The face achieves perfect unity only at arms' length, the minimum distance for the white of the eyes, the iris, and the pupil to coalesce into one. Otherwise the face remains divided, and the expression is seen only in sections. The observer's eye needs a good deal of impressionistic talent to make anything of another's facial expression. . . .

The mouth is the starting point of laughter, with the eye its destination. Long after the mouth is exhausted, the eye continues to laugh. . . .

The imbecile writes his look in space with painstaking penmanship so that everyone may understand what his face intended. An intelligent man's look is finely inscribed right in his own eye while it shapes vaguely symbolic linguistic characters in space as though to keep his intention to himself. . . .

Emotion washes over the cheeks in waves, pulsates on the forehead, spouts in jets on the lips, and curls round itself in the eyes. . . .

Our eyes can never get divorced because their look is one and indivisible. On the other hand, nothing is easier than to have our lips going each its own way: one bristling with irony, the other simple and submissive, one gay, the other sad, one baleful the other placating, one beckoning the other rebuffing. The lips are the most perfect jewel case for the divided ego. The look of our eyes may be all of a piece, but those two lips of ours clamp themselves so closely on our wriggling selves that we can free only one inch at a time.*

* *Sens-Plastique,* pp. 70, 86, 147, 126, 6, 22, 43, 108.

nathan halper*
marshall mcluhan and joyce

My interest is primarily in Joyce. I once read a piece by Mc-
Luhan about Wyndham Lewis, but until last month I did not
look into the books that have made his recent reputation. Yet
since I could not help seeing his name in print, I knew that in
his work he often spoke of Joyce.

It was because of this that I started to read him. To have
made the impression that he has, he must be a worthy fellow.
If, as I gathered, he was a student of Joyce, he might have some
new suggestions, some stimulating thought.

I began with *The Gutenberg Galaxy*. On p. 74:

The work of James Joyce exhibits a complex clairvoyance in these
matters. Leopold Bloom, a man of many ideas and many devices, is
a free-lance ad salesman. Joyce saw the parallels, on one hand between the modern frontier of the verbal and pictorial and, on the

---

* Nathan Halper has devoted most of his literary labors to Joyce's work.
His articles on this manifold subject have appeared in such magazines as
Partisan Review, The New Republic, and The Nation, and in two anthologies of critical essays on Joyce soon to be published in England by Faber
and Faber.

other, between the Homeric world poised between the old sacral culture and the new profane or literate sensibility. Bloom, the newly detribalized Jew, is presented in modern Dublin, a slightly detribalized Irish world. Such a frontier is the modern world of the advertisement, congenial, therefore, to the transitional culture of Bloom.

As it happens, Bloom is not a free-lance salesman. It is stated several times that his job is with *The Freeman's Journal*. Also, in the next sentence, I was baffled by the three "betweens." (I am not sure I can parse it.) It is clear, however, that McLuhan is saying he sees a special significance in the particular employment.

Joyce is a careful worker. If Bloom is a salesman, this is not casual. Bloom is Ulysses, and the city of Dublin is that Mediterranean basin in which Ulysses wanders. His occupation must permit him to do so. It must permit him to "land"—that is, to pause and spend the time that is needed for his 1904 equivalent of the other's adventures. A job as salesman meets these specifications. A salesman is a man of sails. Add that, in the text, he is usually called a "canvasser." "Traveller," meaning salesman, is sometimes used in the same way.

As for what he's selling, one may think of comparable reasons why the item should be ads. Yet no matter how valid these reasons might be, it is not impossible that the choice of ads had a deeper explanation. Especially since McLuhan has presented on the bottom of this page the following quotation from the question-and-answer (Ithaca) chapter of *Ulysses*:

What were habitually his final meditations?
Of some one sole unique advertisement to cause passers to stop in wonder, a poster novelty, with all extraneous accretions excluded, reduced to its simplest and most efficient terms not excluding the span of casual vision and congruous with the velocity of modern life.

If Joyce makes it a point that Bloom's "final" thoughts are on the subject of ads, it must mean that the subject has a special significance. Though I do not know the book by heart, I had thought that I was conscious of its salient points. The many times, however, that I had read this passage, its import had failed to register. So, too, the writers who had written before this had failed to give it its value. This was the kind of insight I had looked forward to receiving. One hears it said of McLuhan, "He certainly knows his Joyce!" If this was a sample, such a comment might be justified.

Still—I had my questions. Take the earlier jobs. Bloom had served, either as clerk or salesman, with Thom, the printer, Cuffe, the Cattle Market, Drimmie, insurance, and Hely, stationer. One would think his present job is of that order. Molly wants him to leave it and, we may be sure, he is going to have another in the fairly near future. On the surface it is one of a series. What is it that allows us to put a finger on this one and say that here is the place where the writer has hidden a message?

And if we answer that there is a *mana*, a radiance, that belongs to canvassing for ads, what are we to do about M'Coy? In the story "Grace," in *Dubliners*, where M'Coy is a minor character, we find he also has had a series of jobs: among them, he was once a "canvasser" for ads for *The Irish Times* and, like Mr. Bloom, for *The Freeman's Journal*. Joyce must have a reason for allowing him this job. Yet it cannot be the one that McLuhan uses for Bloom. It is not because it is "congenial" to M'Coy's "transitional culture."

Professor Magalaner (*Time of Apprenticeship*) has persuasively suggested that M'Coy is a study for Bloom. Is it at all conceivable that Bloom's selling these ads is a vestigial remnant of a story in *Dubliners*?

Yet I could never get around the sentence I have quoted: "What were habitually his final meditations?" The subject of such thoughts has to be of a supreme importance.

I went back to the citation. This time, however, I looked at the entire section. These thoughts of Mr. Bloom are by no means "final." They are his last only in a particular context.

He has narrowed his earlier ambitions: all that he wants is a "2 storey establishment." Then they start to expand. Owning a house may lead to being justice of the peace, a member of parliament. Then he contracts. Even this little house will require more than he has. Again—he expands. He thinks of ways to earn the money he needs. Then (p. 704):

For what reason did he meditate on schemes so difficult of realization?

It was one of his axioms that similar meditations or the automatic relation of a narrative concerning himself or tranquil recollection of the past when practised habitually before retiring for the night alleviated fatigue and produced as a result sound repose and renovated vitality.

It is in this context that, a half-page later, he thinks of the "advertisement." His "poster" is another of his clever-foolish ideas. (*E.g.*, the scheme of goat-vans to deliver early-morning milk.) It is only in regard to this "habitual" session that the ad is his "final" thought. When this topic is finished, he goes on to others. Take the great series of 'reflections" he has about Blazes Boylan.

These are described as "reflections." The earlier thoughts are called "meditations." In that sense only, Bloom's thoughts about a poster are his "final meditations." If this is what McLuhan means, that phrase has lost its magic. It is no longer a key to the meaning of *Ulysses* or the intentions of its writer.

What has happened is this. McLuhan is an advocate. And, as advocates do, has been pushing his case for a little more than it's worth. He is like a lawyer who—even if his case is sound—does not trust the jury's intelligence: so he dishes out a bit of eyewash in order to impress the yokels.

II   This is not heinous. If he is over-zealous, it does not have to blind us to a possible merit in his statement.

In the passage I have cited in the beginning of this essay, he tells us, in effect, that the period exemplified by Bloomsday, 1904, is a period of great transition. So is the Homeric. In terms of these changes, Bloom is also "transitional." The world of advertising is similarly a "frontier." The "modern" world: the Homeric: Bloom and advertising. If we look at them together, they make a meaningful cluster.

And yet—what does McLuhan mean by "modern"? It appears five times on the page I am discussing. And every one of these times it has a different meaning. In a quotation taken from G. S. Brett, "*very* modern" (my italics), seems to go back to the sixteenth century. In the quotation from *Ulysses,* the phrase "modern life" (it is used by Bloom) means a brief period *circa* 1904. When he (McLuhan himself) puts Bloom in "modern Dublin," the word "modern" shares both of these meanings. It is used in antithesis to the ancient or "Homeric." On another level, it is obviously 1904. We might also consider that McLuhan is writing in the 1960s. This is when we read him. When he uses "modern," the reader, willy-nilly, sees it in the sense of "present." Dublin, 1904, may be nearer to the town of a hundred years earlier than to the Dublin of today. But when he calls it "modern," it moves into the sixties.

When McLuhan, in the same paragraph, speaks of a "modern world of advertising," he is presumably speaking of new techniques and media. And in this context Dublin, 1904, is very little different from the Dublin of the nineteenth or even the eighteenth century. Bloom's posters, his copy, the one-column, one- or two-inch ads, even the forward-looking ad on which he "meditates," are closer to that past. Yet when McLuhan puts Bloom into one sentence with "the modern world of advertising," Bloomsday leaves its sluggish neighborhood and somehow finds a place beside the latest method in promoting sales.

And when McLuhan speaks of the "modern frontier" of verbal and pictorial, it is not clear whether "verbal" and "pictorial" are intended as synonyms or antonyms. But either way, the locus of this frontier is rather uncertain.

By the time we come to the bottom of the page, we have the impression that things are related to each other and to Bloom. A part of their connection is this word "modern"; it runs through the passage like a thread. Having looked at this word —is there such a relationship? Or is this impression due to an imprecision of meaning?

The word "Homeric" also brings its problems.

"The Homeric world [was] poised between the old sacral culture and the new profane or literate sensibility." As McLuhan uses it, "sacral" is non-literate; "profane," literate. "Sacral" is auditory; "profane" is visual. It is not clear, however, to what McLuhan is referring when he speaks of a "Homeric" world. The one in which these great deeds supposedly occurred was not the same as that—a number of centuries later—in which the songs about them began to take their definitive form. To which world is he alluding? Or does he mean the one that is *internal* to the two Homeric poems? Does he mean the version in the *Iliad* or the different world that we get in the *Odyssey*? (One would guess the latter; but when, early in the book, he speaks of Homer's world, all of the examples are taken from the *Iliad*.) Or—is McLuhan speaking of what is common to both?

When McLuhan writes of Bloom's "transitional culture," this is not accurate either. Bloom has a culture that's transitional, but it is not the one that McLuhan is discussing. So, too, when he tells us Bloom is "newly detribalized" in a "slightly detribalized" environment. By themselves the words make sense. But as McLuhan uses them the meaning and relevance are minimal.

III   McLuhan knows that his prose does not move in a traditional A-B-C-D progression. In a prelude to his Prologue, he turns this into a virtue:

The Gutenberg Galaxy develops a mosaic or field approach to its problems. Such a mosaic image of numerous data and quotations in evidence offers the only practical means of revealing causal operations in history.

This may well be true. Nonetheless, all mosaics are not equal. There must be some standard as to what constitutes a good one. A writer who uses them is not always "revealing causal operations in history." He who makes a mosaic has to find the proper tesserae. If, after doing this, he puts them into a significant relationship, the configuration may say what a traditional method will not.

Has McLuhan done this? It is difficult to tell. He has not been willing to let his tesserae speak for themselves. He hovers over them—pointing, nudging, interpreting, explaining. (How accurate they are! How well they dovetail!) A sort of salesman —a lot more skillful than Bloom is.

63

The page I have been discussing is the beginning of a little chapter that is headed by, "Only a fraction of the history of literacy has been typographic."

In the text McLuhan goes on to a quotation by G. S. Brett that begins, "The idea that knowledge is essentially book learning seems to be a very modern view." Like the chapter heading, these words appear to be reasonable: not at all tendentious. After this unimpeachable beginning McLuhan says that "Brett here specifies the natural dichotomy which the book brings into any society, in addition to the split within the individual of that society." Normally, on reading this, we might wonder whether the book had that result. After reflection we might decide one way or the other. (Or we might leave it open.) But in this case we do not bother to wonder. Brett has sounded like a responsible gentleman. If he "specifies"—which he doesn't: he does not even suggest—we are ready to accept it.

This helps the credibility of the statement it leads into: "The work of James Joyce exhibits a complex clairvoyance in these matters."

The word "clairvoyance" implies that the "matters" are there to see. In addition, the word has a *cachet*. It is more subtle, sensitive, than a prosaic look. The word "complex" helps to make it even more profound. It is more of a challenge. The "frontiers" are there to see. If we want to keep our self-respect, we had better see them.

He goes on to tell us that "Joyce saw the parallels." The reader is presented with another *fait accompli*. If he "saw" them, they exist. And, what is more, if there is a parallel, each part of the parallel exists. And if Joyce "saw" them—who are we to argue with Joyce?

"Such a frontier is . . . congenial, therefore, to the transitional culture of Bloom." There is no *therefore*. It is not "congenial." But it sets up an illusion of logical proof. McLuhan is getting the benefits without doing anything to earn them.

And, *nota bene*, the words (like "therefore" or "specified") do have an aura of precision. Take a word like "poised." The shift, sacral to profane, audile to visual, was a long and gradual process. No matter how he defines it or how late he places it, the Homeric world was not near the end of this period. There were centuries to go. Yet when McLuhan tells us it was "poised" between the sacral and profane, we think of it on a tightrope: taut, yet graceful, like a spring: or a ballet dancer in a moment's equilibrium, before she takes a step, with decision and finality, into a new area.

When he speaks of a "frontier," the situation is similar. He is alluding to a process that is not finished and, as we have seen, goes back—how far?—maybe to Leopold Bloom. It is a wide, elastic area. Yet the word "frontier" has a rigorous sound. You may see it on a map. (Here is an unequivocal line. On one side of it, France; on the other, Germany.)

When he uses "modern" and "Homeric," they are ill-defined and poorly identified words. But McLuhan says they are "parallel." We get the feeling of a mathematical relationship.

IV   It is not unusual for a writer to dress up a statement. A reader does not believe the moon is queen of the night. Dawn has no rosy fingers, nor does Stephen have a smithy in his soul. Yet—we know what is meant. It gives a bit of pleasure: and no great damage has been done. Here, by contrast, the rhetoric is crucial. The pretense of parade-ground precision acts as a façade for vagueness. As my grandmother used to say, the right scarf makes the dress.

I tend to feel a square when I ask him to dot his *i*s. I would like to make it clear that I think there are occasions when tolerance has a place. Thus, if you say, "Sokrateez is a man. All men is mortal. Therefore, you ass, Socrates am mortal," the unmannerly expression, spelling, and mistakes in grammar do not really affect the validity of the conclusion.

We tend to throw our words in the general direction of the target. As a rule, there is a margin of error. If they fall within it, we do not require that the words should be exact. But, when McLuhan talks, the situation is different. The further he gets from the target, the better it is for himself. If we fail to watch him, he will stake out for himself the entire area between the target and his words.

V   I have been objecting to the way McLuhan has been presenting his case. He has underproved and overstated it. Now, at this point, I want to change my emphasis. It is not a question of McLuhan spoiling his case. It is not likely that there ever was a case at all.

To McLuhan, the Homeric world is a time of shift away from audile values. The visual "literate" values began to have a priority. (With a deep effect on human sensibility.) But did Joyce have this particular turn of mind? Where in his work, his letters, conversation with friends, is there another instance of such a generalization?

Well, there is a first time. But if we insist that he did it this time—what induced him to think of it? How did Joyce manage to see this transition in the *Odyssey*? Where did he get his data? To take one example, there is no mention of writing in the *Odyssey*.

To McLuhan, the time of Bloom is also a decisive period. The visual world was moving into that equilibrium, auditory-*cum*-visual, which is a theme of *The Gutenberg Galaxy*. Now, the first broadcasting service was offered in 1920. Joyce was writing in 1914. He was writing of a day that happened ten years earlier. Is there any reason to think that he saw this day as part of a revolution that was going to happen a number of decades later? (One that is still in the process of happening.) If we answer, "Oh, an artist is prophetic," is there reason to think that he was able to anticipate what a prophet like McLuhan is still anticipating now?

If he was that intuitive, Joyce was able to sense many of the other changes that were implicit or already beginning in the first part of the century. Why should he decide on this one as the subject of his parallel?

McLuhan has a thesis. His topic is communications. In the course of his argument he alludes to many developments, in art as well as technology. He could use any one as a focusing-point for the others. (I am sure that other books have done so.) Yet McLuhan is committed. So that, understandably, he can see them only as secondary to that change—*his* change—the auditory-visual bit of which he is the historian, prophet, and attendant laureate.

Joyce has a choice of options. He is able to weigh the plus-and-minuses and, on the basis of these, he is free to decide what is best for his purpose.

He sought "to recreate life out of life." He saw himself as "a priest of eternal imagination, transmuting the daily bread of experience into the radiant body of everlasting life." Joyce looked for the moment of "epiphany" where a "vulgarity of speech or of gesture" would suddenly show its *"quidditas."* ("Its soul, its whatness" would leap "to us from the vestments of its appearance.")

We are asked to assume that Joyce was able to equate this with an observation of a technological change. We are further asked to agree that he went back three millennia and discovered a comparable change. He saw that the implications of these changes were similar. After which he used the similarity as an important structural girder of a novel about Everyman.

VI   Let us say, "This is what he wanted. This is how Joyce went about the shaping of *Ulysses.*" You would think that having a choice of tools, the craftsman would examine them. The one he took was far from the sharpest.

With his poster, his sorry little ads, Bloom is an adman by courtesy only. He is not suited to be an expressive symbol of this particular "frontier." Let us play we are Joyce and work ourselves into his problems.

Transportation is better. We might notice that Bloom, a "traveller," a "canvasser," is already in that frame of reference. On p. 203, Joyce uses the comparison, "rare as a motor-car is now." Cars were less unusual by the time he was writing. It was also easy to foretell the coming proliferation of these and other vehicles. And if he stopped to think, it would be easy to infer that there would be a proliferation of effects. Bloom could not have a glamorous position. But as part of his line, he might have a minor item that his company is testing:

something that is related to its usual goods—maybe the "motor jerkin" or the "motorgoggles" that Dr. Mulligan wears on p. 483.

(The Homeric field is difficult. But there is nothing in the *Odyssey* apropos of writing. In the area of transportation— even Odysseus' raft is a little more tangible.)

VII   It is more than a matter of relative preference. Joyce may have thought of reasons why, in spite of the above, communications was better for his purpose. Even so—he could not use it in the way McLuhan has suggested.

Mr. Bloom is Everyman. He is modeled on Odysseus (another Everyman). There are other prototypes; but since Odysseus-Ulysses is best for Joyce's purposes, he is the one on whom he centers. The book is called *Ulysses* because, in some ways, it is modeled on the *Odyssey*. There have been many writers who, through the ages, wrote about some aspect of this hero. (Look at *The Ulysses Theme,* the superb book by W. B. Stanford.) Joyce uses some of the others. But because it is best known, most detailed, and most comprehensive, he concentrates on the *Odyssey*.

When he goes to the *Odyssey,* it is in order to select useful incidents and details that will help him bring out the universality of his own *Ulysses.* If he thinks of the Homeric, it is not in the sense of some actual historic period. He did not need to speculate about the kind of world that produced the poet of the *Odyssey.* He dealt only with the world this poet had produced.

If Bloom is Everyman, it is in respect to those of his aspects which are universal. This applies to Ulysses. Each—in his own fashion—is a son, a father, a husband, a lover. Each has troubles and anxieties. Each has certain abilities and, making use of these, he tries to hold on to himself and the things that he considers his.

Bloom is a type of Ulysses only because of the aspects that they share with men in every time and place. The statement that Bloom is Ulysses is a paradigm for an infinite number of similar equations. Everyman—Bloom, Ulysses—lives in a society that, in its essentials, is like every other. It will have some aspect that it does not share with others. The writer may feel this to be a part of the picture. He may therefore keep it in his work, as a bit of local color, as a topical allusion. But he will not use it to structure the book into which he puts it. This function is reserved for something universal.

To McLuhan, these periods—Bloom-Modern and Homeric —are two decisive turning points. He emphasizes an aspect that sets them apart from all others.

Because of this uniqueness, Joyce may not use them as parallels. If he actually saw these audile-visual "transitions," he might put them in his book. But he could not use them as principles. *Q.E.D.* They are not universal.

VIII   Well, if Homer nods, so may his successor. Let us reverse our attitude. "He was a poor workman. Joyce did not realize that his procedure was inept."

But if this is so, how is a reader to see it? Joyce ignored his own plan. He ignored common sense. He went against his own nature. He went against his own theories of art. There is no hint. Joyce said nothing to Stuart Gilbert. He told nothing to Budgen.

If McLuhan sees what nobody has seen before him—more power to McLuhan. Yet somebody may come along and, with equal authority, offer a new mosaic. How are we to choose between them?

McLuhan has been using—is it a coincidence?—the method of presentation we expect to see in an ad. A product may be good. It may be the best in its field. But the advertising is never in terms of the factor that gave it its preëminence.

Something to catch the interest: something to hold the attention. An irrelevant slogan. A potent, mysterious ingredient, one that no one has heard of. A statistic, a quotation, or a testimonial—all of which are irrelevant. There is no prejudice, as such, against truth or precision. Or the article's having quality. It is merely that—like relevance itself—these matters are irrelevant.

A statement has to have the appearance of being plausible.

If you say it fast enough—if you keep repeating it—and, if you do this with a smooth and confident air, nobody will stop to wonder if there is any merit to whatever you are saying.

IX   There is a famous avenue where this method is right. Is it right for Eccles Street?

McLuhan speaks slightingly of those who still write in the old "linear" terms. Yet, as he knows, Wyndham Lewis kept insisting that, at bottom, Joyce was a "school-master." Joyce liked to think of himself as

> Bringing to tavern and to brothel
> The mind of witty Aristotle.

As being "Steeled in the school of old Aquinas."

To some degree, one should try to be "linear" when educing or explaining what the "school-master" is saying. But McLuhan uncovers the inner meanings in Joyce by means of a mosaic. Not only this. He uses Joyce himself as a tessera—a part of a larger mosaic—which McLuhan employs to advance his own argument.

I am not sure whether he is trying to get into Joyce's orbit or if McLuhan wants to draw Joyce into his own. Maybe a little of each. His ideas are realized in Joyce. Joyce, in his turn, is a bearer of good tidings. He gives vivid examples. With McLuhan interpreting, these always bring support to what McLuhan is saying.

But, as we have seen, when McLuhan's words stop spinning, they occasionally lose their balance. He does not interpret Joyce. Joyce does not provide illustrations for McLuhan. And yet, even then, Joyce does have a purpose.

It is something like an ad. The great Irish champion is giving a written testimonial. We do not understand how he has come to do this. We do not understand what the testimonial is saying.

No matter. We're impressed.

X   What McLuhan has done on p. 74 is characteristic of what he does whenever he speaks of Joyce. In talking about this page, I have been discussing all of them. There is no need to keep making the same point. But there are a few things that, because of this book's special nature, come up when he dips into the *Wake*.

Like *Ulysses, Finnegans Wake* is a book about Everyman. It is supposed to be obscure and, indeed, it is. But its universality is clear, even clearer than this is in *Ulysses*. It's a dream and when the sleeper sees himself in terms of his dream identities, the analogies range through all of time and space. The story, such as it is, is rooted in the specific. But the sum of these analogies, H. C. Earwicker, is omnipresent and eternal.

The date of Earwicker's dream is still a matter of discussion, but it is not far from the day of Leopold Bloom. It has been suggested that, once again, the year is 1904. I tend to put it later: 1922. If so, the Dublin world would be higher on the ladder of "modern advertising." No matter who is right, since Joyce wrote it later, he should be aware of the progress. Yet, the emphasis he gives it is no more—in fact, it is less—than the attention he gives to at least a score of other activities.

And when he looks at any of these activities, it is not with the idea of finding a "frontier." Even more than in *Ulysses*, a change is only a variation on the changeless.

This book is full of change. There is a change of cycles: change within the cycle. A new day is coming. There will be the drama, melodrama, of sunrise. But, when this new day comes (new cycle, new minute), it will not be different.

It is the scheme of the book to reflect the scheme of the universe. Joyce looks at this world: at the little worlds—he himself is one of them—of which the big one is composed. What he puts into his book, in continually changing form, is the repeated statement that things are what they are.

"So hath been, love: tis tis: and will be" (p. 116). About himself, what he says is, "Such me" (p. 597).

71

XI   A sun is about to rise. Ireland is becoming a new state. Joyce is writing a new book. The dream sings, with ironic invocation, to a day that is to be. Ironic. He knows that this day, when it appears, will never be as advertised. It will wear the face of Shaun. Shem is the creative brother. Shaun is the organization, Church, State, or Academy that arises and gets the fruits of Shem's creation or discovery. Shaun is superficial, insensitive. The wheeler-dealer. Go-getter. The opportunist. He is the boy who makes it: who goes to the right parties.

To McLuhan, these apostrophes are serious. He is able to decide that the future Joyce is welcoming is the same as the one for which he himself is the cheerleader.

For that purpose, the *Wake* is better than *Ulysses*. It is hard for a reader to apprehend the book as a whole. He is happy if he is told the meaning of a part, of a sentence, a phrase, even of a single word.

A word in *Finnegans Wake* has a large number of meanings. In spite of popular belief, these meanings are precise. At the present time I do not have to prove it. McLuhan apparently knows it. At any rate, he tells us some of his rules for arriving at precision.

On p. 302 of *Understanding Media:*

Joyce puts these matters not so much in cryptic as in dramatic and mimetic form. The reader has only to take any of his phrases . . . and mime it until it yields the intelligible.

This is a good idea. But the trouble is that he does not do the phrase in the context of a larger unit—beginning with its sentence and ending with the book itself. Also, he knows the precise meaning that he wants. He "mimes" until he reaches it. (No wonder that McLuhan adds, "Not a long or tedious process. . . .")

Another of his rules is that it should be read aloud. (The sound of a word is more important than its look.) Another good idea. But when he reads a word, he is once again aware of what he wants it to give him. He uses a great latitude in the way he chooses to pronounce it.

Then—McLuhan is helped by his carelessness in reading Joyce.

XII   On p. 75, he begins his comments by quoting from *The Books of the Wake* by J. S. Atherton.

On p. 20 of *Finnegans Wake* there is an allusion to Gutenberg. Atherton offers a few lines, then makes a few observations about their possible meaning. As usual, what he says is (a rare combination) both sensible and scholarly. So far so good. Then, McLuhan begins to make his own additions: to reinterpret what Atherton has said.

With the usual results.

I would not bother to mention this; but there is an oddity in McLuhan's use of Atherton. The latter is reliable. But, like everyone else, he is sometimes tired when transcribing a citation on a file card. In these few lines there are five misreadings. Atherton is an authority: you have to copy him exactly. So McLuhan does this—including five mistakes.

None of these is serious. (There is only one of them he "mimes." And in this case—though it would have taken longer —the right form of the word would have given him the same result. Same erroneous result.) But it establishes a pattern.

A bit later on this page, he, McLuhan himself, quotes a few lines from Joyce, making two misreadings. These are not serious either. Then, near the bottom of the page, he comes up with a nice one.

The concluding passage is as follows:

As his title indicates, he saw that the wake of human progress can disappear again into the night of sacral or auditory man. The Finn cycle of tribal institutions can return in the electric age, but if again, then let's make it a wake or awake or both.

He thinks enough of this to repeat it on p. 120 of *The Medium Is the Massage*. The rest of the passage is even more important:

Joyce could see no advantage in our remaining locked up in each cultural cycle as in a trance or dream. He discovered the means of living simultaneously in all cultural modes while quite conscious. The means he cites for such self-awareness and correction of cultural

73

bias is his "collideorscope." This term indicates the interplay in colloidal mixture of all components of human technology as they extend our senses and shift their ratios in the social kaleidoscope of cultural clash: "deor," savage, the oral or sacral; "scope" the visual or profane and civilized.

But, as it happens, the word is not "collideorscope." The last syllable is *scape*. The word is "collideorscape." The meaning he finds in *scope,* the meaning he deems significant, is based on a faulty reading, a syllable that is not there. By the same token, he misses the significance of what is there.

In that passage (p. 143), Joyce presents the members of the dreamer's household. They—and what they stand for—are the component particles of life, of the dream, of *Finnegans Wake* itself. They form infinitely changing patterns; but these patterns are based on the finite number of these particles. It *is* a kaleidoscope. But, in this process, there is an element of chance. As he says elsewhere, we "come . . . from atoms and ifs." And in that sense the particles "collide" or "scape."

In addition, McLuhan has transgressed against his own rule of procedure. Whether it is collideorscope or -scape, the first *e* is silent. If you look at the word, the four letters are in sequence. But, if you *hear* it, there is no such sound as "deor." Incidentally, I admit that I lack the wit to see why "deor" has the meaning McLuhan gives it: savage, oral, sacral.

There is also a pun on "colloidal." (This is not Joyce's: it belongs to McLuhan.) The word "colloidal," both by etymology and meaning, is related to such things as gelatin and glue. How, then, is a "colloidal mixture" the "means" for "self-awareness and correction of cultural bias"?

Notice, too, that "collide" has its accent on the second syllable. "Colloid" has it on the first. If, as McLuhan counsels, we give these words an audile rather than a visual inspection, there is no resemblance—no basis for a pun.

XIII   I will take only two more examples. They are not necessarily his most outrageous. I do so because McLuhan likes them enough to repeat them.

On p. 150 of *Understanding Media* he informs us that "For

Joyce, throughout *Finnegans Wake,* television is 'The Charge of the Light Brigade.' " In spite of his quotation-marks, the specific phrase "Charge of the Light Brigade" never does appear in the *Wake.* On p. 474, there is a "light brigade." It is apropos of Shaun. But there is no Charge: no reference to TV. On p. 159 there is a "night brigade." It is apropos of Shem. Shaun wants him "to go and live . . . in charge of the night brigade." On p. 349 we read of "the charge of a light barricade." That is the only time that we find a context of TV. This is what McLuhan means when he tells us that "For Joyce, throughout *Finnegans Wake,* television is 'The Charge. . . .' "

On p. 285 of *Understanding Media,* McLuhan, once again, uses the phrase "throughout *Finnegans Wake.*" "The printed word and its power to create what James Joyce throughout *Finnegans Wake* designates as 'the ABCEDminded.' "

The word used by Joyce is "abcedminded." It is used once— once only—in the *Wake.* And, for that matter, Joyce does not use it in the way that McLuhan suggests.

On p. 313 of *Understanding Media,* he returns to the Light Brigade. "With TV, the viewer is the screen. He is bombarded with light impulses that James Joyce called the 'Charge of the Light Brigade' that imbues his 'soulskin with sobconscious inklings.' " This phrase about the "inklings" appears on p. 377 of the *Wake.* The scene with the television set ended twenty pages earlier. The phrase about the "inklings" is misquoted by McLuhan.

XIV   The first commercial TV program was presented by the BBC late in 1936. At this time, too, Joyce began to work on the sequence, pp. 338-355, where Shaun and Shem, here called Taff and Butt, do a TV-playlet. This was published in *Transition* in the spring of 1938. It is not likely that, in this interval, Joyce learned enough about the medium to make the sort of meaningful remark that McLuhan is able to make in the 1960s. (Something like, "Television is 'The Charge of the Light Brigade.' ")

As for Mr. Earwicker—I do not know if they had reception in Dublin. And if they did, would there have been a set in a lower-middle-class pub like the one that he had in Chapelizod? (I may be wrong, but I do not remember having seen one in such a pub more than twenty years later.) What is the reason for having a set in his dream?

On the simplest level, *Finnegans Wake* is universal. The set is a part of the paraphernalia of the world. It is also universal in that it shows the patterns of all that happens—and could possibly happen—in the world. No matter where you look, no matter where you listen: in gossip, in reminiscence, a letter, lecture, sermon, in testimony in court, in children's games or sport, in homework, an interview, a guided tour in a museum, a seance, an inquest, a riddle, song, quiz program, a pantomime. Equally with these—there is a TV-playlet!

Joyce begins with personal material. His father had in his repertoire a scatological story of how, in the Crimean War, Buckley shot a Russian general. Against a background of Sevastopol, Balaclava, the Charge of the Light Brigade, this occurs in the playlet.

In 1951, in *Partisan Review,* I showed that this story, as used in *Finnegans Wake,* is a retelling of the Oedipal killing of the Father. Young Buckley is the Son. The Crimean War is the archetypal Crime.

All through *Finnegans Wake* (I use the phrase advisedly) the coming of the sun implies that of the Son. The *Light* Brigade is a part of the same pun.

Now, television allows the viewing of battle scenes. The word itself means "seeing from afar." The skit looks back to the Crimean War. Back to the Primal Crime. The killing of the Father—the breach of Authority—is the dreamer's image of guilt. He looks at his Sin. At the same time, he looks into the future. To a time, perhaps, when he may be having such a set in his pub. What is more important, he looks forward—in fear. The dream is that of the Father who fears the Oedipal Son.

In the 1920s people knew of TV. Once commercial radio started, it was anticipated that TV would be the next development. There was an article about it in the 1926 *Britannica.* "Television" was used by Joyce in September, 1927. (It was in *Transition, 6;* p. 150 of *Finnegans Wake.*) Here is how the writer continued. "This nightlife instrument needs still some . . . betterment."

He also referred to Buckley. Joyce considered using this theme before he even began the actual writing of his book. He referred to Crimea and Balaclava. Also, to the Light Brigade (p. 474, we have noted the citation). It appeared in *Transition*, February, 1929. Prof. David Hayman, who has studied the manuscripts, tells us that this phrase was written in 1924.

Joyce was marking time. He used 11 as a number of renewal. (The series of digits is finished. A new series begins.) He reserved the eleventh chapter to the story of Buckley. He waited till it was definite what form video would take. Late in 1936 a program finally was shown. Joyce put Taff and Butt upon the screen.

They are component parts of Buckley. Taff is outer brawn. He is sterile Shaun. Butt is inner drive. He is creative Shem. Before they change the cycle, they must first unite. Ere they kill the Father—they must form the Son.

On p. 349, they do this. Butt and Taff interpenetrate, becoming *Tuff* and *Batt*.

The phrase "light brigade" is associated with Shaun. Its opposite, "night brigade," is associated with Shem. When they come together, the phrase is related to both. It is here that we have "the charge of the light barricade." (A barricade being a traditional symbol of revolt.)

Their union lasts a moment. It is like a moment of conception. After this, they uncouple. But the seed is planted. On p. 353, the old general is killed. We see—we hear—"abnihilisation of the etym."

The "etym" is the Adam. The old Adam goes—*à nihil:* into nothing. A new Adam comes—*ab nihil:* out of nothing. The "etym" is the atom. And—in addition—the "etym" is the *etym*. The Greek word for meaning.

This refers to Joyce. He is exploding meaning. He is recreating meaning. In other words—*other words*—he is writing *Finnegans Wake*.

XV   If we read an account of what happened at Balaclava, we learn that, beside the Light, there was also a Heavy Brigade. The Charge of this Brigade was in every way the finer. It had won the battle when the Light Brigade came charging in a showy meaningless attack. As the observer said, *"C'est magnifique, mais ce n'est pas la guerre!"* The Light Brigade undid all the other had accomplished.

Of course, the Light Brigade is what the public knows. It gets the attention of a Tennyson or McLuhan. (Since it fits his theme, Joyce has a number of allusions to the Charge of the Heavy Brigade. To reflect what happens in the world, the allusions are concealed.)

In television, too, what we see is the superficial. What is new, when it appears, always wears the face of Shaun—The creative is undone.

If this is what McLuhan means when he tells us that TV is the *Charge of the Light Brigade*—there are those who will agree with him.

XVI   As a rule, though McLuhan wanders, we can see the port he starts from. (Bloom *is* an ad man. The Light Brigade *is* mentioned in the story of the Russian general.) There are times, however, when even this is difficult.

On p. 193 of *Understanding Media,* he has this comment:

Joyce knew more about the effects of photography on our senses, our language, and our thought processes than anybody else. His verdict on the "automatic writing" that is photography was the *abnihilisation of the etym.*

How is McLuhan able to relate this phrase to photography?

I have looked at not only the paragraph and page. I have been through the playlet. I may be wrong, but I notice only a single reference to photography. This is *fourteen* pages before the *"abnihilisation of the etym."* On p. 339 it is Taff (Shaun) who distorts the observer's statement.

"Say mangraphique, may say nay por daguerre."

XVII   After many delays, here is my last example. On p. 35 of *Understanding Media* we find this by McLuhan:

. . . the Western world is going Eastern, even as the East goes Western. Joyce encoded this reciprocal reverse in the cryptic phrase:

The West shall shake the East awake
while ye have the night for morn.

On p. 143 of *The Medium Is the Massage* McLuhan is a bit more accurate.

The west shall shake the east awake . . .
while ye have the night for morn . . .

This is repeated on p. 145. McLuhan has removed the capitals from East and West. But, to compensate, he has added a quotation from Lao-tse plus the statement that "Electric circuitry is Orientalizing the West."

Now, in *Finnegans Wake,* this is not a couplet. It is set as prose. There are two consecutive sentences and McLuhan has deleted the first word of the second. The text—p. 473—is as follows: "The west shall shake the east awake. Walk while ye have the night for morn. . . ."

The first sentence is impersonal, declarative. The second sentence is imperative. It is directed to Shaun. Earlier in the chapter Shaun has made his sanctimonious, prurient, and worldly sermon, one of the best-known sections of the book. At this point, he is addressed with a contemptuous irony.

The "reciprocal reverse" is one that Joyce often uses in the *Wake.* It has nothing to do with "electric circuitry." Since the movement of the sun is from east to west, the west is the future: the east is the past. Yet the east is sunrise. The west is sunset. Each is thus a symbol of both beginning and the end. Joyce is saying, as he always does, that old gives birth to new: the new revives the old.

As for Lao-tse—the page has no reference to China. There are allusions to Ireland. One of them is to De Valera. . . . The new state is pedestrian. Its face is De Valera. "All through *Finnegans Wake*"—De Valera is a Shaun.

There are also allusions to Joyce. "The west shall shake the east awake. Walk while ye have the night for morn. . . ."

After the word "morn," the text has a comma, followed by "lightbreakfastbringer." As a rule, in this book, James Joyce is a Shem. But he is writing *Work in Progress*. He is the idol of his claque. The Boy Most Likely to Succeed. When they read the chapters in *Transition*, both his admirers and detractors see only the outer surface. Who sees the latent meaning? They see the face of Shaun.

On p. 473, when Shaun is addressed, he is also Joyce. One of the phrases said to him is, "Work your progress." *Finnegans Wake* deals with the night. He has the "night for morn." The future is about to bring the east a *Wake*.

"Lightbreakfastbringer" is a reference to *Ulysses*. "Light-bringer" is Lucifer, with whom Stephen is identified. Bloom habitually brings her breakfast to Molly in bed. He is the "breakfastbringer." The combination is Bloom-plus-Dedalus. James Joyce himself.

XVIII If these imprecisions were a part of his plan, it would take McLuhan too long to work out the machinery of every paragraph and page. It is rather that the prose just flows from his fingertips. He has a general idea of the effect he wants. He glances at his material and, not looking too hard, he picks any colorful swatch that happens to strike his eye. Joyce is a favorite cupboard. He is a treasury of phrases on which McLuhan can improvise. A word is Aladdin's ring: it brings him all that he can possibly desire.

By and large, the many allusions to Joyce are not relevant to his discussion. It is a form of snob appeal. If the quotations were accurate, if interpretations were sound, it would not help McLuhan to validate his case. When they are not, it does not —essentially—disprove it.

Besides this, I cannot judge, I am not qualified to decide (or speculate) on the virtue of his theories. (Though, I must admit, what he does with Joyce has given me grounds to wonder.) As I said in the beginning, I am interested in Joyce. My concern with McLuhan is only with McLuhan as the "man who knows his Joyce"—the man who, potentially, might tell us something about Joyce.

Alas, he fails to do this. He has read his Joyce. He reads books about him. (*Books of the Wake* is a good one.) He has Joyce on his mind and, certainly, on his tongue. As the word is nowadays used, he may be called an expert. But McLuhan is not a scholar. He is not even a man who, though he is careless, sometimes has a brilliant idea. All he does is dabble. This does not give him authority. A man who is *always* singing in the shower is not necessarily a tenor at the Met.

When it comes to Joyce, McLuhan is a doodler. He does not bother to think.

michael j. arlen*
marshall mcluhan & the
technological embrace

Marshall McLuhan, who, as just about everybody ought to
know by now, is the Canadian agricultural expert and author
of "The Romance of Wheat"—No. I am mistaken. Marshall
McLuhan, who, as just about everybody ought to know by
now, is the Canadian communications whizbang and author of
a number of books about media, was on TV the other Sunday
afternoon, on one of the new "NBC Experiment in Television"
programs, and although McLuhan didn't say anything he hasn't
said before (actually, he almost never says anything he hasn't
said before, although sometimes he says it differently, and very
reassuring is this note of constancy in a world gone mad), it was
a mighty hippy, moderny, zim-zam-zap performance all the
same, complete with the full Pop ritual of flashy, splashy
lighting, electronic sound, fancy cutting, zooms, lots of stop action—in fact, the whole art director's kit of exciting-visual-
effects: go-go girls zazzing away but as if the film ran sidewise
(why do they never show go-go girls dancing straight up, the

* MICHAEL J. ARLEN *is the television critic for* The New Yorker. *The two
articles here reproduced were originally television reviews in that periodical.*

way their mothers would want them to?), and, toward the end, a cute little bit of I-can-be-as-cool-as-you-are-buddy contemporary graphics, showing an H-bomb exploding in the shape of an exclamation point as the narrator intoned, "The hydrogen bomb is history's exclamation point." (Once, I remember, McLuhan was pleased to describe a hydrogen-bomb explosion as "information," which goes to show you the sort of pressure the dictionary-revision people have to work under.) It was a snappy show, really. Interesting. But, for all its snap and flash, it was awfully reverential in tone—reverential toward McLuhan and reverential, more especially, toward the whole idea of modernism and technology. I don't know that it was supposed to work out that way. I don't know that McLuhanism is supposed to work out that way. Now and then, McLuhan will waft out to us a sentence ("There is absolutely no inevitability as long as there is a willingness to contemplate what is happening") that gives the impression, or maybe gives *him* the impression, that he is making some sort of evaluative confrontation of the onrush of technology. But a sentence like that doesn't ever appear to be connected to anything else, to any other thought—to any other sentence, even—and when you get right down to cases, it seems to me, the confrontation turns out to be largely illusory, turns out to be instead an almost bland embrace. The NBC program provided a fairly broad embrace, as these things go. "The electric age is having a profound effect on us," intoned the narrator, paraphrasing McLuhan. "We are in a period of fantastic change . . . that is coming about at fantastic speed. Your life is changing dramatically! You are numb to it!" And "The walls of your rooms are coming down. It is becoming a simple matter to wire and pick out of your homes your private, once solely personal life and record it. Bugging is the new means for gathering information." And "The family circle has widened, Mom and Dad! The world-pool of information constantly pouring in on your closely knit family is influencing them a lot more than you think." Well, o.k. But it all sounds rather too much like the revival preacher, who doesn't really tell you anything about hellfire you didn't know before but who tells it to you more forcefully, with all the right, meliorative vogue words ("fantastic change . . . fantastic speed . . . dramatically . . . numb"), and so makes you feel appropriately important and guilty in the process. In this instance, McLuhan tells us, the fire next time will be technological and lit by an electric circuit, but, having told us that, the preacher seems content to take up the collection and walk out of the church, leaving us with happy, flagellated expressions and a vague sense of having been in touch with an important truth—if we could only remember what it was.

For myself, I'm not so sure about McLuhan's truths. He has the Big Idea, which he pushes, about the effects on Western man of the alphabet, movable type, print—how this visual-mental dependence on little letters all in a row, lines of type, lines, one word right after another, has created in man a linear response to the world, has created specialization, compartmen-talization, civilization even, mass production, and sundry other evils. It's an interesting idea, all right, and there's a lot of sub-stance to it, but, in the first place, it seems plain foolish to try to rest the full breadth and weight of man's linear sense of or-der on a single factor even as large as the alphabet and print. Art, after all, imitates life, and life is surely, among other things, intrinsically geometric. Nature is geometric. Trees, tides, plants, planets don't move psychedelically, they move geometrically, and as long as nature exists in any recognizable form the paths of force and tension and, consequently, the or-der that man intuitively responds to will in the main be linear, too. In the second place, it seems worse than plain foolish to be so modernistically airy about man's sense of logic. McLuhan seems to have the idea that man's dependence on print has been constricting and unnatural and has resulted in an imbal-ance of the senses, and that, with the disappearance of print and the concomitant rise of electronic information-feeding technology, man will once again come into a fuller life of the senses. "Television . . . reintegrates the human senses, thereby making books obsolete" is one of the ways he put it that after-noon. Oh, boy, some life of the senses is my thought for the week, with Brother and Sis upstairs in the kids' communication room watching "Uncle Don's Visit to the Fulton Fish Market," which they can't smell, and Mom and Dad curled up on Acrilan grass in Dad's windowless information center holding hands and watching a twenty-four-hour weather program. In any case, just because an electronic circuit looks circular, or sounds circular, and just because the hippy teen-agers that McLuhan admires so much (by gosh, fellows, I admire them, too) go floating about absorbing sense impressions and otherwise having a fine old time doesn't seem to me much of a reason for supposing that we're going to start wanting to do without logic—intuitive, deductive, analytical, linear, call it what you will. After all, logic, brains, intellect, sustained formal thought are how we splendid, wonderful people got to be so splendid and wonderful in the first place, and when a philosopher-king like McLuhan starts saying things like "The way you react to them [television and computers] is what is important, not what is in them or on them," it's hard to forget that the first thing that boring old Gutenberg printed was the Bible and the first thing television gave us was Uncle Miltie—and, on present evidence, there doesn't seem to be any very pressing basis for tossing out the first because of the second. McLuhan is so cheery and accommodating to the hard bewilderments of technology. I don't know, maybe he worries like hell about them, but he comes on cheery and accommodating. ("There is nothing sterile about television, except in the eye of the beholder.") I guess if you live here and now, you might as well enjoy it. Still, there's an appalling inevitability to this onrush of technology, and since much of it is likely to bring secondary effects that will just as inevitably diminish the possibilities of natural human life, I don't really see that you're doing much of anything when you toss up a line like "The new electronic interdependence recreates the world in the image of a global village," or "We have begun again to structure the primordial feeling," or "Our new environment compels commitment and participation," and leave it hanging. I don't really see that you're doing much of anything except, possibly, trying to ride with the winners.

It seems a pity, because McLuhan is an original man. A lot of people, I know, are down on him these days, because he's been so much in the public eye (all those cover stories; even

Family Circle had something on him this month, in which it referred to McLuhan as "the most sought-after dinner guest of our time in New York") and because, they say, he's inconsistent, which he is, and often wrong, which he is, and unfunny, which he certainly is, and even (they say) unoriginal. The thing is, about fifteen years ago, when McLuhan—then, as now, a teacher of undergraduate English courses—began writing about print and communications and media, he didn't claim to be entirely original. Most of these notions about print and type and Western man had been written about for a number of years by a number of people (even though the editors of *Life* may not have been reading them then). What McLuhan did that *was* original was to put them together in a new way and add a sort of twist of his own that gave them relevance—and expansiveness. One got a feeling, in reading those earlier books, of rooms being opened up. But that was a while ago. These days, I get the feeling, especially watching McLuhan on something like the NBC show, which was content to present his views pretty much at face value (as, indeed, most of the mass magazines have been), that, for all his talk about how he's mainly an investigator, a prober, how he's interested in getting people to think about their environment, the principal result of what he writes and speaks—partly because of what he says, partly because of how he says it—has been to diminish discussion. When he touches something ("The technology of the railway created the myth of a green-pasture world of innocence." "Pop Art simply tells you the only art form left for you today is your own natural environment"), he seems to do it in such a way that although there's often substance or interest in his thought, the effect is somehow to close the subject off, to leave it in the end (despite the aphoristic crackle) more dead than alive. At least, it's odd that for all the talk of controversy surrounding his work, most people trying to come to grips with it, in conversation or in print, rarely ever seem to do much more than helplessly paraphrase what he's already said. On the NBC program that afternoon, he appeared sometimes in darkness, sometimes in light, sometimes with a red light flickering on his face. He appeared, disappeared. Sentences hung in the air. Print. Electronics. Technology. The alphabet. Western man. Life. Death. Pop Art. The motorcar. The Beatles. Gutenberg. Civilization. Quite some time ago, Archimedes said, "Give me a lever long enough, and a place to stand, and I will move the world." McLuhan seems to be intent on moving the world, all right, and thinks he has found the lever—"the clash between print and electric technologies." But the lever keeps bending, and it's hard to find a place to stand. At least, he hasn't found one yet, which is perhaps why he keeps skittering all over the place. Maybe, one day, he'll settle for something less.

the bodiless tackle, the second-hand thud

Jack Whitaker, the gray eagle of CBS sportscasting, jaunty as a Hudson riverboat gambler in his Balliol Old Boy's blazer, held himself gracefully upright in the empty press box of Baltimore's Memorial Stadium the other Sunday, the camera alternating fondly between Whitaker, the near-empty stands around him, and the spectacle of a dozen or so soccer players (all those shorts and knobby knees—nothing totalitarian about *that* uniform) milling about on the baseball field below, and observed that we were shortly to become witnesses to history. He may have said hostages, but I think it was witnesses. The history, in any case, referred to the approaching debut in this country of the National Professional Soccer League, a hastily assembled federation of ten teams (many of which are owned by the owners of baseball teams) and the only sports organization I know of that seems to have been put together expressly for the purpose of making a potful of money out of television—the baseball (now soccer) owners expecting to make their potful by television contracts and by having a few people come out to the parks on non-ballplaying days, and the TV people expecting to make theirs by buying rights to televise soccer games on the cheap, promoting the game into a big TV attraction, and then selling the commercial spots at a profit. Who is to knock People's Capitalism these days? The only drawbacks to this glorious plan, or plot, seem to be that there may not be an awful lot of people in this country right now who think they want to watch soccer, and that since the International Soccer Federation has refused its sanction to the CBS-sponsored league, with the result that only young unknowns or old-timers (the word usually favored is "veterans") are willing to play in it, the soccer played isn't likely to be especially brilliant. But who knows? Soccer is a good sport—in fact, as knowledgeable people are forever kind enough to remind one, it is the most popular sport in the world this side of South African Frog Rolling (perhaps that side of South African Frog Rolling) —being fast-moving, fluid, and televisable in a way that baseball, for example, isn't, and maybe eventually it will catch on here. Televisable seems to be the key word. Baseball still has a big TV audience, all right, and a good team still draws people out to the ball park, but the audience seems to be mostly a kind of holdover audience—baseball doesn't *pull* people (the way football now does), because the game just doesn't come across really well on television. Television distills baseball down to moments of action, but in baseball the heart of the game isn't so much in the isolated instances of action (the hit, the catch, the put-out) as in the number of moves that may be taking place at a given time: the runner leading off base, the pitcher in his windup; the ball hit, fielded, thrown; the flight of the ball and the flight of the runner, and the measurement of both. Much of what baseball is about is centered on this awareness of measurement, and television usually can't cover it—can't look in many directions at once, can't really see the game as well as someone in the stands can see it. The other thing that baseball is about, of course, is the feel of being out there at a ball game, and although it's easy to sound like a retread Lake Poet burbling on about bleachers and hot dogs and dust blowing in across the infield and the sharp, sweet crackle of Dolph Camilli's windbreaker, the fact is that these things are real, this appeal to the senses is real (as real, certainly, as the rhythms of the premotorized American summer that gave shape to it)— and not only is it real but it provides a substance to the game that, so to speak, fills out all the intervals of inaction, and gives the intervals meaning. Football appeals to the senses, too, but less than baseball. (The action distilled through the camera eye in a football game is a much larger natural part of the game than it is in a baseball game.) What seems to account for football's immense rise in popularity in recent years isn't so much this fact of its being an action sport (although that has a lot to do with it) as this simpler, or at least more technical, fact of the television viewer's finding the game much more intelligible on his set than from the stands; by this I mean that the key to understanding, and therefore liking, football is in the play—what goes on after the ball is snapped—and that now, with imaginative camera positions and stop-action, you can follow the moves in a way that you simply can't from Row Q on the twenty-yard line, or even the fifty-yard line.

There's no doubt, really, that television has to some degree affected just about every sport of consequence that is being played in this country. In fact, the only sports I can think of that it hasn't affected are the ones, such as yachting and bridge, that are virtually TV-proof. In a relatively short time, it has turned minor sports into major sports—golf, say, and, for heaven's sake, bowling. It's true that the present mass popularity of golf derives in good measure from the natural consequences of "the new leisure" and "disposable income"—from the whole trend toward the proletarianizing of sport. But it's just as true that this popularity was polarized and accelerated by television, with its showering of prize money into the game, its dramatization of the money glamor as well as of the actual drama (all those Arnold Palmer clutch finishes a couple of years ago), and also—you notice this especially on color TV—of the real beauty of some of the great courses, such as Pebble Beach and Augusta. In the same relatively short time, it has practically destroyed other sports, such as boxing, which doesn't seem to have recovered at all from TV's greedy insistence, in its early days, on presenting three or four big fights a week, with the predictable, and predicted, result that the fights ran out of fighters, and so new fighters were rushed up from the club level to the big time, where they had no business being (I'm reminded of an amiable left-handed welterweight from Michigan State who bumbled along for a while until one night he was more or less literally chopped to pieces by Kid Gavilan—a lousy business), and so gradually the club fights disappeared (people could watch supposedly big-league stuff on TV, so why should they go to a club fight?), and finally there was no place for boxers to develop. And TV has placed baseball, the National Pastime, in a precarious position, forcing it into an ever closer alliance with the entertainment business (Judge Hofheinz's Astrodome in Houston seems a long, long journey from Commerce, Oklahoma) and requiring the all too willing owners to constantly alter the structure of the sport by such essentially TV-pleasing gestures as the introduction of peppier, more hittable baseballs, the lengthening of schedules (from a hundred and fifty four games to a hundred and sixty-two), and the expansion of the leagues (from eight teams apiece to ten)—as if baseball, like any good sport, didn't depend on a carefully evolved, carefully balanced arrangement of internal rules, tensions, dynamics that simply can't be fiddled around with like a boxful of building blocks if the game is to not so much "stay alive" as continue to have meaning to itself. In 1911, for example, Home Run Baker set the year's record for home runs. In 1927, Ruth hit sixty, with a peppier ball. Yet the remarkable thing about Ruth's feat wasn't merely the number but the fact that in those days there were mighty few players who could just plain hit the ball so far. Nowadays, since people like to see home runs, and since, as a result, the ball has become still lighter and faster, there are mighty few shortstops so thin-wristed that they can't, and don't, hit a handful of homers each season. So, although it's true that sports should and do evolve, like anything else, it's also true that the evolution of most American sports is now being effected, for the most part, heedlessly and meretriciously from the outside—from television—and that a sport like baseball, which, whether one is bored by it or not, has such a strong, deep connection with many of the fundamental rhythms of American life, is gradually being gimmicked into becoming something quite different, a sort of neo-baseball, whose connections are largely with show business. In a way, of course, for all the increase these days in the numbers of people watching sports, for all the increase in the numbers of people supposedly engaging in sports, it's hard to see, really, how even the concept of sport is going to survive into this eerie and unphysical era of technology and technocracy. Right now, we stay at home and watch Notre Dame play Michigan State and still manage to inform the disconnected photographic image of the game (itself an image) with an animating nostalgia—a nostalgia that seems to go deeper than the more conscious "Wouldn't it be nice if life were still so simple and beautiful that one could care half a damn for Notre Dame and Rockne and the Gipper?" It's a nostalgia, probably, for a time when physical conflict between teams, players, athletes, men, meant more, because the physical quality of life meant more. In football, the brute, uncomplicated nineteenth-century flying wedge (those masses of mustached, open-countenanced Protestant boys mashing into each other) gave way to individual blocking; then came the introduction of the detached, more cerebral and technical forward pass; and now the game is so solidly given over to passing that a line-plunging runner like Jim Taylor seems almost an anachronism. Life evolves, sport evolves, each becoming more technical, drawing further away from nature, and, in the case of sport, which drew its original meaning from natural sources, the disconnection seems to be abetted by an audience that now observes sport largely through a machine that filters out the senses, that somehow makes all baseballs travel at the same speed, that silences, and so renders nearly meaningless, the thud of hockey players against the boards, and that places us finally in the position of watching, with a peculiarly modern sort of bland, detached excitement, the leaps and strains and prowess of modern athletes as if from the other side of a pane of glass. Athletes evolve, too. Babe Ruth, who, in answer to a question from a radio interviewer about the speed of Walter Johnson's fast ball, slammed his fist into his leather windbreaker, then blurted, "Jesus Christ, I bust the goddam cigars," gives way to Maury Wills, articulate, grammatical, natty (not too natty), talking smoothly in a post-game interview about his off-season business career. At any rate, where once people went, almost instinctively, to sporting events (perhaps in the same sort of way that other peoples once went to the drama) because both the facts and the sensory appeal of these conflicts corresponded to their own view of the world, now, it seems, they go to them, or watch them on TV, in part because of "excitement" but mostly, as a guess, out of memory, as if looking at a Colts-Packers game on TV, with all its stylized confrontations, with its lack of smells and touch and heat and cold, with its lack of any sense of what a forty-two-yard pass feels like to throw or catch, with its lack of any sense, really (except for the disconnected clack of shoulder pads), of bodies touching one another—as if even this distilled, unsensual experience could somehow take one back, back to a time when life was more densely centered on human bodies and on nature, and when men acted out things that were important to them, rushing at each other across open fields and meadows, rowing on rivers, and skating on frozen lakes.

Oh, yes. The soccer game between Atlanta and Baltimore. It was pretty ragged—I think that's the word—but it wasn't too bad. A large player from Trinidad called Guy St. Vil scored the only goal of the game (for Baltimore) on the only good pass. The Atlanta goalie was Sven Lindberg, presumably also new to the South.

john simon*
pilgrim of the audile-tactile

If there is anything that characterizes this rather characterless age in which we live, it is its inability to make choice. In politics, it seems impossible to choose between disarmament and an arms race, and perfectly well-meaning people find themselves embracing both. Gone are the simple-minded days when one talked peace and meant war; now one talks peace and *means* peace, yet also prepares for, and prepares, war. Socially speaking, one dares not choose anything but conformity; but publicly speaking, one cannot choose to extol anything but independent thought. Emotionally, to choose a mate becomes harder and harder, but to opt openly for noncommitment is harder still. The great advocate of the supremacy and goodness of science spends most of his time writing bad novels, and the practitioners of that purest of all arts, music, expend most of their efforts on reducing it to mathematico-physical laboratory experiments. Under the sway of nuclear physics and Freud, the

* JOHN SIMON *writes regularly on the movies for* The New Leader *and covers plays for* Commonweal. *He has just published a collection of movie reviews,* Private Screenings.

93

would-be artist paints the dance of the electrons or the hostilities of the subconscious; and the brilliant intellectual is consumed by his desperate attempts to be both a guiding light and the plainest of regular guys. We dare not choose either specialization or breadth, but dream of a magic formula combining both, and in the pursuit of this Both-in-One, our highest mathematics become an abortive poetry, and our poetry an aborted algebra.

The inability to choose is probably nowhere more evident than in the current English language, in which structural linguistics is by way of creating a new, organized "chaoticism," vastly superior in confusion to any former, merely disorganized, chaos. Before *Webster's Third New International Dictionary* arrived on the scene, it was possible only—to various degrees, to be sure—to know or not know English. Thanks to this masterpiece of noncommitment, however, it is now possible, by memorizing twenty equally endorsed pronunciations of one word, to know exactly how not to know; or, by not being able to accept twenty choices, not to know how to know. And this triumph of relativity need only be accepted absolutely to enable us presently, by making us both relativists and absolutists, to shirk even that last remaining choice.

As might be expected, the apologists of the choiceless society were hardly likely to keep us waiting for their appearance. As might further be expected, the gigantic task of defending the choice of choicelessness was not going to be undertaken by any casual casuist, but would require the emergence of men with considerable resourcefulness, erudition, and authority. Such a one is Professor McLuhan of the University of Toronto whose press has just published his new book *The Gutenberg Galaxy*, a study of the starring role typography played in the shaping of human thought and life. The thesis of the book is that man was once tribal and fully developed in all his senses, *i.e.*, in the jargon of the trade, "audile-tactile." "Touch," McLuhan suggests, "is not so much a separate sense as the very interplay of the senses." But the invention of the phonetic alphabet and, particularly, of printing, stressed man's visual-conceptual orientation and development, until everything from his politics to his art, from his science to his commerce, became lineal, sequential, organized according to a perspective and logic that were merely the hypertrophy and hegemony of the visual or conceptual. But the coming of the telegraph, films, radio, television, and other mass media, which demand the use of various senses and which reduce the world to a tribal village, creates a new revolution comparable to the typographic one but in the inverse direction. McLuhan claims that if we can understand the nature of this revolution, we can avoid being its victims. Perhaps, then, it would be more accurate to describe him not as the apologist, but as the dupe of the new technologies.

As McLuhan summarizes his book, the typographic world "is the method of the fixed or specialist point of view that insists on repetition as the criterion of truth and practicality. Today our science and method strive not toward a point of view but to discover how not to have a point of view, the method not of closure and perspective but of the open 'field' and suspended judgment. Such is now the only viable method under electronic conditions of simultaneous information movement and total human interdependence." It follows that McLuhan's hero and model should be Harold Innis who, he alleges, "was the first person to hit upon the *process* of change as implicit in the *forms* of media technology. The present book," McLuhan continues, "is a footnote of explanation to his work." Innis, we are told, "is not reporting anybody's point of view, least of all his own. He is setting up a mosaic configuration or galaxy for insight." And what sort of thing does Innis arrive at with his galactic or "field" method of no point of view? McLuhan quotes him: "The effect of the discovery of printing was evident in the savage religious wars of the 16th and 17th Centuries. Application of power to communication industries hastened the consolidation of vernaculars, the rise of nationalism, revolution, and new outbreaks of savagery in the 20th Century." (One hates to think what Mr. Innis' statements would be like if he had a point of view.) Late in the book,

McLuhan announces, "The present volume to this point might be regarded as a gloss on [this] single text of Harold Innis."

Let us consider, for the sake of our survival as readers and writers in the global village of the structuralist age, how Mr. McLuhan's book without a point of view is put together. It is, as he says himself, a footnote, but a footnote made up of footnotes. I would guess that it is about three quarters quotations, with the remaining quarter chiefly a connecting text introducing and commenting on the quotations, but also slipping in some assertions startling in their boldness and, occasionally, their irreconcilability. To turn his book "audile-tactile," he divides it into short, overlapping chapters which tend to have as little beginning and end as possible, and which may consist, for example, of quotations from Dom Jean Leclercq's *The Love of Learning and the Desire of God,* W. W. Rostow's *The Stages of Economic Growth,* Frazer's *The Golden Bough,* and the Opies' *Lore and Language of Schoolchildren* cheek by jowl. Such chapters are introduced by superscriptions in twenty-point boldface italics, and may read—or roar—as follows: *"Heidegger surfboards along on the electronic wave as triumphantly as Descartes rode the mechanical wave."* Or, yet more "audiac" (to use a term from the book): *"Pope's* Dunciad *indicts the printed book as the agent of a primitivistic and Romantic revival. Sheer visual quantity evokes the magical resonance of the tribal horde. The box office looms as a return to the echo chamber of bardic incantation."* Such configurational headlines, reminiscent of Joyce's Cave of the Winds, but meant quite seriously to reach the inner ear, are further removed from the visual and sequential by sometimes having precious little to do with the chapter itself. To make the book more of a "field," page numbers appear only on the rectos, so that one must frequently swivel one's head (a tactile phenomenon) to find out on what page one is. The book, moreover, is full of the new words of the electronic tribe: analogate, auditorially, haptic, specialisms, decentralism, etc.; as well as phrases like "civil defense against media fall-out," "Greek celature as a take-off strip for medieval manuscript culture," or "the Montaigne kodak trick of snapshotting moments," and other such felicities, meant, perhaps, to activate our olfactory sense as well.

Underneath it all McLuhan plays the history-of-ideas game, and plays it, I am afraid, none too well. Though he avers that what is bad is not print culture but only its effect on those who do not comprehend its bias, distinctions certainly become blurred when McLuhan blames "the Gutenberg galaxy" for everything from the "compartmentalizing of human potential" to the French Revolution, and speaks of "the natural victims of print" and "people reduced to things" by it. Furthermore, McLuhan does not have the encyclopedic learning with which to back up his generalizations: often we feel that a single book on a large topic holds him in thrall, and a vast historical question is supposed to be resolved by a single contemporary quotation. With medieval deference to authority, McLuhan keeps making his obeisance to this or that "major work" or "grand study"—favorite critical terms of his. One's confidence is further shaken by references to the Bavarian composer Carl Orff as a Viennese musician, or to Umberto Boccioni, whose painting was far more important, as just a sculptor. It is, then, typical for McLuhan to make a contestable generalization about Spanish culture on the basis of two books (one a collection of essays by various hands), quotations from which are used, to say the least, deviously; thus Casalduero's statement that Don Quixote and Sancho "are of the same nature with a difference in proportion" is supposed to demonstrate that print in Spain was "effecting a new ratio in the senses."

Indeed, this is McLuhan's worst failing: the wholesale reinterpretation of texts to prove his preconceived argument. He offers lengthy misreadings of *King Lear, The Dunciad,* and *Finnegans Wake,* among others; but let me cite here a few of the numerous shorter ones. Thus he quotes Dyer's well-known poem, "My Mind to me a Kingdom is;/ Such perfect joy therein I find/ That it excels all other bliss/ Which God or Nature hath assigned" as evidence of "the power of print to install the reader in a subjective universe of limitless freedom and spontaneity." Again, Shakespeare's Sonnet LX, in which

JOHN SIMON

our minutes "Like as the waves . . ./ Each changing place
with that which goes before,/ In sequent toil all forwards do
contend," is proof to McLuhan that Shakespeare was against
"lineal denudation of language" and the "mechanical repetition" inaugurated by print. If Adam Smith says that in commercial societies thinking becomes the business of a few people
who furnish the public with reason, to McLuhan this means
that "the intellectual is to tap the collective consciousness,"
which two lines later becomes "the massive unconsciousness";
forthwith Adam Smith's meaning is that the Gutenberg society
casts the intellectual "in the role of the primitive seer." Irre-
sponsibility becomes absurdity when, for example, McLuhan
quotes the octave of Sonnet LXXV from the *Amoretti* as alleged proof of a point, but omits the sestet, a palinode in
which Spenser himself refutes what went before.

Even more remarkable are Mr. McLuhan's contradictions, as
when Euclidean geometry is still so "tactile-muscular" that
later scholars criticized it for its pusillanimity, but Euclidean
space is "linear, flat, straight, uniform" and a product of that
literacy which, in turn, produced print culture. Film, which is
sometimes viewed as part of the new electronic age, at other
times becomes part of the Gutenberg galaxy: "Montaigne had
all the experiences and techniques of the impressionist film
. . . both modes . . . are direct extrapolations of typography." It will take a few decades to understand fully the impact
of TV—"today it is futile to discuss it at all"; but we learn
that Professor McLuhan is already at work on *Understanding
Media,* in which he addresses himself to this and similar matters. Such inconsistency is one form of abdication of choice;
another one is the hiding behind an alter ego like Harold
Innis.

McLuhan's conclusion is that visual orientation resulted in
the fiasco of "mechanical matching, not imaginative making
. . . in the arts and sciences, in politics and education until
our own time." But when it comes to suggestions for dealing
with the present cultural crisis, which, true apologist or dupe
that he is, he does not fully recognize ("Today we live on the
frontier between five centuries of mechanism and the new elec-

tronics, between the homogeneous and the simultaneous. It is painful but frutiful."), he offers no more help than he did in his previous book *The Mechanical Bride*. There we read, "Why not use the new commercial education as a means to enlightening the intended prey? Why not assist the public to observe consciously the drama which is intended to operate upon it unconsciously?" Like Poe's sailor, we are supposed to study the maelstrom, and so discover the way out. But that is a faulty analogy. Beyond Poe's maelstrom was safety; beyond the trends that engulf our world there is no terra firma, no other world. And it is not topography or the sequential view that does us in, but any multiplication and vulgarization of ideas: the fact that the masses demand mass production—in a way which Ruskin and Morris could not foresee, and which McLuhan's "field" view avoiding choice cannot concede—spells the end of culture, typographical or otherwise. I do not know just what about television, for example, Professor McLuhan would have us understand. How the tube works? The shoddiness of sponsors, agencies, and programs? The cloddishness of the public, which dooms attempts at improvement? How would that help us to anything but choiceless acquiescence? It seems preferable to hold on to the pitifully individualistic, non-audile-tactile values of print culture: for the betterment of life, it is not death that needs understanding, but life.

christopher ricks*
mcluhanism

"You've heard money talking? Did you get the message?" That query from Marshall McLuhan's *The Mechanical Bride* has a satisfying timbre in a month when *The New York Times* reports that the State Attorney General is holding up—and may reject—the contracts for McLuhan's $100,000 professorship at Fordham University.

The State Constitution bans aid to sectarian schools (Roman Catholic, in this case). Not that McLuhan will need to pack his bags: Fordham have said that they will find the money themselves if need be. It would be unworthy to feel that a salary of $100,000 can't be right—but all the same there is something heartening about the possibility that McLuhan (for whom laws and politics are mere shadow-boxing, with the media really packing the punch) might be pummeled by an impact which has little to do with media. Not that all of the

* CHRISTOPHER RICKS *is a Fellow of Worcester College, Oxford University, and contributes regularly as a critic to the literary reviews. He has written a book on John Milton entitled* Milton's Grand Style.

$100,000 is just for kicks—some of it is for McLuhan's side-kicks.

We now have all of McLuhan to play with. His first book, *The Mechanical Bride* (1951), is the last to be published in England, which must please the spokesman for the new electronic discontinuity against the old sequential literacy. McLuhan's books all say the same things, often verbatim, and the closer they are to anthologies the better. *The Mechanical Bride* is an anthology of words and pictures about American advertisements, newspapers, comic strips, films. It is witty and provocative, and hardly ever cogent.

Then comes *The Gutenberg Galaxy* (1962, now in paperback). McLuhan looks back to see what printing did to the whole nature of man, forcing him into an inordinate respect for the eye and for everything which is linear, sequential, regular, repeatable, and into an inordinate numbness towards all other areas of the "sensorium," especially the ear. But now the eye-intoxicated men are angry with our new age—ours is (to mimic McLuhan's ceaseless mimicry of Joyce) a *Zeit* for sore eyes. Since there are no pictures in *The Gutenberg Galaxy*, and since McLuhan is an outrageously false historian, this is a maddening book. But it has *aperçus*, and a running anthology from those historians of ideas who really did the work.

Understanding Media (1964, now in paperback) is his worst book—and the best-selling. No pictures, no anthologizing, just repetitive non-arguments about the media (from TV to the wheel and the nylon stocking) held together by the incantation: "The medium is the message." It's not what a medium overtly says that matters, it's what it does to your sensorium. He faggoted his notions as they fell, and if they rhymed and rattled, all was well.

Last, and least, *The Medium Is the Massage*, "An Inventory of Effects," about how the media work you over. It is an anthology from McLuhan, tricked out with clever (-clever?) photos and typographical showmanship. It "may shatter one's sense of what a book is for ever." When is a book not a book? When it only numbers the pages when it feels like it. Plenty of fun here, and worth the twenty minutes (though not perhaps the 42s.) It offers—and with the appropriate franticness—the gists and piths of McLuhan's "thought."

Not that the insights are as new as he makes out. McLuhan on "the impact of machines on human rhythms and social patterns": "The throbbing of the gasoline motor and the rhythm of printing presses have much to do with the everyday thoughts and feelings of ordinary people." T. S. Eliot in 1926: "Perhaps the conditions of modern life (think how large a part is now played in our sensory life by the internal-combustion engine!) have altered our perception of rhythms."

The case against McLuhan is soon going to lapse out of sheer wearied repetition, but it ought still to stand. That he has no respect for evidence or history. That he shores up his inability to argue by claiming that arguing and rationality are yesterday's bric-a-brac, and by always changing the subject. That he claims to be neutral ("stating without approval or disapproval") while continually using a vocabulary which works on behalf of the electronic culture (which is said to create organic wholeness, heightened human awareness and humble involvement) against the culture of literacy (whose literacy "victims" are schizophrenic, crude, numb, and mutilated). That he makes out that he has to contradict himself because he contains multitudes. "What if he's right?" asked the thrilled Tom Wolfe, as if McLuhan could be anything but right since by now he's committed himself to contradictory opinions on everything.

But the line of such accusations ought to stretch out to the crack of McLuhan's doom. That his style is jargon-ridden—all this talk of "heuristic probes," as if a probe could be anything but heuristic since that's what the word means. (The medium is Mr. Sludge.) That he is high-handed and offhand about what he chooses to know—a media expert who was unaware that Asa Briggs had published two important volumes of a history of the BBC.

Like a writer whom he much admires (rightly), G. K. Chesterton, all too often he doesn't master paradoxes but they master him—"crucifying truth head-downwards." He uses his religion as if it can be potently flashed like a badge behind the lapel. To the question "Why should the most important pressure exerted by a medium always be the subliminal pressure?" he has replied with a guided missal, *"Grace* is subliminal."

By now he is an Unsinkable Molly Brown. Possibly because there is no gravity in that "noosphere" which he shares with a writer whom he admires, Teilhard de Chardin. "People of literary and critical bias," complains McLuhan, "find the shrill vehemence of De Chardin as disconcerting as his uncritical enthusiasm." But it was not a literary gent, it was P. B. Medawar, who launched on Teilhard de Chardin an attack which would have been lethal if any rockets could ever reach up to the noosphere.

But if you think that there ought to be serious investigation of the media, do you want McLuhan to be sunk? On the one hand, it could be said that if it weren't for McLuhan nobody would ever have got round to these questions. In some ways *The Mechanical Bride* is very like Mrs. Leavis' *Fiction and the Reading Public,* another book which doesn't argue well and is in the end historically false, but one which looks incisively at popular culture and which did precipitate some thinking. And yet the most important point against McLuhan is precisely that his antics are enough to give media studies a bad name.

Still, even if media studies are so rich a field that they can afford even a McLuhan (and I don't mean just that $100,000), by now McLuhan's insistence on "massage" alone, his indifference to "message," is as stultifying as the old indifference to everything but message. The media, after all, are *both* the subrational or subliminal massage, *and* their contents or programming. One parlor game makes the point: you phone McLuhan "collect," and when he answers the phone you say, "This is the message" and replace the receiver.

A newspaper is not *only* what McLuhan so effectively shows us that it is (a montage which replaces continuity by simultaneity, and so presents the globe in juxtaposition, "cramped into a planisphere"), but also actual news items, which say some things and not others. McLuhan's isolation of the medium (the front page itself, not the news items) may once have been a reasonable strategy. But he is now trapped in his strategy, so that he has practically nothing to say about the really difficult question: the *interplay* between what a medium does and what it says. McLuhan now denies that any medium says anything at all, which certainly makes his job easier, but only at the expense of replacing the old evasiveness with a new one. *The Mechanical Bride* is a better book than *Understanding Media* exactly because it does try to talk about interplay. So McLuhan is obliged to disown it: "a book that was completely negated by TV."

The other evasion is about inevitability. Can we do anything about our environments and about the massage which the media exert on us? The cover of *The Medium Is the Massage* proclaims: "There is absolutely no inevitability as long as there is a willingness to contemplate what is happening." The trouble is that he never explains what could be done. Or rather, he can't make up his mind whether *understanding* media makes much difference.

But most of the time he talks as if contemplation, understanding, were enough. Again and again he reverts to Poe's sailor in "The Descent into the Maelstrom" who "staved off disaster by understanding the action of the whirlpool." But Poe's sailor had to act as well as understand. McLuhan prefers to gloss over this, as if understanding were enough—otherwise he'd be back with "mere politics." Elsewhere he does a Joycean pun on that whirlpool and calls it the "worldpool." In that case what is the difference between Poe's sailor and someone who cries "Stop the worldpool, I want to get off"?

If the media batter the sensorium directly, like radiation, what difference does consciousness make? McLuhan argues two different ways, and he never builds a road across. (1) The media affect every part of you whether you like it or not; there is no taking them or leaving them alone; they don't give a damn for the controls of rationality. (2) "Its baneful effects are at present entirely dependent on its being ignored."

Can we escape or not? Is the Mechanical Bride as transfixing as the Iron Maiden? McLuhan makes a lot of play with Perseus' mirror ("the mirror of conscious reflection") as the only protection against Medusa—but Perseus' mirror wouldn't have been very much use if he'd forgotten to bring along his sword.

neil compton*
the paradox
of marshall mcluhan

I have been following the career of Marshall McLuhan for
some years, and have never found him at a loss for an explanation of any phenomenon about which he is asked. But even he
must sometimes be nonplussed by the extraordinary thrust,
which, after years in the decent obscurity of a solid academic
reputation, has carried him to heights of fame exceeded only
by such semi-divinities as the Beatles or the late Marilyn Monroe. Last spring, it was almost impossible for any inhabitant of
North America to escape from the man or his image: his photograph appeared on the cover of both a major American news-
magazine and Canada's largest weekend supplement; cartoon-
ists in *The New Yorker* and *Saturday Review* joked about the
McLuhan craze (McLuhanacy?); NBC-TV presented an hour-
long documentary on his work, and the CBS interviewed him

*NEIL COMPTON *is at present a Professor of English and Department
Chairman at Sir George Williams University in Montreal. He writes frequently on the subject of popular culture as well as on more serious academic subjects.*

106

at length on its top-rated Sunday night public affairs show. Meanwhile, *The Medium Is the Massage* was piled high in every paperback bookshop and reviewed in all the major media. After this sort of ubiquity even the sweet felicity of a jet-age academic chair, the $100,000 Albert Schweitzer Professorship in the Humanities at Fordham, must have seemed anticlimactic.

McLuhan owes his celebrity, of course, not to his formal scholarship and literary criticism, but to the apocalyptic pronouncements that have established him as "the first pop philosopher" (*The New Yorker*) and "the prophet of the New Life Out There, the suburbs, housing developments, Astrodomes, domed-over shopping centres, freeways, TV families, the whole world of the new technologies that stretch out to the West beyond the old cities of the East" (Tom Wolfe). Fame and adulation of this proportion are granted only to someone who tells people something they already want to hear. McLuhan would certainly deny any such intention and rightly insist that his roles as scholar and prophet are indivisible: both arise from a lifelong concern for the quality of life and art in our time and a long and passionate dedication to one or two governing ideas. Nevertheless, he is obviously winning disciples at a rate and on a scale that cannot be explained by mere rational persuasion.

The paradox is that this darling of marketing associations and the switched-on set idealizes the twelfth century, dislikes almost everything about the twentieth century to date (except its art), and has never really wavered in his loyalty to one of the most orthodox and conservative (not to say reactionary) of intellectual traditions. In his earliest published essay,* he praised G. K. Chesterton for seeking "to re-establish agriculture and small property, the only basis of any free culture" and blamed the intellectual confusion of the 1930s upon "Luther's anathemas against Reason, and Descartes' expressed contempt for Aristotle and Aquinas." In his later work he drew heavily upon the Tory triumvirate of Eliot, Pound, and Wyndham

* *Dalhousie Review*, XVII, 1936.

Lewis, and upon Joyce's version of Thomist aesthetics and Viconian philosophy (though not, naturally, upon Joyce's political liberalism).

Because he held such views, it is not surprising that McLuhan at one time gave the impression of being a bitter man who scornfully contemplated the world about him. Today, however, he embraces the universe with an almost alarming eagerness and zest. His system of values remains very much what it has always been (at any rate since his conversion to Catholicism) but recent history has apparently transformed his pessimism into a kind of millennial optimism. In spite of repeated claims to detachment and impartiality, he has clearly invested a great deal of emotional as well as intellectual capital in his faith that we are entering an era which bears the promise of paradise in the form of an undissociated electronic culture. How this improbable conviction came to take hold of him is the subject of this article.

II   McLuhan was a pioneer in the revival of interest in rhetoric that has characterized literary scholarship during the past generation. As a result of his studies (which began with a Cambridge thesis on Thomas Nashe, the Elizabethan pamphleteer and novelist), he came to see the history of Western culture in terms of an all-embracing dualism in which "grammarians" are ranged against "dialecticians." According to this theory, the conflict began with the confrontation between the Sophists and their great antagonist Socrates. The Sophists, believing in the primacy of action over knowledge, consistently subordinated the study of logic to that of rhetoric or persuasion. By contrast, Socrates, Plato, and Aristotle insisted that "dialectics should control rhetoric, that knowledge was superior even to prudential action."* On the whole, subsequent history has been on the side of the dialecticians, but McLuhan clearly sympathizes with the Sophists. For him, the achievement of a theoretical separation of knowledge from action or eloquence was not a great moment in the history of thought, but the first

* "An Ancient Quarrel in Modern America," *Classical Journal*, XLI, 1945–6.

step in a long progress toward the fragmentation and dissolution of the human personality. (Later, as we shall see, he was to find an explanation for this development in the rise of phonetic literacy.)

McLuhan traces the opposition between exponents of the two traditions throughout two and a half millennia. On one side are the grammarians Isocrates, Cicero, St. Augustine, Erasmus, Thomas Jefferson, and Woodrow Wilson (I confine myself to names mentioned by McLuhan); on the other are the dialecticians William of Ockham, Peter Abelard, Peter Ramus, Descartes, and John Dewey. The former tend to be encyclopedic (*i.e.*, nonspecialist), forensic, practical, and find their ideal image in Cicero's *doctus orator,* whose highest value is eloquence; the latter are specialist, speculative, introspective, and analytic. Prince Hal, Ulysses (in *Troilus and Cressida*—at least in I, iii), and Leopold Bloom belong with the grammarians; Henry IV, Hamlet, Sherlock Holmes, and Stephen Dedalus (much of the time) are dialecticians. (McLuhan's fondness for dualistic categories—hot and cool media, visual and acoustic space, dialecticians and grammarians—always tempts me to offer prizes for further lists of imaginatively paired opposites.)

Around this dichotomy McLuhan builds a theory of American culture and, hence, of modern culture generally. He sees the South as a direct inheritor of the encyclopedic Ciceronian tradition.* By virtue of its conservative, Anglican heritage, the South was able to maintain vital connections with the eloquent and humanistic European ideal represented by Castiglione, Sidney, and Spenser. Passionate, nonintrospective, devoted to public life (as distinct from private life, which was nonexistent in the South), the educated Southern gentleman never became alienated from his humbler and unlearned fellow citizens. Consequently, says McLuhan, the South has the only tradition of real political thought in America.

In contrast to this vision of balanced civility, McLuhan paints a black picture of New England culture, founded as it is upon "the most destructive aberration of the Western mind—

* "The Southern Quality," *Sewanee Review,* LV, 1947.

autonomous dialectics and ontological nominalism." Northern thought is repressive, impatient, fragmentary, and suffers from "elephantiasis of the will." Henry James epitomizes its materialistic individualism; in his sick world almost all the characters are tourists, females are dominant and luxuriant, while males are timid and meager. The denatured submen of Northern cities, according to the McLuhan of two decades ago, "best express their helplessness by means of Negro music." He explains that "while ostensibly setting about the freeing of the slaves, they became enslaved, and found in the wailing self-pity and crooning of the Negro a substitute for any life-style of their own." (Clearly, McLuhan's reputation for being hip must postdate this essay.)

In a world in which Southern civility was doomed by Northern barbarism, McLuhan found little to please him. Complaining of a time "when a triumphant technology croons the sickly boasts of the advertising man, when the great vaults and vistas of the human soul are obscured by images of silken glamor, and when it is plain that man lives not by bread alone but by toothpaste also," he called for a return to the values of St. Thomas.* His idea of political sanity was so remote from current practice that he seemed condemned to impotence and despair. In the course of a perverse but brilliant essay on detective fiction (for McLuhan, the epitome of debased modern literature), he suggested two improbable exemplars of political prudence: Shakespeare's Ulysses, whose speech on Order is "a scientific formula for what was happening and what continues to happen"; and Charles I, who, for the English world, will always be "a symbol of opposition to the tradesmen ethos." †
Judging the world by these standards, he had to conclude that "today we not only live barbarously (human community is little more than a memory) but emotional illiteracy is almost universal." That characteristically shapeless sentence draws attention to a pathetic anomaly in McLuhan's intellectual equipment. This man who regards eloquence as one of the

* St. Louis University Studies in Honor of St. Thomas Aquinas, I (1943).
† "Footsteps in the Sands of Crime," *Sewanee Review*, LIV, 1946.

highest values is himself a notoriously inarticulate and inelegant stylist.

At this point, the reader might well conclude that McLuhan is no more than an extreme reactionary of a familiar type. His hatred for specialization, abstraction, and the hard urban ego, and his nostalgia for an imagined womblike pre-industrial Eden might seem to presage a career of splenetic irrelevance. However, he never allowed the apparent hopelessness of the situation to drive him to despair. His passionate love of literature (which he tends to read as prophecy or revelation) and his Catholic faith (an implicit element in his value system) presumably helped to preserve him from so deadly an intellectual sin. On the contrary, he has always insisted upon the absolute importance, first, of recognizing the existence of a crisis that involves us all willy-nilly; and, second, of trying to understand what is really going on. McLuhan's contempt for Marxism is unbounded, but he would certainly assent to the Marxist axiom that freedom lies in the recognition of necessity.

III   His favorite exemplar of this attitude, one who makes an appearance in virtually all McLuhan's books, is the sailor hero of Poe's "Descent into the Maelstrom." Caught up in an irresistible process, the sailor does not panic, but saves himself by studying the action of the whirlpool and learning to cooperate with it. McLuhan conceived *The Mechanical Bride* (1951) in this spirit. This study of "the folklore of industrial man" (in other words, advertisements, comic books, radio, and other popular media) attempts "to set the reader at the centre of the revolving picture . . . where he may observe the action. . . ." Like Poe's sailor, who finds amusement in speculating on the relative velocities of objects floating by him (and thus discovers how to escape from his predicament), the reader is invited to contemplate the images and the sardonic commentary in McLuhan's picture book as a first step toward developing a strategy for survival as an "integral" human being in the modern world.

In *The Mechanical Bride,* McLuhan repudiated the moral

indignation and the nostalgia that had heretofore charaterized his work. Like his exemplary hero, he tried to use the destructive energy of his environment in the service of his own creative purpose: the wisecracking, jazzy headlines and the flip, knowing tone are simply heightened versions of the language of the media tribe—as though a severe moralist were writing for a kind of uncorrupt *Variety*. The result is McLuhan's most successful act of communication, even though he now repudiates the hostile, disdainful spirit of this book. (Al Capp and Chic Young are among the few popular artists to emerge unscathed.) There has never been a more devastating analysis of the latent content of dozens of contemporary myths and images, ranging from Blondie to Superman, Best Sellers to Great Books, Humphrey Bogart to Emily Post, and from sexy automobiles to the assembly-line femininity of drum majorettes, pinup girls, and nylon-stocking models.

The energy and aplomb with which the author went about his exegetical task almost disguises from the casual reader the fact that *The Mechanical Bride* is a rather bleak and gloomy book. The maelstrom of commercial culture is wittily charted, but there are no very convincing hints about how to escape from it. On the contrary, the idealization of twelfth-century philosophy, the sneers at coeducation, feminism, and working mothers, the dubious assertion that the rich were once more socially responsible than they are now, and the rather Victorian attitude toward corsets, brief skirts, and high heels would depress the *Bride* to the level of silly Tory propaganda if they were anything more than digressions from the main concern of the book.

Between *The Mechanical Bride* and McLuhan's next book, *The Gutenberg Galaxy* (1962), there is a gap of ten years during which his interpretation of contemporary culture (but not his basic value system) underwent a radical revision. I have no privileged knowledge of what influences wrought this transformation, but three factors were obviously important.

The first was the development of network television. Though it was published near the dawn of the TV age, most of the exhibits in the *Bride*'s chamber of horrors are drawn from the pre-video press and radio of the forties. In a sense, the book was out of date on the day it appeared. McLuhan would certainly say this, though most readers would probably agree that the book stands up remarkably well after sixteen years. After all, there are no sharp breaks in the history of culture, and the *Bride* herself will almost certainly still be around to celebrate her golden wedding in 2001.

Another potent influence was the work of the Canadian economist Harold A. Innis, who died in 1952 at the age of fifty-eight, just as he was adumbrating a brilliant theory of political and cultural change, based upon shifts in communications media. *Empire and Communications* (1950) and *The Bias of Communications* (1951) were published too late to influence *Bride,* but McLuhan's acknowledged debt to Innis is apparent in everything he has published since 1952.*

Finally, there is McLuhan's collaboration with the American anthropologist Edmund Carpenter (then at the University of Toronto), which extended throughout most of the 1950s and recently has been renewed at Fordham. Together they published *Explorations* (1953–1959), a brilliant, eccentric, and imaginative periodical devoted to the study of communications in the wildest possible definition of the word. (A selection from the journal, *Explorations in Communications,* was published in book form in 1960.)

Even if one is aware of these influences on McLuhan during this period, it is quite a shock to pass quickly from *The Mechanical Bride* to its successors, *The Gutenberg Galaxy* (1962) and *Understanding Media* (1964). The most startling difference is the change in the author's attitude toward the contemporary world. Not only has his contempt for many of the media and those who control them almost evaporated, but he tries (without complete success) to avoid assuming any intellectual posture that could be mistaken for a "point of view." His animus in both books is reserved for the civilization of the

* For an excellent account of Innis' ideas and a comparison with those of McLuhan, see James W. Carey, "Harold Adams Innis and Marshall McLuhan," *Antioch Review,* XXVII, 1967. [See pp. 270–308 of this book. —Ed.]

recent past and for contemporaries who are so "stunned" by their commitment to its values that they cannot see reality as in itself it really is. Above all, these books radiate confidence that history has taken a sudden shift toward the kind of society McLuhan could admire.

IV *The Gutenberg Galaxy: the Making of Typographic Man* expounds a revised standard version of the gospel of history according to McLuhan. The works of Innis and a variety of lesser influences (including H. J. Chaytor, Tobias Dantzig, Siegfried Giedion, E. H. Gombrich, William Ivins, and Walter Ong) have been assimilated without altering the author's basic credo. In essence, *Galaxy* identifies McLuhan's old heroes, the "grammarians," with a tradition of discourse based upon the spoken word; and his old enemies, the "dialecticians," with the cult of knowledge based upon alphabetic literacy. The whole theory is worked out in detail, with a wealth of quotations from primary and secondary authorities. Even those who are immune or antipathetic to McLuhanism may find a great deal of fascinating and out-of-the-way information in the pages of *The Gutenberg Galaxy*.

There are already too many explanations of McLuhan's explanation of what Western culture is all about, and I have no intention of adding to them. Nevertheless, a résumé of the argument of the *Galaxy* is necessary if we are to follow McLuhan's development from glum reaction to eager apocalypse. In a prefatory note, he eschews the linear form of a consecutive argument for his book, and claims that it "develops a mosaic or field approach to its problems. Such a mosaic image of numerous data and quotations in evidence offers the only practical means of revealing causal operations in history." To dramatize this intention, he has arranged the main body of the book in the form of two hundred and sixty-one more or less self-contained sections, each headed with what a composition teacher would call a topic sentence—a punning, epigrammatic, or summarizing statement in large, bold, italic type—not unlike the chapter headings in early-nineteenth-century novels. Theoretically, the sections might be read in any order, like those experimental novels that come with pages that can be shuffled like a pack of cards. However, I don't recommend that anyone try this with *The Gutenberg Galaxy*. The truth is that the alleged mosaic or galactic form is little more than window dressing. McLuhan has a good old-fashioned story to tell, and those who want to understand it had better begin at the beginning in the square old way.

The introductory note also repudiates the idea of offering "a series of views of fixed relationships in pictorial space"—what McLuhan elsewhere calls a "fixed point of view." But here again, his claim to have made free and impersonal arrangements of evidence, without bias or commitment, cannot be accepted for a moment. Anyone who reads McLuhan's books with a degree of care will have no difficulty in deciding where the author's sympathies lie.

In form, the *Galaxy* follows the classic pattern of tragedy. McLuhan begins with a preposterous interpretation of *King Lear* as "a working model of the process of denudation by which men translated themselves from a world of roles to a world of jobs." Wisely, he relies upon literary intimations of a pre-alphabetic cultural Eden, rather than attempting to prove that such a condition ever actually existed; but that does not inhibit him from describing the emergence of modern culture in terms of "the anguish of the third dimension," "the madness and misery of the new Renaissance life of action," and "schizophrenia [which] may be a necessary consequence of literacy." Like all proper tragedies, the book closes with intimations of restored order in an improbable electronic Arcadia of tomorrow.

In McLuhan's mythology, the Fall that alienated man from his naïve acoustic paradise (a fortunate Fall, he sometimes almost admits) was the change in the ratio of his senses brought about by the development of phonetic literacy. As more and more knowledge and experience came to be transmitted from generation to generation not by the spoken word but by its visual equivalent in inscription or manuscript, men moved farther from the muddled, communal, and involving culture of the ear toward the sharply defined, isolate individualism of the eye. Gradually, the linear, sequential, and segmented ordering of syllables and words on the page came to serve as a model for all thought, and Western culture began to take on its characteristic individualistic, analytic, and visual form—literally, its point of view.

Until the fifteenth century, aural and visual modes of thought continued to coexist in relatively fruitful tension. However, with the invention of printing (a characteristically "visual" attempt to achieve quantity, uniformity, and repeatability) the visual bias of European culture began to assume murderous proportions. All values that could not be reconciled with mathematical order, utility, or empirical rationalism were undermined and subverted. From the triumph of Gutenberg technology stems everything that McLuhan most detests about the modern world—capitalism, secularism, industrialism, nationalism, specialization, and socialism. Worse than that, those who ought to lead their fellows back to a saner mode of life—the intellectual and academic elite—are so "stunned" and brainwashed by their dependence upon print that they are incapable of understanding what is happening to them. These "bookmen of detached and private culture" mistake for reality what is really the pre-packaged, homogenized, and denatured product of assembly-line Gutenberg thought processes.

Whether or not this interpretation of Western culture is a valid one is a question that cannot be answered in a sentence or two. McLuhan's fallen visual world is similar to Blake's "single vision and Newton's sleep," Pound's "usura," and Eliot's "dissociation of sensibility." No doubt all four myths stem from the same sort of dissatisfaction about the way things are. However, did the catastrophe occur in the fifth century B.C. or the fifteenth century A.D. (McLuhan), the sixteenth century (Pound), the seventeenth (Eliot), the early eighteenth (Blake)—or are we right to doubt that any of these mysterious disasters ever occurred in real life?

Those who are obstinately skeptical are unlikely to find themselves convinced by *The Gutenberg Galaxy*. McLuhan unwittingly epitomizes the shortcomings of his own style of

THE PARADOX OF MARSHALL MCLUHAN

argument when he quotes Ashley Montagu on primitive man: "The trouble with the nonliterate is not that he isn't logical, but that he applies logic too often, many times on the basis of insufficient premises." When generalizations are erected upon isolated examples, when syllogisms often have missing or undistributed middles, when connectives such as "thus," "therefore," and "in this way" are used to link tenuously related propositions, then precisians are likely to dismiss the perpetrator of such solecisms as beneath serious consideration.

Yet most people who have read *Galaxy* are unable to dismiss it. After every objection has been made, the book still contains a wealth of fascinating and novel material about the culture of the past twenty-five hundred years. McLuhan may be wrong to blame the alphabet and Gutenberg for all the ills of Western bourgeois culture (for a man who attacks the idea of linear cause and effect as an illusion of literacy he is sometimes surprisingly simple-minded about it himself), but the "galaxy" he describes certainly does exist. Most of the out-of-the-way information comes from secondary sources, often quoted verbatim and at length; yet for a literary scholar to discover this heterogeneous material and perceive its relevance to the contemporary condition is a creative achievement in itself. The theoretical (though not the ideological) framework of the *Galaxy* is derived from Innis, but the detailed applications—some of them brilliant, as in the discussions of *Gargantua, Don Quixote,* and the *Duncaid*—are all McLuhan's. Finally, if *The Gutenberg Galaxy* is a maddening and undisciplined contribution to the study of the role of printing in Western culture, it is also virtually the only work of its kind. Until one of us writes a better book we should be grateful to have this one.

V   In a kind of postscript, "The Galaxy Reconfigured," McLuhan suggests that we are at last beginning to understand the Gutenberg era only because "we have moved into another phase from which we can contemplate the contours of the preceding situation with ease and clarity. . . . As we experience the new electronic and organic age with ever stronger indications of its main outlines, the preceding mechanical age becomes quite intelligible." McLuhan also finds that our period of transition is not only "richer and more terrible" than that described by Patrick Cruttwell in *The Shakespearian Moment* (1955), but it is moving in the opposite direction—from fragmentation and dissolution to community and involvement. The last sentence of the *Galaxy* promises to carry on the story with another volume devoted to *"Understanding Media* in the world of our time."

In spite of the fact that it is the book that led to McLuhan's contemporary fame, *Understanding Media: The Extensions of Man* came as a disappointment to those whose interest had been whetted by *Galaxy*. Its main ideas had been briefly outlined in the earlier volume, and their detailed application to twenty-six different "media" (including number, clothing, clocks, motorcars, typewriters, and weapons) often illuminates the subject less than it reveals deficiencies in the theory or eccentricities in the author. (I must apologize for all these visual metaphors, which perhaps betray my unfitness to cope with the phenomena under discussion.) Once again, McLuhan planned the book as a configuration of chapters readable in any order; but this made necessary a great deal of repetition, the tediousness of which is not relieved by the slapdash prose style.

Having already written at length about *Understanding Media,** I shall not rehearse here the arguments for and against McLuhan's famous division of media into "hot" and "cool," his contention that television is "haptic" or tactile rather than "visual," or his "explanations" of Kennedy's electoral victory over Nixon, the assassination of Lee Harvey Oswald, and the sensuous superiority of mesh over sheer nylons. The aspects of the book that are relevant to our interest in the "paradox" of its author are its extreme optimism and the equally extreme determinism epitomized in the slogan The Medium is the Message.

Though something of a determinist, Harold Innis was certainly not an optimist. Some of the melancholy of his mentor's somber, clotted prose attaches to McLuhan's account of the rape of oral culture by typography in *The Gutenberg Galaxy*

* *Commentary,* January 1965.

—though McLuhan's compulsive paronomasiac cheerfulness keeps breaking through.

Understanding Media is different. It deals with a series of phenomena that had hardly become apparent at the time of Innis's death and about which (by McLuhan's own testimony) there is far less possibility of writing authoritatively—until we move far enough into the post-electronic age (if there is to be one) to see the present era more clearly. Furthermore, no one, least of all Marshall McLuhan, can contemplate the present and the future with the same Olympian detachment we can bring to the past. In this book, he explicitly confesses a faith concerning "the ultimate harmony of being," and commits himself to that "wholeness, empathy and depth of awareness [which] is a natural adjunct of electric technology." It is easier to share his admiration for these values than his confidence that they are somehow implicit in a postliterate culture based upon the computer and the microwave relay.

McLuhan's optimism arises out of his theory that media are extensions of human organs—wheel extends foot, gun extends eye and teeth, radio extends mouth or ear, writing extends eye, and so on. In the past, every new technological development has disturbed the balance or "closure" between the various faculties. Because the extended sense exaggerates or intensifies only one element in a complex process, it leads to a systematic distortion of all experience. Eventually, men cease to be conscious that this has happened to them: like Narcissus, they mistake their own distorted reflections for reality itself. During the Gutenberg era, hypertrophy of the eye was the chief source of error. However, because electric technology differs from all other "media" by extending the whole nervous system rather than just one faculty, we are on the verge of a new era in human history, in which a proper, harmonious ratio between the senses will be restored. What is more, while the older mechanical technology was "explosive," fragmenting the personality and increasing the psychological distance between men, the new order is "implosive," healing the breach in the psyche and joining all humanity in a huge "seamless web" of instant electronic communication. McLuhan halfheartedly warns of the danger that we may sink back into a preliterate "Africa in the mind," but he is obviously much more hopeful that we shall all become secure and contented members of a utopian "global village."

What must we do to be saved? The answer is Nothing. Like a kind of megalomaniacal New Critic who takes the whole world for his poem, McLuhan insists upon the inseparability of content from form. The true content or "message" of any medium is "the change of scale or pace or pattern that it introduces into human affairs." What we usually think of as "content"—paraphrasable arguments, plots, or ideas—is "like the juicy piece of meat carried by the burglar to distract the watchdog of the mind." Those of us who worry about horror comics, TV violence, the lack of controversy in news media, and the Vietnam war are wasting our time on irrelevancies. All these "problems" (some of them illusory, in McLuhan's view) will be solved without our intervention by electronic technology. Our sole duty is to understand what is happening (even if this involves reading *Understanding Media* in which the Gutenberg medium seems hopelessly at odds with the McLuhan message).

VI   The two invariables that have helped to shape McLuhan's strange odyssey from straitlaced and pessimistic conservatism to his present euphoric and approving interest in everything from *Naked Lunch* to topless waitresses are his dislike of Protestant and capitalistic individualism, and his Catholic faith. The first is quite explicit in his early works and clearly implied in the later; the second is never allowed to intrude formally into any of his books, though it presumably accounts for McLuhan's lack of interest in ontology and his confidence in the essential harmoniousness of the creation. Only someone who believes that he has already *got* the message could be so indifferent to the problem of what it is that media mediate. He discusses the universe in the same spirit as a theologian might discuss the development of dogma or the evolution of the liturgy.

But even (or, perhaps, especially) from the standpoint of

120

orthodox Catholic theology, there are serious lacunae in Mc-Luhan's account of the way things are at the dawn of the electronic era—his inadequate psychology, his lack of interest in social structure, and his apparent inability to perceive the full tragic dimensions of some of the phenomena about which he writes with such flip assurance.

McLuhan appears to regard the Freudian unconscious as a simple product of Gutenberg technology. There is perhaps something to be said for this idea, but the man who would convince us of it ought to offer at least the outlines of an acceptable alternative theory of human behavior. This he does not do. On the contrary, he seems to see man as a ratio of five senses whose balance is wholly determined by outside circumstances. Granted that "elephantiasis of the will" is (or was) an endemic modern disease, it is surely going too far to try to save the patient by amputating his selfhood. McLuhan's account of how media extend our "outer" human faculties likewise makes some sense, but it is certainly no less simplemindedly mechanistic than any of the Gutenberg absurdities at which he jeers. His analogy between electric technology and the central nervous system seems a useful one until we realize that he means it literally, and he really does envisage a kind of universal electrical organism into which all men will be plugged—a prediction that involves not only bad psychology, but even worse theology.

Associated with McLuhan's strange idea of the psyche as a kind of Lockeian *tabula rasa* upon which media record their messages is his indifference to problems of political and economic power. This was not always so, as we have seen: he once expounded a kind of Chestertonian or Southern agrarian conservatism. Now, however, he seems to embrace an equally extreme and impractical utopianism in which his old enemies Big Government and Big Business have become the allies of avant-garde artists in the cause of electronic togetherness. Presumably, this new confidence in the humane potentiality of the economic status quo owes something to McLuhan's avowed preference for the iconic over the analytic mode. ("Icons are not specialist fragments or aspects but unified and compressed images of complex kind. They focus a large region of experience in tiny compass.") Advertising, television, and Cold War ploys such as the space race all appeal to him more than old-fashioned forms of communication or persuasion because of their iconic character. The fact that these media may be controlled and exploited by men with petty or sinister motives, such as speculative financiers, cosmetic manufacturers, or the military establishment does not appear to interest him. He sees contemporary history as a kind of cosmic *Finnegans Wake* in which some mysterious force is at work to harmonize and reconcile the apparent conflicts. Often he tries to clinch a dubious argument by quoting an enigmatic sentence or two from *Finnegans Wake*—but even Joyce's most ardent admirers will feel that one does him a disservice by using his superb evocation of Europe's collective unconscious as a kind of politico-cultural primer of the atomic age. In fact, treating writers and artists as though they were prophets in the vulgar Tiresias or Jules Verne sense of the word, rather than as Isaiahs or Jeremiahs, is one of McLuhan's last defensible habits.

While McLuhan places his faith in this kind of cosmic aestheticism (a modern equivalent of eighteenth-century "cosmic Toryism"?), the society in which he lives shows signs of lapsing into technologically sophisticated chaos. Although he occasionally evinces an awareness of this, most of the time he appears to be so stunned by his vision of electrical Nirvana that he misses the living reality as spectacularly as any Gutenberg somnambulist. Certainly, it would be hard to match the cocksure impercipience with which McLuhan sets us right about many of the more agonizing issues of our age.

Civil rights? "Many people have observed how the real integrator or leveler of white and Negro in the South was the private car and the truck, not the expression of moral points of view." Southern Negroes will be astonished to learn that General Motors really deserves the credit usually given to lunchroom sit-ins and voter registration drives, and flabbergasted to note the tense in which McLuhan couches his remark.

Rigged TV quiz shows? "Any play or poem or novel is also rigged to produce an effect. . . . But . . . So great was the audience participation in the quiz shows that the directors of the show were prosecuted as con men. . . . Charles Van Doren merely got clobbered as an innocent bystander. . . . Regrettably, [the investigation] simply provided a field day for the earnest moralizers. A moral point of view too often serves as a substitute for understanding in technological matters." This line of reasoning opens up tremendous opportunities for imaginative television producers: what about rigging the World Series to provide a suitable number of ninth-inning tie-breaking homers? With electronically controlled balls, and Nicklaus and Palmer cast as good and bad guys, the PGA tournament might be made even more exciting than it is. Instead of having to share riots with other networks, a progressive news producer could foment his own private disturbance in some unexpected city where only his cameras were ready for action. One would like to hear St. Thomas' views on this bit of moral analysis by his disciple.

War? This is really "a process of achieving equilibrium among unequal technologies." Nowadays, "the cold war is the real war front—a surround—involving everybody—all the time—everywhere. Whenever hot wars are *necessary* [my italics] . . . we conduct them in the backyards of the world with the old technologies." The Vietnam war is unpopular with the American people [unlike the Korean War?] because this hot conflict is being waged before the cool eyes of television cameras. I do not think that it is merely my hot liberal heart that is repelled by the cool glibness of these formulations—particularly that casual "necessary," the Western arrogance of "backyards," and the idea that helicopters, defoliants, guided missiles, and "Lazy Dog" shells are merely fragments of the "old technologies."

These defects in McLuhan's emotional and intellectual equipment were almost as discernible in his early work as they are in *Understanding Media* and *The Medium Is the Massage*. However, when he wrote in the character of a lonely defender of eloquence and reason in the midst of a debased and commercialized culture, his occasional crudities of thought or feeling did not detract from the general brilliance of his insights.

Lacking any particular hope for the future, he was concerned less to proselytize than to maintain a detached and ironic awareness of what was happening.

Now that McLuhan foresees the triumph of electronic technology, dramatically reversing the cultural processes which prompted his pessimism, his intellectual energy is naturally diverted not merely from contemplation of the past to prediction of the future, but also from detachment to commitment. It is quite clear that his deep emotional investment in the expected new order stems from motives of which he himself is only partly aware and about which it would be inappropriate to speculate. He would be the first to heap scorn upon an opponent who allowed wish fulfillment to have such a distorting effect upon his view of reality. It would be better for McLuhan if his oversimplifications did not happen to coincide with the pretensions of young status-hungry advertising and television executives and producers, who eagerly provide him with a ready-made clacque, exposure on the media, and a substantial income from addresses to sales conventions. The Marshall McLuhan who wrote those classic articles in the *Sewanee* and *Kenyon Reviews, The Mechanical Bride,* and *The Gutenberg Galaxy* deserves a better fate than to become Madison Avenue's favorite philosopher.

milton klonsky*
mc² luhan's message *or:*
which way did the
second coming went?

That snake seems to have bitten its tail again, another age come full cycle, *in saecula saeculorum,* and lo, from the bogs of the undermind, certain primordial fears and superstitions have emerged, oozing, into our own enlightened times, resurrected by the same science that was supposed to have buried them forever. *For instance, what are those spectral presences (or UFOs) that appear and disappear at will, being and not-being both here and there and now and then? Where do they come from? What do they want? And those strange signals recently detected by radiotelescopes, the so-called "mysterium phenomenon," emanating from somewhere within the Milky Way, do they contain a message for us? And for how many billions of years has the phone been ringing unanswered? Also, what about the discovery by subatomic physicists of antimatter, which has led to the conception of an anti-universe that mirrors our own, Ahriman to our Ormuzd (or the other way*

* MILTON KLONSKY *is a student of poetry and civilization whose articles have appeared in such magazines as* Commentary, Partisan Review, *and* Esquire.

around), with both mutually annihilatory? Or the equally mind-spinning theory of Russian scientists that the two small moons of Mars, Demos and Phoibos, are really artificial satellites, relics of a vanished Martian race? What happened to them? Can it happen to us? Once more, does the sin of having plucked the nuclear apple mean that Cosmic Man, like the old Adam, has been cursed with mortality? And how will we be saved this time? . . . And so forth. God or no God, it figures the universe must be haunted.

A generation, born since World War II, for whom science fiction has become science, can hold no truths to be self-evident, no speculations too far out. So where, *dictes-moy où,* are the old-time peepers and mutterers, seers and aurists, apocalypsos and doomsdaters who used to be around? All snowed under. Instead, as the millennial countdown approaches 2000, an entirely different breed of prophets, "new hatcht to th' woeful time," prophets out of the academy and the laboratory, have taken their place; and for them the Word has now been swaddled in other words, the jargon of psychoanalysis, cybernetics, celestial physics, sociologistics, and so on, just as the various conflicting political and social ideologies during the Age of Faith had to assume the guise of religious dogma. *Olev hasholem* and/or *Sartor Resartus.*

Among these oracles the most celebrated at present are: Norman O. Brown, author of *Love's Body,* who has attempted to psychoanalyze Man himself, treating his entire history from the Pleistocene to the present as an ever-deepening neurosis; Dr. Timothy Leary, who has proclaimed a New Dispensary, with LSD as a more up-to-date Eucharist for ecstatic liquefaction and communion with OM; and, of course, Marshall McLuhan, the media man, who preaches the coming of a new electronic Age of Gold in which Man will be redeemed and transfigured. And of these three, it is McLuhan who has Made It most spectacularly, turned (or put) more people on, given the kaleidoscope a new shake.

One globe-eyed critic (*Zip-zap! Ten thousand volts!*) has compared him to Pavlov and Darwin, Freud and Einstein, and Sir Isaac Newton. His famous slogan "the medium is the message" (or "massage") has already become as proverbial as "nice guys finish last" or "history is bunk," part of American folklore. And though he disapproves of the medium of print, four of his books have become best sellers, while his theories have been expounded in universities and seminaries as well as on TV and the radio and in all the mass magazines. Most of the converts to McLuhanism came with minds already well equipped with the latest thought-saving ideas, from *Angst* to Zen, and accepted it as a new and shinier intellectual gadget. But he has also found support among distinguished writers and professors and experts in various fields. And to many young McLuhanites, tired of squinting through the Freudian-Marxist bifocals of their elders, he seems to provide a periscopic view into the next millennium . . . though there are others, too, who think it's a rearview-mirror image of the millennium before this one.

The germinal idea, or genesis, of the McLuhan gospel can be found in one compacted metaphor: "All media are extensions of some human faculty—psychic or physical," as the computer is to the mind, radar to the ear, the H-Bomb to the fist. To extend the metaphor, then, suggests that we are all members of a single hypostatized Man in whose body we have our being and in whose mind we participate. ("The godhead is broken," as Melville once wrote, "we are the pieces.") If one accepts Anselm's ontological proof of God—that the idea of Him necessarily implies His existence—then the existence of a "deified" Man can likewise be "proved." And, McLuhan adds, since the media are changing rapidly from the mechanical to the electronic and the nuclear, Man's faculties are also changing.

With only mynah variations, this repeats the French Catholic philosopher Teilhard de Chardin's conception of a planetary "noosphere"—the psychic layer of mankind above all other living things—and of a "noospheric brain, the organ of collective human thought," which result from the evolutionary "convergence" and "super-cerebralization" of human society. And yet, Teilhard asserts, "Man is only now, after a million years of existence, emerging from his embryonic phase." But the ultimate source of this idea may lie even deeper, in the

Gnostic and Pauline vision of the "Pleroma" (or "fullness of God"); and it also has affinities with Plotinus' "world-soul," Hegel's "Zeitgeist," Jung's "collective unconscious," and so on. Cosmic Man, in the guise of H.C.E. (Here Comes Everybody), has been celebrated as the hero of Joyce's *Finnegans Wake*.

No one would care to quarrel with so grand and ultimately poetic a conception of the human species, yet it does tend to exalt Man at the expense of ordinary men, whose lives are still as nasty, brutish, and short as ever. "Between the idea," wrote T. S. Eliot, "and the reality . . . Falls the Shadow." And when McLuhan, alas, brings his metaphor down to earth and applies it to the quiddities, the hard little facts, of existence, he sometimes stumbles into absurdity. Everybody nowadays believes the world is round, but no one wears arc-shaped shoes.

McLuhan, following Joyce, seems to believe that history repeats itself in a "commodious vicus of recirculation." In the mid-fifteenth century, then, a second fall of Man took place as the result of Gutenberg's fatal invention (the stuttering thunder of the printing press reiterated and gutenburbled by Joyce as "bababadalgharaghtakamminnarronnkonnbronnton-nerronntuonnthunntrovarr . . ." like pied type); after which Man was thrust out of the "sacred" oral and tribal culture of the past, where all his senses were in harmony, and into the "profane" and sensorily unbalanced mass culture we live in today, dominated by the eye with its fixed "point of view," thus causing our anxiety-ridden time sense, our robotized work schedules, and all our other woes. (Even the Bible says of the first fall: "And the eyes of both of them were opened. . . .") What T. S. Eliot and the old New Criticism in its heyday once characterized as a "dissociation of sensibility," between thought and feeling—which is supposed to have occurred sometime in the seventeenth century and to have led to our present schizophrenized society—might have influenced McLuhan's own ideas here, since he is by profession a literary scholar. ("You wipes your glosses with what you knows," as Joyce said.) However, McLuhan affirms, now that the Electronic Galaxy has arrived to challenge Gutenberg's, the dominance of the visual will be broken, the human sensorium balanced once more, and Man himself retribalized and reredeemed. A family today watching the flickering shadows on the TV screen would thus be reaching across the millennia to commune with savage ancestors squatting around a campfire. The "all-at-oneness" of the electronic media (according to McLuhan's weird parody of Scripture) is atonement for the Gutenbergian sin of "single vision."

Naytheless, the mind boggles at the thought that the entire economico-technico-scientifico and social and cultural complex of society has been determined by the printing press, which is, after all, only its product. But McLuhan is fond of such metonymous *presto-changos*—viz., "the medium is the message." Granted that a medium such as TV affects us in its own way, for good or ill, there is also a message . . . from the Sponsor—commercial in the United States, political in the Soviet Union, but total, exclusive, and pervasive in both. (One might even say that it is for the sake of this "message" that the medium has been developed and sustained in the first place.) Again, in his chapter on "Roads and Paper Routes" in *Understanding Media,* McLuhan writes that "the use of papyrus and alphabet created the incentive for building fast, hard-surfaced roads," and, consequently, made possible the Roman Empire. How come, then, that the otherwise highly advanced Incan culture before the Conquistadores, had no alphabet, no means of writing—not even a vague surmise of what it might be—yet constructed hard roads and suspension bridges from one end of Peru to the other, which are considered by engineers to equal those of the Romans?

McLuhan's need to build his system and get his "massage" across—his own sin of "single vision"—tempts him to overlook and to disparage the visual sense on every occasion. For instance, he insists on calling TV a "tactile-kinetic" (or sometimes an "audile-tactile") medium when it is, plainly, visual —as any late viewer with rectangular eyeballs can tell him. Though the eyes (as the blind John Milton complained) are "so obvious and so easy to be quenched," it is sight—not smell, hearing, touch, or taste—that is the prime human sense and source of knowledge, now and as in primitive times, and will

129

remain such until the advent of ESP. ("You wipes your glosses with what, your nose?") Then again, why must the movies be labeled a "hot" medium (one that extends a single sense in "high definition") and TV a "cool one" when, after all, not only is the quality of the TV mosaic bound to be improved by technology (consider the dim, jerky, and scratchy movie image circa 1900) but also so much depends upon the individual's own far-, near-, or clear-sightedness, anyway? Men see through their eyes, not the Eye. . . . But 'twould require Occam's cleaver to hack one's way through some of McLuhan's wilder exfoliations. Like some medieval alchemist, he tends to regard symbols as somehow more real than what they symbolize and to transmute base facts into glittering half-truths. With so much mental smog around, why pollute the noosphere any further?

Since McLuhan prefers to consider himself an "explorer" ("casting my perils before swains," as he tells us), and used to ranging at large through conceptual galaxies, a mere pedestrian critic has no right to carp if McLuhan sometimes loses his way in one universe of discourse or other. Nevertheless, as several of these ungrateful "swains" have pointed out, the medium he must use for these intergalactic explorations is words, words arranged in syntactic order and in uniform lines stamped out by the printing press. How, then, avoid the "single vision," "serial time sense," "fixed point of view," and all the other evils that Gutenberg flesh is heir to? The philosopher Wittgenstein saw this paradox clearly: "Propositions cannot represent the logical form: this mirrors itself in the propositions. That which mirrors itself in language, language cannot represent. That which expresses *itself* in language, *we* cannot represent."

To unhoist himself, McLuhan has lately published a picture book (with Quentin Fiore), *The Medium Is the Massage,* that strives for a "mosaic effect," the "simultaneity" of the electronic, with the words confined to a few slogans and cryptic remarks; more recently, he has even made a long-playing record for people who want to get the "massage" through their ears; and the next step may be a version in Braille or even in a futuristic Des Esseintes-type taste-and-smell package, just to cover the whole sensorium.

But understanding McLuhan, unfortunately, still necessitates reading *Understanding Media,* no matter how onerous or old-fashioned the experience is; and if words fail him, think how he's failed them.

For all its idiosyncrasies, there is a curiously impersonal though shrill tone to McLuhan's prose, as if the intention were to harangue a crowd of readers rather than to persuade a single one. Certain key words and phrases, such as "audile-tactile," "single vision," "high intensity" and "low intensity," "tribalized" and "detribalized," and so on, recur throughout and are repeated insistently like Tibetan *mantras* or radio commercials; and should the reader's attention be lulled at times by the predictability and repetitiveness of the argument, he is liable to be jabbed awake by unexpected puns, some of them painful. It is a "hot"—to use McLuhan's term—rather than a "cool" style, somewhat reminiscent in its messianic fervor of Ezra Pound's and Wyndham Lewis' magazine *BLAST* during World War I. This sometimes causes him to overload and thus short-circuit his sentences, as in the following from *The Gutenberg Galaxy:* "The art and scholarship of the past century and more have become a *monotonous crescendo* of *archaic primitivism*" [my italics]. Or in this, from *Understanding Media* (which must have been intended solely for the eye, since no one could possibly mouth it): "Only the visceral and audile-tactile Teuton and Slav have the needed immunity to visualization for work in the non-Euclidean math and quantum physics." His two chief works (which are really integral) contain a number of such howlers and, in addition, stagger under a load of scholarly jargon as well as his own peculiar brand of academic jive, with hundreds of heavy tomes epitomized, so that in a way it is a kind of left-handed tribute to Gutenberg: Never has there been so bookish a book against books.

Actually, the secret of the printing press was discovered by Gutenberg (born Gensfleisch, meaning "gooseflesh") after he took part in a grape harvest in his native Rhineland, and suddenly saw that the wine press could also be applied to seals, or movable type, thereby producing his great invention. A bibulous bibliomania, endemic among writers and scholars of all sorts, may thus be traced back to the press itself, though McLuhan himself claims to have taken the pledge. Both Gutenberg and McLuhan, it turns out, have much in common. For the chief talent of the author of *Understanding Media* may lie not in weaving metaphysical systems but in compounding intellectual metaphors, rare bisociations of ideas, like Gutenberg's, from seemingly unrelated fields.

Some of these metaphors, which abound in his work, may strike the reader as frivolous or even silly, such as this: "An army needs more typewriters than medium and light artillery pieces . . . suggesting that the typewriter now fuses the function of the pen and the sword"; or this: "What we call the 'French phone,' the union of mouthpiece and earphone in a single instrument, is a significant indication of the French liaison of the senses that English-speaking people keep firmly separate." But once in a while he comes up with something exceptional. One memorable example is his analogy between the medieval monk's private reading booth in the monastery and the contemporary phone booth.

As McLuhan indicates, the old illuminated manuscript, like our telephone directory, was bulky and hard to come by, and so it had to be chained to the wall; and since the monks could read only by reading aloud (for there were no punctuation marks in their books and no divisions of words), each monk had to have a separate nook, just as we need individual phone booths, so as not to disturb one another. (In synagogues today, incidentally, the Torah is still chanted aloud by the congregation.) But silent reading—which makes possible the public rooms of libraries—was a later development in the cultural history of mankind.

For a touch of the marvelous, the Argentine poet Jorge Luis Borges in an essay entitled "The Cult of Books," claims to have found the exact time, A.D. 384, when this event took place. Borges cites St. Augustine's account in the *Confessions*

(Book VI) of his teacher St. Ambrose reading in his cell in Milan:

> When Ambrose read, his eyes moved over the pages, and his soul penetrated the meaning, without his uttering a word or moving his tongue. Many times . . . we saw him reading silently and never otherwise, and after a while we would go away, conjecturing that during the brief interval he used to refresh his spirit, free from the tumult of the business of others, he did not wish to be disturbed, for perhaps he feared that someone who was listening, hearing a difficult part of the text, might ask him to explain an obscure passage or might wish to discuss it with him, and would thus prevent him from reading as many volumes as he desired. I believe that he read that way to preserve his voice, which was easily strained. Whatever the man's purpose was, it was surely a good one.

This feat by St. Ambrose—actually swallowing the biblical thunder, the Word, and allowing it to mutter away into silence inside him—which so astonished Augustine, marks a stage in the transit of mankind from what McLuhan terms the oral and "sacred" to the visual and "profane."

A profane reader can almost forgive the author for leading him up the garden path of his metaphysics when there are such real toads hopping about. Another step, though, and McLuhan would be out of the familiar everyday world (as Alice once passed through the Looking Glass) and into the noumenal realm of Art, or Imagination, which might be the proper medium for much of *Understanding Media;* yet for some reason he holds back, teetering, and tries to stand on both sides of the Looking Glass at once. How he does this provides a valuable clue to McLuhanism, though it gets us there by labyrinthine ways.

There is a famous poem by Yeats, called "Fragments," which McLuhan cites in order to illustrate the "hypnotic trance induced by stepping up the visual component of experience until it filled the field of attention":

> Locke sank into a swoon;
> The Garden died;

> God took the spinning-jenny
> Out of his side.

If we unlock the symbols of this cryptic little poem, which compresses an entire cosmology into just seventeen words, its "meaning" can be paraphrased as follows: John Locke, the contemporary of Newton and celebrated Whig philosopher ("but what is Whiggery?" asks Yeats in another context. "A levelling, rancorous, rational sort of mind . . ."), denied and refuted the doctrine of innate ideas taught by the medieval schoolmen as well as the neoplatonists up to his time. (Plato's and Plotinus' system of Ideas rooted in the Mind was once regarded as the pagan counterpart of the Garden of Eden.) By advocating the experimental method in science, religious skepticism, and a broader political and social economy, Locke thus became the source (Adam) of the Industrial Revolution (the wicked Eve being the "spinning jenny" taken from Adam's side) and of modern democracy.

However, McLuhan follows relentlessly the gleam of his own "single vision," and interprets "The Garden" to mean "the interplay of all the senses in haptic harmony," though that is merely one of the posies in it. Yeats goes on to ask in the second part of the poem:

> Where got I that truth?
> Out of a medium's mouth,
> Out of nothing it came, . . .

He got it from neither place, but (whether aware of the fact or not) from a poem similar in form by William Blake:

> When Sr Joshua Reynolds died
> All Nature was degraded;
> The King drop'd a tear into the Queen's ear
> And all his Pictures Faded.

Blake's quatrain was written in the margin of a copy of Sir Joshua Reynold's *Discourses,* next to an account in the Introduction of the painter's death in 1792. At his State funeral, attended by the royal family, King George himself is supposed to have wept. Reynolds was to Blake what Locke was to Yeats

—a worshiper of the physical world of appearances ("Satan's wife, the goddess Nature," according to Blake), who denied the all-creating Spirit of the Imagination.

On another page of the *Discourses,* Blake wrote: "Mind and Imagination are above Mortal & Perishing Nature. Such is the End of Epicurean or Newtonian Philosophy; it is Atheism"; and then, further on: "Man is born like a Garden already Planted & Sown. The world is too poor to produce one Seed." Finally, next to an editorial footnote in the *Discourses* that the colors of certain pictures by Reynolds were fading, Blake comments: "I do not think the Change is so much in the Pictures as in the Opinions of the Public."

The status of Nature was thus diminished, or "degraded," by Reynolds' death. And if we recall that to Blake "tears" (like the tears shed at Reynolds' funeral) were mental ("For a tear is an intellectual thing/ And a sigh is the sword of an Angel King"—"The Gray Monk"), then the literal-symbolic meaning of this druidic little poem becomes clear.

The prophetic vision of Blake—and, by seeing through his eyes, of Yeats—stems ultimately from the author of the book of Daniel in the Bible, who was the first to have comprehended world history symbolically as a divine drama moving toward some final consummation. The four great beasts in Belshazzar's dream—the LION with eagle's wings; the BEAR; the LEOPARD with four heads; and the unknown MONSTER with four heads—were interpreted by Daniel as emblems of "four kings which shall arise out of the earth." So also, the LOCKE and REYNOLDS imagined by the poets were not the actual physical beings Locke and Reynolds, but mythic characters who played great roles in the *theatrum mundi.* As personifications of historical forces and abstract human values, they seem to sustain the theory of the Greek philosopher Euhemerus, who held that the gods and demigods were merely the deified great men of a long-forgotten time.

Finally, after this long "commodius vicus of recirculation," to return . . .

The historical Gutenberg (or Gensfleisch), blown up by Mc-Luhan's afflatus into GUTENBERG, who deranged the

135

human sensorium and profaned the Word, takes his place alongside Blake's REYNOLDS and Yeats's LOCKE. But since this godling is contained neither in a religious myth nor a poem, but presented as a historical reality, then he must be judged as such; and in that case, what emerges is a spook, an hallucination bred from the fumes of literary scholarship, and of the sort beloved by those mystagogues described in Butler's *Hudibras*:

> Those busy, puzzling stirrers up of doubt,
> Who frame deep mysteries, then find 'em out.

McLuhan could have attempted a poem in the manner of Yeats and Blake, maybe something like this:

> Gensfleisch pressed the Word like grapes;
> Man's mind was pied;
> Jehovah took His fatal law
> Out on his hide.

Perhaps then all the evils attributed to the invention of printing might be more comprehensible.

When Blake later came to write his prophetic and symbolical works (*Jerusalem, The Four Zoas, Milton, The Book of Ahania*), such mythic personae as Los, Enitharmon, Albion, Urizen, and the rest were cast with Voltaire and Socrates, Milton and Abraham and Benj. Franklin, erasing the border between poetry and fact, for by then he had come to believe that Imagination was the sole reality. James Joyce, as well, expounding the dream of Earwicker in *Finnegans Wake,* unites conscious and unconscious and so gives equal billing to Don Quixote and Cervantes, Hamlet and Shakespeare, Mutt and Jeff and Romulus and Remus, et al. in his cosmic drama. As a scholar and critic of Joyce, McLuhan has borrowed much from the Meister in his own glossolalia on the media. "We are following the track of the old Finn," he writes, "but wide awake this time as we re-enter the tribal night. It is like our contemporary consciousness of the Unconscious." The Joycean puns, the palimpsestic style, the cyclical recurrences—"vicous circles"—and cross-references of theme, all are present in Mc-

Luhan's own work . . . and also a propensity to forget that he is not supposed to be writing literature but social criticism. As a result, we have neither one nor the other, but a kind of Delphic gibberish, in which metaphors turn into facts and facts are transsubstantiated into symbols and symbols blur into myth . . .

In an essay on McLuhanism, Dwight MacDonald quotes the following: "The computer promises by technology a Pentecostal condition of universal understanding and unity. The next logical step would seem to be . . . to bypass language in favor of a general cosmic consciousness which might be very like the collective unconsciousness dreamt of by Bergson." Upon which Macdonald comments: "Only McLuhan would see the conscious as 'very like' the unconscious; in his case, the resemblance may be close." So be it. Freud's Olympian pronunciamento: "Where id was, there ego shall be," has here been strangely reversed.

And there's something else, too. McLuhan is well known as a convert to Catholicism (now teaching a course in Millenniary Ecstatics at Fordham); therefore his bias in favor of the "oral" and "sacred" medieval Church may have led him to anathematize Gutenberg and the Bible-reading Reformation he helped bring about. An old-fangled profane reader sometimes has the feeling that underneath the persiflage of print versus electronics, serial order versus instantaneous galaxies, "hot" versus "cool" media, and all that jazz, a weird allegory is being produced in which the Senses Five are personified as actors engaged in a struggle for the human psyche, with Sight finally exposed as an agent of Lucifer, racked up, and made to confess.

The Catholic Church, as it should, has responded nostalgically to this message, but also with its newly acquired electronic pep. (What hath Pope John wrought?) Among McLuhan's most fervent acolytes, spreading the good news about the media, are numerous priests. The Reverend John Culkin, S.J., Director of the School of Communications at Fordham, has proclaimed: "The linguists are doing it for languages. The anthropologists are doing it for culture. McLuhan is doing it for the media." The late Prophet Jones once said almost the same thing, though somewhat more eloquently, in praise of Father Divine: "I know that the chassis of your divine mind has been lubricated with divine lubrimentality." Should this new modernizing trend persist, it offers hope that the Church, which in time came to accept the Copernican system and the plurality of worlds, and now, it seems, has even made room for McLuhan's electronic galaxy, may some day find a little niche, so to speak, in its vast theological corpus, for the insertion of Mrs. Margaret Sanger's humble, but humane device.

Outside the Church, McLuhan's disciples among the young have already started to build their own temples. These are the new stomp-and-salvation "intermedia kinetic environments," discotheques that provide a multisensory *Schwärmerei*, the next thing to acid, in which to get McLuhan's massage. For those who don't, or who have tired blood, it's like being trapped inside a jukebox, an imploded Coney Island, and reduced to a state of zomboid catatonia. Perhaps they may serve a benevolent purpose—who knows?—as decompression chambers for the Orwellian future. Like they say, man, God's tripped out . . .

One engineering firm called "Sensefex," that designs such places, has recently declared its faith: "Our three muses are Tim Leary, the Beatles, and McLuhan. In our daydreams we approach every project with: How many senses can we involve?"

The Beatles have their own daydreams to dream; but if we substitute the name of Norman O. Brown (cited at the start of this trip into McLuhanland), then our original trinity of mystagogues, all homooisian if not homoousian, will be complete. The author of *Love's Body* can jump from ergo to ergo to ergo with as much slippery facility, and has the same prestidigitational expertise with symbols as McLuhan himself. And as for Dr. Leary, the author of "Tune in! Drop out! Whack off!" has much in common with the inventor of "The Medium Is the Massage." As McLuhan states: "In business as in society, 'getting on' may mean getting out. There is no 'ahead' in the world that is an echo chamber of instantaneous celebrity." *Ipso dixit.*

Their conclamant voices, amplified by all the media, Gutenbergian as well as electronic, proclaim:

If LSD can offer instant hallelujah, without any moral or spiritual effort required, why not just freak out? . . . If all social institutions are nothing but giant cribs to prevent us from enjoying our god-given rights to polymorphous perversity, why not rip them all down? . . . If the media can massage our heads with divine lubrimentality, at the expense of no mental exertion whatever, why read dull tomes by old fogies?

Having come so far around, we can now change the famous conclusion of Hume's *Enquiry Concerning Human Understanding* (which the philosopher had intended, ironically, to banish the smog of superstition) to read:

"If we take in our hand any volume, let us ask: *Will it help make me high?* No. *Will it help me make out?* No. *Will it help me Make It?* No. Then commit the book to the flames, for it can contain nothing but abstract and dreary reasoning or boring speculations on matters of fact and existence, and who the hell needs it?"

tom nairn*
mcluhanism:
the myth of our time

The difficulties of interpreting Marshall McLuhan are notorious. Academics hate him, ad-men love him, most people feel he is perversely and uncomfortably important.† The problems and the discomfort appear to arise from an unusual aspect of his work: he is not merely "difficult" in the sense familiar from any college education (obscure, long-winded, technical, etc.), but expresses his ideas deliberately in a manner that outwits our normal categories for understanding theoretical discourse. There is an unusual relationship between content and form in his writings, in other words, that poses an unusual semantic

* TOM NAIRN *teaches sociology at the Hornsey College of Art, one of London's important art schools. He has published reviews and articles in the* New Left Review, Les Temps Modernes, *and* New Statesman. *He is presently writing a book about Scotland.*

† Good examples of academic hate and publicitarian adoration attending the introduction of McLuhanism into Britain are "McLuhanism" by Christopher Ricks, in *The Listener*, September 28, 1967 [see pp. 100–105 of this book.—Ed.], and the Lintas Advertising Agency brochure "I'm the only one who knows what the hell is going on," September 1966.

problem to the reader. The aim of this essay is to suggest some ways of elucidating the problem.

McLuhan's distinctive style and way of arguing generates "McLuhanism," the cult, as has often been remarked (usually with a sneer). But what is a cult, in this sense? It is the contagious, uncritical diffusion of ideas felt to be important, and through it new notions and attitudes can emerge and impose themselves almost before we are fully aware of their meaning. A spontaneous "ism" can only arise like this, however, where there *is* meaning. There is little point in sneering at the PR slickness of McLuhanology or the vested interests that have made McLuhan number-one speaker on the U.S. after-dinner circuit: such success is possible only because of the wide, genuine appeal of his ideas.

It is more important to see the sense of the whole process than deprecate it. That is, to see that McLuhan's odd way of expressing himself and the social form his ideas have assumed amount to a kind of contemporary *mythmaking*: this would seem to be the appropriate semantic model. Then one must ask *why* such an important movement of thought, dealing with such central issues, should assume the guise of myth (and a new sort of myth, at that) in our time. Myth was once the natural way of making sense of the world, in spite of its limitations and conservatism; in the twentieth century it has become a way of imposing such conservative limits on thought, a strategy of evasion as well as a way of grasping reality. Why is *this* the way we have to consider such vital questions?

What is the principal subject matter of McLuhan's writing? It can be defined as the means or media of human communication, mostly in the sense of *language* communication (the conveying of meanings) although sometimes the argument overflows into a treatment of "communications" in the sense of transport. Now, the simplest question one can ask in this field (which also provides the best avenue toward grasping McLuhanism) is: Why was there no such subject matter to perplex intellectuals until so recently? In the great thought syntheses of the nineteenth century, for instance, Hegel and Marx, communication does not appear as a "problem" or even a distinct area of interest. Yet now it has become a dominant theme of culture. Why?

There seem to be two reasons for this. Firstly, there is a "problem" of communication that has arisen from general social development since the latter part of last century; and secondly, there are certain new facts about communication itself, also arising from this development and familiar to us in themselves, but which present peculiar difficulties of comprehension when one attempts to relate them theoretically to other social phenomena.

Traditionally, there was no "problem" of human communication for the simple reason that men's means of communication fitted society like a glove. By and large, given the over-all stability of the social framework or structure (underneath wars, dynastic changes, plagues, etc.), there was no necessary disparity between social reality and ways of speaking about it. This must not be taken to mean that communication and its content reflected social reality accurately, of course; but distorted or false consciousness ("ideology") fitted naturally into the system, for historical reasons that have been studied. Men found no problem in conveying the meaning of their experiences to one another (even if the meanings were false ones, often).

Since then, however (and more and more dramatically since 1914), the rapid development of social structures within the permanent industrial "revolution" has tended to break through the infrastructure of communication. Reality has evolved faster than languages. A strain is imposed upon consciousness, upon our ability to grasp the meaning of experiences (that is, upon our ability to communicate their meaning to one another). The social class most affected by this situation is naturally the intellectuals, the professional formers of awareness. Oriented primarily towards the past by their lengthy cultural formation, but feeling new meanings pressing in around them continuously from below, they find that:

> . . . Words strain,
> Crack and sometimes break, under the burden,
> Under the tension, slip, slide, perish,
> Decay with imprecision, will not stay in place,
> Will not stay still.*

The breakdown and fragmentation of the more complex cultural "languages" (easel painting, or the theater, for instance) has become a familiar phenomenon in this situation. The basic conventions of such modes of communication fall out of touch with evolving reality, and must be constantly and radically restructured in the struggle for meaningful speech.† Although this is characteristic of Western capitalist society, comparable crises have occurred in Communist countries; and perhaps the most drastic "problem" of all exists in "underdeveloped" lands dragged forcibly into history by the alien development of the world economy. Customarily the forms of alienation expressed in modern culture are attributed to the basic material conditions of civilization—to a schematic image of either "capitalist" or "communist" estrangement of humanity from its real potential, to the tyranny of commodity-reification or the tyranny of the State and its bureaucracy. How far it may, instead, be attributed to various forms of estrangement of language from reality has not been duly studied.

Yet clearly it ought to be. It is precisely in the shadow of this problem that "communication" has begun to seem of central significance, in sociology, in anthropology, in psychiatry. It is in this situation that the notion of society as language, of human personality as speech, has become plausible and appealing. In a world in which (as a thousand dramas, novels, poems, and films have shown) nobody can communicate with anybody else any longer, communication has become all-important:

---

* T. S. Eliot, "Burnt Norton," in *Four Quartets* (1935).

† These "conventions" are language, "langue" in the sense defined by Saussure, and followed, *e.g.*, by Roland Barthes: "A language . . . is a social institution and a system of values . . . the social part of language . . . like a game with its own rules." (*Elements of Semiology* [1964, English edition 1967], p. 14.)

> . . . The word is so little,
> so little, all space, in these raw
> misted, new-grown moons: what is wanting
> and twists our hearts and stays me here
> among the trees to wait you is a lost
> sense, or the fire, say, that prints on earth
> parallel outlines, shadows at peace,
> hands of the one dial . . .
> . . . Too torn is the human wood, too dull
> that year-to-year voice, too anxious
> the cloud-gap that tatters on the snowed
> ridges of Lunigiana.*

These considerations alone explain a lot of McLuhan's appeal. There have been many poets of the "lost sense," many expressions of the loss of language and meaning, from Beckett to Godard. McLuhan is the first mythmaker of the dilemma —at an intermediate stage between poetry and theory, as it were, half expressing and half theorizing a common, fundamental problem.

Within this problem-situation, new facts about communication have arisen to complicate it still further. These are the novel techniques and possibilities of communication associated with "the electric media," such as radio, telephone, television, telex, and so on. They are obviously the main focus of McLuhan's argument.

In relationship to the abovementioned "problem" of communication, the chronic split between social experience and means of speech, these means have a peculiar role. They represent, as it were, a colossal *technical* solution to communication problems of all sorts. Humanity has found an immense loudspeaker in its hands, capable of carrying the movement of an eyelid instantly to the moon and back, at the very moment in history when—like the guest in Ionesco's *The Chairs*—all that can be uttered is a strangled cry, a groping for new sounds of meaning. The technical solution is potential only, because of

* Eugenio Montale, "Personæ Separatæ," in *Poems* (trans. George Kay, 1964), p. 169.

course the problem is not technical, but social and human in character. Deprived of speech, we are compelled to invent languages, not only to speak in the old way, but to fill these new vehicles of communication worthily, according to the new conditions they impose. In our estrangement we are forced to communicate, the world is drenched with words as a new "informational environment" constitutes itself. This has turned the problem of communication into a sort of crisis.

But what sort of crisis? This raises the question of how we are to understand the modern phenomena of communication themselves, in the widest sociological terms. And the point about them seems to be their transcendence of certain of the terms employed in traditional conceptions of society.

The most important model of society in this respect is the one associated with Marx which since him has penetrated very widely into the common understanding. According to Marx, historical societies (but not necessarily prehistorical ones or the societies of the future) are composed of an identifiable substructure of "economic" realities, usually called simply the "structure." This may be seen on the analogy of a skeleton, or the underlying and possibly invisible foundation and frame of a building, which nevertheless shapes all the rest. Around this "basis" there is a "superstructure" organically linked to it and made up characteristically of, for instance, legal institutions, political institutions, and forms of culture and consciousness. In the alienated societies of history consciousness is in a sense confined to the superstructure—which is everywhere informed by society's false consciousness of itself, and of course is precisely *not* the consciousness of the "structure" and the "structure-superstructure" relationship, of society's true nature. Instead, it is a consciousness of "Man," of "God," of the "Nation," and so on. Marxism, by contrast, was to emerge as the break-through of this consciousness to reality; and the revelation took the shape of this general model of society's working.

No one can deny the immense usefulness of the model, or the genuine demystificatory function it still performs for us. It is and will remain what Marx saw it as: the beginning of a more adult and realistic human self-awareness. However, one

145

need only recall it like this to see how badly it needs to be rethought in the contemporary situation. The "structure" was the power of society, the roots of authority; the "superstructure" was the consciousness of society, and naturally included the means of communication. But these were traditional media of communication which fitted into the social interstices in the way mentioned above. Modern media of communication no longer fit into such a pattern.

The economic substructure was the transformation of nature through labor, man's control over the world. But with modern media, the industrial revolution of structures attains to an intervention in nature which is *itself* a massive development of human consciousness. Conscious culture does not echo or transform such a change, as it did the cotton mill, or the railway, for instance: it *is* the change. The traditional social power structure was founded upon the basis, and worked through the agency of the distorted consciousness in the superstructure, through faith, fear and myths. No instruments comparable to the modern "mass" media were available. A complex, subtle hierarchy of cultural forms transmuted the meaning of society and bound it together, a counterpoint of reverberations which often defies analysis. Insofar as power was an essential part of social structure, thus defined, the new media are "structural": their colossal power over mind immediately renders them relevant on this level. The old model pictures consciousness as being basically a product of structure, a reflection, a justification, the mirror of social being. This remains true in spite of the emphasis placed by Engels and many later thinkers upon the positive function of consciousness and its effect upon the basis. The change of scale and dimension brought by modern media, on the other hand, makes consciousness a direct part of the "structure" (in addition of course, one must remember the extent to which modern communications is itself economy, big business in the West, etc.)

The *potential* effect of such communication systems is to nullify, or bridge, the gap between "structure" and "superstructure" posited by the classical model. They are superstructural consciousness which is much more than just this; they are structural elements in society different in kind from any other previously known. In relation to the ancient patterns of alienation, they occupy an ambiguous role. Obviously, as instruments of rule, their potential is inconceivable and renders superfluous or invalid many traditional forms of estranged consciousness; but this very power, the expansion of consciousness on such a scale, is no less obviously dangerous to any system of false consciousness. Not grown to match the alienated grain of the social structure, the indiscriminate, indifferent, "mass" media of communication are potentially able to *unite* society in a hitherto unknown way, to cast a white light into every recess. Marx pictured a century ago, in *The Communist Manifesto,* how in the bourgeois era "All fixed, fast-frozen relations, with their train of ancient and venerable prejudices and conventions, are swept away. . . . All that was solid melts into air; all that was holy is profaned. . . ." But in fact only later forms of capitalism have evolved instruments capable of such traumatic liberation of consciousness (just as only later capitalism has envolved the unified world market and rendered nationalism archaic).

According to Marx's panorama of world history (echoed in McLuhan) primitive societies are without alienation internally: society is united in consciousness, against the fearful, unknown environment. Historical societies achieve power over this environment, at the cost of internal disunity, a stratification of class and consciousness. The society of the future will regain its conscious unity, but on a higher level, on the basis of its complete power over environment. Many thinkers have pointed out how the capitalist industrial revolution has already made possible the *material* foundations of such a development, and so both holds the future within itself and prevents this future from being born, because of its archaic social forms. With the growth of modern communication systems, however, capitalism has also begun to anticipate the *form* of the future, it has created agencies that already, in their own nature, reconstitute the conscious unity of society. Capitalism has moved from constituting the *preconditions* of the future (the productive machinery of material abundance, able to end

147

scarcity) to constituting an anticipation of this future in actual experience, a *condition of the future*.

Surely this is the sense in which the "medium *is* the message." And the message is somewhat different from the one conveyed by McLuhan.

According to McLuhan, what is happening is "the recreation of the world in the image of a global village," through the "electronic interdependence" of modern communications. This is the ultimate phase of a long historical process. It began everywhere in what he calls "tribal society." There the dominant medium was of course the spoken word, and men inhabited "the implicit, magical world of the resonant oral word." This close, organic society of the ear, with its intense collective feeling and low intellectual definition, was disrupted by the invention of the phonetic alphabet. The latter turned sounds into visual forms and "gave tribal man an eye for an ear."

However, the full potential of the written word could not be realized in Antiquity or the Middle Ages. Concentrated in the hands of a small class, the alphabet remained a technique of domination rather than a total form of social culture, and coexisted with the remains of the older aural culture. The next basic change was the universal extension of the phonetic alphabet, after the invention of printing. This is the revolution described in *The Gutenberg Galaxy*. The printed book "provided the first uniformly repeatable *commodity*, the first assembly-line, and the first mass-production." The typographic explosion thrust a more uniform culture into the interstices of society, and made possible the mode of social unity we know as the nation-state: it was "the architect of nationalism," as well as the original model of industrialism. The triumph of the neutral, calculating eye was complete, and was symbolized in the glorious perspective of later Renaissance art. At the heart of the Gutenberg revolution lies the modern, detached individual, the "cold fish" Western intellectual, muttering silently to himself in a corner, with *his* book.

This print era was analysis, fragmentation, repetition, the

victory of a certain sort of rationality. But this era is really over, nowadays, although we are unable (or unwilling) to grasp the fact. It has been ended by an even more drastic upheaval: the "implosion" of instantaneous electric communication has thrown back together what Gutenberg sundered, and brought about a new multisensible world of wholeness and all-at-onceness. Intellect is no longer isolated in a corner, or on a professorial rostrum; it can be literally everywhere at once, in the "cosmic membrane that has been snapped round the globe by the electric dilation of our various senses." The different aspects of this process are interestingly discussed in McLuhans' third book, *Understanding Media,* and are also re-emphasized in the more recent *The Medium Is the Massage:*

We now live in a *global* village . . . a simultaneous happening. We are back again in acoustic space. We have begun again to structure the primordial feeling, the tribal emotions from which a few centuries of literacy separate us.

A part of McLuhan's thesis is that this social history is not the history of a constant "human nature." Because the communication media are "extensions" of the senses (or even of the nervous system as a whole, in the case of the electric media), they shape our psychology as well as the fabric of society. Thus, the generational gap in Western society today is partly due to the formation of younger people by the media, to the different attitudes and feelings, the different employment of the senses arising from this situation, and so on.

The contemporary age made by the new forms of communication is an age of *myth.* By contrast, the age of the printed word was one of literalness, and books were the original "square" things. The new media environment we call "popular culture" is one in which the mind reaches for an immediate, sensible explanation, an image, an involving experience— for a "mythic dimension" of knowing, a new totemism. McLuhan's own work is—and is seen by him—as part of this dimension.

The mythical aspect of his notions is easily demonstrable,

with reference to any part of his theory. Take the example of the so-called "global village." To anyone who can extricate himself from the McLuhanite trance for a few seconds, it is reasonably clear that the existing global village was created by European imperialism, not by television; that it is not a "village," but a cruel class society tearing humanity in two; that the techniques which made it, and sustain it, are overwhelmingly pre-electronic—private property and the gun; and that the *actual* use made of media like television in our society, far from pushing us toward a healing of the gap, reinforces our acceptance of it. That we now *could* live in a "global village," that our actual experience prefigures this more and more in its form, thanks to new media, is another and different point. The *potential* of electric media is, in fact, in *contradiction* with a great deal of the actual social world. And the actual, historical and social grasp of the meaning of such media depends more than anything else upon seeing the contradiction.

McLuhan's mythical history and sociology consists precisely in evading such contradictions. And, by this evasion, what is lost is the very idea of a *historical* understanding of social phenomena. McLuhan behaves as though, with our new modes of communication and sensibility, we had escaped from history —so that it is now possible to compose a myth-history, in which communications are seen as the *causes,* the main levers of all change. This is not merely unscholarly. It is an attack upon the best achievement of human thought: our capacity to understand ourselves as social and historical beings, the work of generations to demystify our consciousness and confront our own reality. By an absurd (and characteristic) confusion, McLuhan identifies explanation of this kind with a bygone linear rationalism, with the illusions of print mechanism. In reality, the dimension of myth in the existing media world is not a natural product of "electric media," but of the *frustration* of such media by the outdated social framework they have emerged into. Unable to generate the global consciousness that would correspond to a real "global village," our societies produce instead a new totemic consciousness. The end to alienation would imply a healing of the rift between fantasy and social reality. Although we now have the means to do this, our existing society cannot employ these means; hence, they must expand and enclose us within fantasy still unrelated to reality. A stultifying myth-consciousness conditioned by this dilemma is seen by McLuhan as the meaning of the future, and re-expressed in his own celebrated style of composition.

It is not possible here to attempt a more extensive examination of Marshall McLuhan's work. But perhaps one may try to define—in the light of the above remarks—what form such an examination ought to take.

McLuhan's myth-world is a mythical process of a new type. Older bourgeois myths were focused upon "Human Nature," the unchanging substratum of the social drama, and so ". . . transformed reality into an image, History into Nature."* McLuhan's mythology has gone beyond the stage of projecting a fixed human or social "essence" to mask the unstable change of bourgeois society: it mythicizes process itself, in the form of the media. It still accomplishes the essential task of myths, the abstraction of our consciousness from real history; but it does so in a novel way, by seizing upon one aspect of the historical process and making it the determinant of the rest (like a force of nature). The truth in the myth lies in the real, and growing importance of the aspect in question; the false consciousness of the myth prevents us from grasping this importance historically. The exegesis of McLuhan therefore consists in attempting to separate the genuine historical meaning of the phenomena he discusses from the (literally) reactionary form in which he disguises this meaning. To put it crudely: after Hegel, Marx put history on its feet, right way up; McLuhan has turned it upside down again; criticism of McLuhan must inevitably try and put it on its feet once more.

The mythical side of McLuhan's thought is also plainly derived from a certain North American tradition of thought, not very well understood in Europe and consequently neglected in appreciations of him. He belongs to what one writer recently

* Roland Barthes, "Le Mythe, Aujourd'hui," in *Mythologies* (1957), p. 250; see also pp. 258–268.

called the tradition of ". . . the popular or populist sage, the cracker-barrel Socrates, the lofty or ribald annunciator of values moral, national, cosmic. . . . Watcher at the gate or monologuist by the molasses barrel in the general store, vatic bard or television humorist—there is a distinctive brand of American writers and 'talkers' who carry on with the tradition of the frontier publicist travelling the wide land with his grammars, recipe books, shreds of apocalypse and nostrums for spirit and bowels." * In this respect, clearly, like Mumford or Emerson, he is an inspirational sermonizer who assumes a very conventional relationship to his public, and this must be taken into account in unraveling his ambiguities.

McLuhan's view of modern communications is located halfway between being simply an expression of them, as they now are and appear to us in contemporary Western society, and being a theory of them, in the realm of pseudo-theory, or myth. Hence, one could say that a main task of social theory is now to debunk this mythology, and go on to construct a real historical theory of communications, a true consciousness of the new phenomena of consciousness.

But the fact that this is a main task is itself the best index to Marshall McLuhan's real importance. In the end, he only compels one to feel the need to rethink all that he has thought. But this is a great achievement. For a rethinking of the area whose significance he realized more vividly than anyone else cannot stop short of a revision of all our ideas about men and society.

* Review in *The Times Literary Supplement,* November 9, 1967, p. 1060.

geoffrey wagner*
misunderstanding media:
obscurity as authority

In the beginning was the word. Or, rather, the word was the word, and it was with God. Now, as we know, it is with Herbert Marshall McLuhan, and "the medium is the message." The very alliteration of the catch phrase is suspicious, exhibiting that predominance of sound over sense characteristic of the new experts in "communications media." It is resonant with the wonders of technology, and anyone who opposes the emotional reversion, who still believes that the word is the word rather than a medium, is automatically reactionary, *arrière-garde*, square and/or dead.

It is all most convenient, and the Container Corporation can subsidize the new apostle of conformity under the banner of experiment. Since, for a variety of reasons, the new is more likely to agitate as the authentic in America than elsewhere—

* GEOFFREY WAGNER *is a Professor of English Literature at Barnard College, New York, and is well known for his novels and critical essays. His most recent novel,* The Sands of Valor, *described the desert campaign fought by British troops during the Second World War.*

Margaret Mead contending that "Americans have substituted anthropology for history"—technology replaces the genuine magic of old, and Donald Duck now travels not on his carpet but on Uncle Scrooge's airline to his gold, diamond, emerald, and titanium mines. The Marx Brothers used to fool around in an operating room with scalpels, bedaubing themselves with blood, until a real doctor peeped in, and cried out, "Hey, you guys must be crazy." To which Groucho replied, "That's what they said about Pasteur."

Literary intellectuals—old-fashioned bookmen, that is—haven't felt exactly galvanized by the new myths about media. The meetings at which writers discuss the implications of radio or TV are generally centered on marketing problems. Language is for listeners, in a code of awareness from which media result. Such new frames for our world pictures are both self-protective and self-identifying. They cannot help but be so.

Thus, to attach some significance to the clarion call from Canada that "the medium is the message," we must be given something more than a worn cliché. For, to the literary scholar, this is simply to restate that style is vision, that man evolves new forms to answer the non-animal stresses of his environment. And to Marshall McLuhan, it must be said, nearly all these forms seem good, meliorative—although, as stated by one manufacturer at Senator Long's subcommittee hearings into snooping devices, it was human "needs" that developed wall listeners, and phone monitors, and the rest of the repertoire of repulsive bugs we are trying to kill by technology as soon as they spawn before us.

Needless to say, the world does change; everything does not always stay the same. Jet travel, electric daylight, and a telephone that (to date) imposes blind discourse—all interfere with biological rhythms within us. We include our perceptions of such disturbances in the truth of understanding them. Much of McLuhan's work seems, indeed, an (unacknowledged) application of Benjamin Lee Whorf's "metalinguistics," his contention of the need for a synthetic "grasp" replying to Whorf's theories about ideograms and phonograms. In his comments on the phonetic alphabet, Whorf phrased a dislike for any dissociation of sense and function such as we find popularized by the Canadian "thinker."

For there is the matter of how much thinking is going on in this instance. The intrinsic contradictions of McLuhan's reasoning, or prose, have been pointed out on occasion.* Even Hugh Kenner, a former student of the master, has expressed some reserve, putting his finger on how, in this mystique, "everything, alas, is something else," adding, "and if content is negligible, so are facts."† Plato's dialogues are not media, or manner, because spoken in one age and written in another. In both cases they were "sequential, linear," and the rest of the epithets of the new anathema.

The reply is always the same: McLuhan's insights are not meant to be right or wrong so much as stimulating. Such has, in fact, become his principal platform gambit of late. This is again awfully convenient—one wishes one could satisfy one's students in the same way. One is (you know) just running it up the antenna and waiting for Mrs. Front Porch to come out panting for enlightenment.

Thus McLuhan can mistake an effect for the true cause of that effect, without incurring challenge—he has provoked the liaison, or zeugma, and is simply asking questions. And while it seems certain that he does not, from his writings to date, understand the difference between electric and electronic (the first the grosser, power-carrying aspect of electricity, the second the finer, sensory or switching aspects involved), it is to be debated whether he, or his numerous followers, knows what a medium is in the first place.‡

* See especially, Ross Wetzsteon, "The Doubtful Necessity of Understanding McLuhan," *The Village Voice*, May 12, 1966. Also Kenneth Burke, *Language as Symbolic Action* (University of California Press, 1967). As Burke well puts it of *Understanding Media*, "Any analogy, however lax, between an invented medium and some part of the human body can be presented as an 'extension' of that part, whether or not it actually is so. We here confront a mere matter of terministic policy." [See Kenneth Burke's article, pp. 165–177 of this book.—Ed.]

† Hugh Kenner, "Understanding McLuhan," *National Review*, November 29, 1966. [See pp. 23–28 of this book.—Ed.]

‡ The medium is the message—"Give your child better grades by Christ-

155

The medium of a radio program is its "carrier" frequency, ten twenty megacycles on your friendly dial. The message is the music that is "modulated" or superimposed on the carrier. Radio theory stresses the distinction between medium and message, and any licensed radio ham will rhapsodize on it for hours. McLuhan is here hardly revising communications theory.

Similarly, if I receive a letter from my Auntie Loo, the medium is not the postman, it is the written word. Yet it is the former for McLuhan whenever such suits his purpose ("with the telegraph came the integral insistence and wholeness of Dickens," or, again, "print created individualism and nationalism in the 16th century"). If you do not observe separate rules for the nervous and physical functions, you can get as glib as *Time* in no time.

Indeed, the ease with which these lucubrations about participational culture were assimilated by popular journalism was quite enough to make them suspect to the serious. The whole "psychedelic" craze (a women's-wear store advertising "psychedelic knits" as I write) should surely alert one to the fundamentally innocuous and frivolous nature of this literary Lysistrata. That the world is watching television hardly proves the world is right. It's happening, man, froths McLuhan in answer to such objections; I'm just telling it the way it is. But *is* it happening? In fact, by McLuhan's book, and it is the Bible of the educated or half-educated conformist, almost anything that happens *should* happen. It is all a slap-happy ad man's dream come true.

Thus, the total confusion between the chicken and the egg makes it possible for McLuhan to point to TV as a "medium" stirring participational desires in the young. In actual fact, any

---

mas. Start his school year off right with a Royal Galaxy portable typewriter. For typing improves grades . . . and report cards prove it. When students start typing assignments, school work (and grades) start to improve almost immediately. Educators acknowledge it. Classroom tests have proved it. But for truly first-class work, a student needs a portable that's easy to type on, easy to learn on . . . a Royal Galaxy" (advertisement in *The New York Times*).

concern for involvement aroused by this new force—by no means as new in its semantic ratio to culture as all that—is likely to have been caused by a disgust with TV as yet another ideological treachery.

I am not denying that a cause can be a previous effect. Orwell cites the man who boozes because he thinks himself a washout, and promptly becomes one because he boozes. This is the familiar *post hoc* fallacy: my income goes up, I buy more stock, my income goes up. Loss of appetite increases anemia, anemia increases loss of appetite. But what happens *chez* McLuhan is that the point of departure suddenly becomes, by bogus sleight of hand, the thesis proved ("With the arrival of electric technology man extended, or set outside himself, a live model of the central nervous system itself"). In this way we learn that it was really the fishes that discovered water.

In truth, "medium" and "message" are terms that can be used interchangeably, coterminously, by McLuhan, as can his catchall categories of "hot" and "cool." (After all, you have to fill in a lot of radio from other senses than the ear, so it should logically be "cool" rather than "hot," but it isn't because McLuhan says it isn't.) In a sense, everything can be made into a medium—including, of course, poor old print. McLuhan's misunderstanding of the audiac, a device that allegedly deadens the pain sensors by "superstimulation" of the aural, might show what I mean.

McLuhan cites the "autoamputation" (of Jonas and Selye) as being that technique whereby, when the source of irritation cannot be located or avoided, the sensory apparatus is deadened, "amputated" so far as the central nervous system is concerned. McLuhan extends this: under the stress of "superstimulation," the nervous system protects itself by "amputating or isolating the offending organ, sense, or function." (Of course, an organ is not a sense, nor a function, so that their cutting-off can hardly be metaphorized under a general heading like this; but one can parenthesize in such a manner on almost every page of McLuhan.)

According to this argument, then, the dentist's drill should be *more*, not less, painful under audiac, since the other senses are said to become more receptive after "amputation." The tautology is anticipated in McLuhan's *The Gutenberg Galaxy* (1962), where we read that "no sense can function in isolation" but that a kind of audiac hypnosis can be produced by "the filling of the field of attention by one sense only." Interestingly, McLuhan here adduces a quotation from Edgar in *King Lear* that should tell him *the opposite* of what he gets out of it ("Why then, your other senses grow imperfect/By your eyes' anguish . . ."). What McLuhan is really referring to, in his characteristically cavalier fashion, is audioanalgesia, in which the sense of hearing is insulted, chiefly by "white sound" (massively cascading water, and the like), in order to anesthetize another sense. Audioanalgesia has, after some initial enthusiasm, largely fallen by the wayside since, in common with hypnosis, it requires unusual cooperation from the patient, and since it introduces more problems than factors of advantage over routine anesthesia. But this last does not, of course, invalidate McLuhan's speculation.

Still, perceptions must remain poor assumptions with as low a level of rationality as this, without some sense of reality, or what is plainly going on. It is in this way that, far from being some new messiah for the young, McLuhan emerges as a man of the study, monkishly substituting metaphor for equality and mistaking abstraction for universal truth whenever it suits his book to do so—not to mention misreading literature right, left, and center. He takes Buckminster Fuller's metaphor of tool as extension of man, with no reference that I can find to the originator, and restates it as equality. Such a confident detachment from concretion must seem like so much intellectual balloonism. In *Tristes Tropiques,* Claude Lévi-Strauss in fact identifies this sort of thing as the real vice of our intelligentsia in America, the sickness of the *philosophe:* namely, mere playing with ideas.

If we have evolved color and closed-circuit TV, and now visual telephones, it is because our relationships to reality demand some such, not the reverse. We answer a disrupted cycle somewhere. In effect, the movie emerges in literature, print, long before McLuhan sees it doing so on the screen (take the early work of Willy Busch or "Bonaventura"'s *Nachtwachen* in Germany). It is poor semantic harmony that has driven our young to seek out more participational responses, in poetry-reading cafés and the like.

Indeed, McLuhan's attack on general semantics as "obsolete" (so reported by Tom Wolfe) is significant. For it says no more than that modern man is obsolete. And in a sense this is another truism, or cliché, of communications. Our biological cycles become daily more out of phase with our environment—thus throwing up, by the way, distortions like McLuhan. Cults of impermanence in the arts are of this order, for to be perpetually impermanent is scarcely to exist. We live in an age in which animals have been made to eat their young by the thunder of passing jets—here is more direct echo of *Lear,* if you want one.

Newness as a norm, or criterion of value, is the quickest and most convenient concession to the dominant technology. "Beaujolais 1966 is here!" yodeled a Bordeaux Wines & Liquors Corporation ad . . . in 1966. Newness, ahead-ofness would dignify the dreariest academic eruptions of various past days. "Works of art aren't eggs," T. E. Hulme objected. The emphasis on the ahead-of race of technology causes McLuhan's misreading of literature to attain at times a kind of genius. What does his repeated catch phrase "Hopkins and the symbolists" mean? Which "symbolists"? When? Though of course we should not forget that "symbolism is a kind of witty jazz." Nor that Freud would "have carried no interest" unless "the West had long been processed by print." The seventeenth century (where? which part of it?) "emerged into a merely visual science in its conscious life"—note the *merely.* Meanwhile, as we move on, the "painterly strategy" [*sic*] of Cézanne has been "to paint as if you held, rather than as if you saw, objects."*

---

* The quotations in this paragraph are from *The Gutenberg Galaxy.* There is space for only one final clobbering of truth by these kinship terms: "The miseries of conflict between the Eastern and Roman churches, for example, are a merely obvious instance of the type of opposition between the oral and the visual cultures, having *nothing to do* with the

The apogee, or nadir, of antiprint mania is to be found in McLuhan's *The Gutenberg Galaxy*, neglected in assessment of the author today. It is an anthology of other people's ideas, for the most part—the ideas on which he erected his medium-message structure. The galaxy supposes that "the eye has none of the delicacy of the ear" and that "speech is an outering (utterance) of all our senses at once." It is an attack, a fairly bloodthirsty one, on the habits of printed literature in favor of something called the ear, which is axiomatically excellent. (As Harry Levin has put it, "oral literature" is really a contradiction in terms.) The Initial Teaching Alphabet (or "augmented Roman"), devised by Sir James Pitman and utilizing forty-four letters and digraphs, is currently under evaluation by the Reading Research Unit of London University, and at Leeds University, where it serves as a kind of intermediary alphabet for children, showing the phonetic possibilities of script.

Since McLuhan's confusions are becoming institutionalized daily, *The Gutenberg Galaxy* is worth a second look, in the character of their genesis. The book assembles an arsenal of weaponry critical of the development of print. The whole edifice relies on the cornerstone statement, "The auditory field is simultaneous, the visual mode is successive." Yet McLuhan had just told us, before we came to this proposition, that savages cannot generalize their visual experiences, a prerogative of the sophisticate. Therefore, the "mosaic" of the latter can hardly be "successive."

It is highly debatable, to say the least, that the eye is any more "successive" than the ear—physiological formulations are not aesthetic results—and to go on to say that " 'writing' to a medieval student was not only profoundly oral but inseparable from what is now called oratory" is quite another tack altogether. That the Chinese "written character does not separate speech and visual code in our way" may be an equally unexceptionable, and unexceptional, statement. I do not know Chinese well enough to say, and doubt if McLuhan does, either.

Faith" (my italics). And yet McLuhan can still quote Sidney's sonnet which concludes, " 'Fool,' said my Muse to me, 'look in thy heart, and write!' "

But the Chinese students to whom I have put the theory do not seem immensely excited by it, and of course China is happily alphabetizing its script (or, at least, adopting the Cyrillic), no doubt making it "visual, sequential, uniform, and lineal."

Nor is it clear that McLuhan understands the printing process at all. He talks about something called "print," and that is that. In fact, the first wood blocks, laboriously cut to simulate the writing of scribes, barely speeded the process of script. Moreover, though presumably "sequential," the linotype machine used in newspaper work casts individual *lines* of type, while the roll taken off the monotype machine to the caster is non-predicative since it "plays back," unwinding backward.*

Although McLuhan ducks out from specific evaluation, everywhere asserting that he is only studying what is happening in media, the "visual, sequential" is, we note, *uniform* and disliked. "We have spent much energy and fury in recent centuries in destroying oral culture by print technology so that the uniformly processed individuals of commercial society can return to oral marginal spots as tourists and consumers, whether geographical or artistic." It is hardly likely that man would have proceeded with this "destruction" for century after century if it were not in some manner necessary for him to do so. And indeed McLuhan has to admit that it is print that has kept funny little principles like *freedom* in the forefront of man's political dialogues.

Once more, the truth is that McLuhan's terms "visual" and "oral" are, like his terms "hot" and "cool," in *Understanding Media,* so hypergeneralized as to be applicable at will, and even interchangeably. They are self-suffocating classes. We are

* There is no space to evaluate here the capital McLuhan has acquired out of the theory of J. Z. Young, the British anatomist, concerning language "feedback." It is a sort of semantic translation of, or shorthand for, the phenomenon of nature following art. Wilde mentions Turgenev's nihilism producing real nihilism at the end of *The Decay of Lying.* Today, America exports rock-and-roll and then stands hypnotized by the Beatles. France plays fashion to Anglo-Saxony and gets mesmerized by the *mini-jupe.* It was not McLuhan who remarked on the attraction of a reflection over the reality, but it was McLuhan—who else?—who called it "Narcissus-narcosis."

told that unlike "visual" English and American audiences watching *The Bridge on the River Kwai,* Frenchmen are "oral." Ah, come off it. *Is* the ear more sensitive and multiperceptual than the eye? Who says so? McLuhan says so, just as McLuhan decides at the end of this study of "print" that "lineal specialisms and fixed points of view" are dissolved in 1905, with, presumably, Einstein and Planck.

Similarly, we are told that "with film you are the camera . . . But with TV you are the screen." This sounds delightfully adroit, smooth cocktail patter indeed, until you realize it was written at a moment when about 80 per cent of most TV consisted of film, and the remainder of technically analogous material. However, we are quickly reminded of the heresy of such objections—"This, of course, is to consider only the 'content' of new theories." TV soaks up dud film, McLuhan alleges, because any new medium needs matter; the early printing presses pleaded for manuscripts, and so forth.

This argument, like so many others, is legerdemain, a schoolman's trick. We are assured that form produces its own content at will. Thus, McLuhan once again answers himself by his own question, confusing origin and import, cause and effect. His tautology on television boils down to this: bad TV is merely the "content" of a past, demoded form, being temporarily borrowed, as it were, by the new form—until this throws up new content itself. But, as there is virtually no other content available to examine as yet, one is left to speculate on the basis of form alone. So we end up (like *Life* magazine) conceding that only McLuhan can predict the future. We are back with the familiar cultural ahead-of-ness race. Only the pundit is supposed to know what is avant garde—*i.e.,* in the position of possibly being permanent: in the position of one day being great art. But the pundit is ineluctably part of his time, and his criteria of prediction thereby contaminated; they can be forced to fit almost anything. "Works of art aren't eggs."

It would, lastly, be tempting to go further and run down the basic antipopulism of McLuhan's whole approach, ending, as it does, in a Nietzschean *furor Teutonicus* or surrogate bookburning that sends advertising executives braying with delight down Madison Avenue, while the Ballet Luce curtsies in genuflection at the side. (McLuhan's work is, like the later Nietzsche's, aphoristic and percolated with contempt.) But to do this would require a further attack.

Suffice it to say here that: unlike Chinese, and despite Herbert Marshall McLuhan, our language is enumerative. Word order is for us a primary signal (and word order does not mean a *certain* word order, it means the order of words). If we regard predication as a social relationship, rather than as a problem of bookish study, we shall not, I think, be overenchanted by this attack on the "sequential." Predication is the characteristic mode of our experience. Speech is *not* purely "oral"—whatever that means (one cannot form close categories out of human sense systems). Literacy itself is multisensory, as Pitman's "augmented Roman" acknowledges. Speech is largely sequential and is only fully speech, as Sapir showed, in a contextual situation of which it takes full cognizance. Beyond exceptional instances, such as Maurice Grammont's sound-metaphors (tonal forms instinct with, say, the cuckoo's cry, the owl's hoot), the sounds of words give no clue to their meaning.* *Rock* means a jacket, a year, or fate, according to which national boundary you happen to be crossing, and even in the same language it has a semantic refraction; a British rock is different from an American. We note that the pop group didn't call itself the *Rolling Rocks*. The only writing I can think of that appeals wholly to the eye is mathematics, and perversely McLuhan calls number "an audile-tactile code." If seventeenth-century punctuation was "for the ear and not for the eye," it was still sequential (and I would like to know much more about printers' habits of the time before accepting this) .

McLuhan is really rather like the man who apologizes first

* In *Scientific American* for June 1960, James Cook Brown discusses the synthetic language called Loglan. This goes beyond mere revision of the alphabet into the kind of differentia of meaning that Charles Peirce tried to organize into his complicated system of qualisigns, legisigns, semes, and so on. Loglan's grammatical apparatus is determined by 112 operators predicated on phonetic familiarity. Its most readily learnable word is *matma* (with a score of .94). *Matma* means mother. This is hardly a surprise to linguists, but Loglan is what McLuhan might properly call "oral."

GEOFFREY WAGNER

and then steps on your toe second. His vogue evinces how
dearly we love a pundit, especially when he is polysyllabic. But
his whole confusion of form and content is dangerous epistemology, since it is yet another force disrupting harmony and
leading to excitable action. As Alfred North Whitehead gently
put it, "Error is the price we pay for progress." Or, in the squib
by fellow-Canadian A. J. M. Smith,

> McLuhan put his telescope to his ear.
> "What a lovely smell," he said, "we have here."

kenneth burke*
medium as "message"

Some thoughts on Marshall McLuhan's
Understanding Media: The Extensions of Man
[and, secondarily, on *The Gutenberg Galaxy*] †

There are many loci of motives. For instance, an act may be attributed to the nature of the agent; Marxists lay major stress upon the motivating force of the "objective situation" (the Dramatistic nomenclature would call it "scene"); McLuhan's book on "media" necessarily puts the main emphasis upon the role of *instruments* (means, agencies) in shaping human dispositions, or attitudes and habits. And though men's technical innovations are but a fraction of the "human condition" in general, the great clutter of such things that characterize modern life adds up to a formative background. Thus, we confront the pragmatistic trend I discussed in my *Grammar of Motives*,

* KENNETH BURKE *is one of the deans of American literary criticism. His most important books include* Counter-Statement, Permanence and Change, Attitudes Towards History, Philosophy of Literary Form, A Grammar of Motives, *and* A Rhetoric of Motives. *This essay is a chapter from his latest book,* Language as Symbolic Action.

† Much of this material parallels part of a paper on "Dramatism" presented at the Second International Symposium on Communication Theory and Research, 1966, the proceedings to be published in a volume edited by Lee Thayer and issued by Spartan Books, Washington, D. C.

whereby the accumulation of agencies becomes viewed as the major aspect of man's motivating scenes (or, as I put it in my Definition, man is "separated from his natural condition by instruments of his own making").

But though McLuhan's title features Agency as a locus of motivation, his subtitle provides a different twist. The agencies, in turn, are derived from the *agent* (namely "Man"). Thus, as the title suggests a brand of *pragmatism,* the subtitle suggests a somewhat *idealistic* modifier. (As explained in my *Grammar,* the Dramatistic perspective classes as "idealistic" all terminologies that have for their *Ausgangspunkt* some intrinsic aspect of "man" or his "consciousness.") But even here, the initial pragmatist emphasis ultimately prevails to the extent that by "extensions" is meant such instruments as are to be found *primarily* in our technical devices, such as wheels, printing presses, radio, television. (I say "primarily" because the category has some vague edges. For instance, there is a chapter on Games as extensions of man; and language is called "a human technology." But it is typical of McLuhan that whereas, from the full Dramatistic point of view, one would necessarily include a chapter on "War" when discussing the problems of human culture, he writes instead on "Weapons." This shift permits him to end on the sunshine thought that "weaponry is a self-liquidating fact," whereas alas! a fully developed Dramatistic way of meditating on such matters goads us to realize that *any* new power, or mode of control (such as control over the weather), is potentially an instrument of war.

Obviously, when man's "extensions" are viewed thus narrowly, insofar as most of the instruments considered are physical (things in the realm of sheer *motion*), they will be viewed as extensions of human *physiology*. But this pattern is impaired somewhat, and for the better, in the chapters on language and games, which impinge upon the Dramatistic in the full sense of the term. (Basically, I am contending that since Agency is one member of the Dramatistic pentad, McLuhan's bright book is at least inconsistent enough to keep straying beyond the realm of motion into the realm of action—and, of course, this step shows up most clearly when he turns from such mere technical mechanisms as the *wheel* to such media as newspapers printed on a rotary press.)

The word "dramatic" keeps turning up at many points in the text, and at least once there is a shallow reference to the "cathartic." But drama and its motives get head-on treatment in only about three pages of the chapter on games. This omission is particularly important because the stress upon the media in the narrower sense reduces to a minimum such considerations as we find in *The Gutenberg Galaxy* (with regard to the dialectical nature of the medieval manuscript). Fundamentally, the term "extensions" is used along these lines: Instruments prior to the "electric" age are said to have been extensions of *particular* bodily parts (such as eye, hand, or foot), but the inventions of the new "electric age" differ from those to the extent that electricity is viewed as an extension of the "central nervous system" in general. This distinction serves as a quasiphysical basis for McLuhan's claim that the electric media (by "extending" the nature of the nervous system *in general*) will eliminate tendencies toward specialization characteristic of the earlier "mechanical" inventions that were extensions of *particular* bodily parts.

We should introduce two admonitions here. First, we should note that man's symbolic prowess in general is not derived from particular bodily parts, but in its own way reflects the central nervous system as source. Hence, throughout the whole era of "mechanical" specialization, there has been a realm of motives grounded (by his scheme) in physiological beginnings that *naturally transcend* such specialization, even though it may include specialized terminologies. (I would contend, of course, that McLuhan's great skimping on *drama* as a "medium" necessarily leads to an overly simplified view of media in general and their role in our culture.) I would also call it to your attention that although many human inventions conceivably might *not* be "extensions" of the human body, the whole subject is sufficiently vague to allow for McLuhan's mediumistic genealogy. I mean: Maybe the sight of birds flying is what induced man to try to invent flying machines. Nevertheless, by McLuhan's derivation the airplane would be an "extension" of the human body. A club could be thought of as a kind of "extended" arm and fist; but when McLuhan puts major emphasis upon the notion that the wheel is an extension of the feet, I can't help recalling a newspaper dispatch that observed: "Your body contains virtually every engineering device except the wheel." And it gave this list: "The cylinder, ball joint, dome, tripod, hinge and reinforcing beam." But no matter. What is really involved here, as viewed from the standpoint of sheerly terministic resources, is: If, instead of saying that certain media are *analogous* to parts of the body, you say that they are "extensions" of such parts, and if you allow for great latitude in the use of analogy, anything will fit in somewhere. In fact, since the body is itself an aspect of nature, and thus embodies the same kinds of goings-on that we can observe in other parts of nature, even if an invention did happen to arise from observation of nature rather than by "extension" of the inventor's body, lax rules for the application of analogy here would allow you to find some analogical process in the body itself—whereupon, in keeping with the prime resources of the McLuhan nomenclature, you could call such an *analogy with* the body an "extension of" the body, that is to say a *derivation from* the body. The wheel could conceivably have been derived from looking at a disk like the sun or moon; or it might conceivably have been derived by slicing a log, or whatever. The main point is that even though the body has no wheel, this major invention in McLuhan's scheme is, by terministic fiat, derived from the "circular" motion of the feet (a derivation made easy by the fact that if you treat analogy with latitude enough, the *repetition* of a *reciprocating* motion can be called "circular," or even more broadly, the regular repetition of *anything* can be called "circular"). To haggle with McLuhan on this point is necessarily a waste of time. All we should do is recognize what's going on here. And what *is* going on? Simply this: Any analogy, however lax, between an invented medium and some part of the human body can be presented as an "extension" of that part, whether or not it actually is so. We here confront a mere matter of terministic policy. And since the body does, beyond question, affect our thinking by providing us with analogies, to that extent the policy can serve. We'd go along with him, just for the ride, were it not that he later uses this terministic device to the ends of faulty interpretation as regards our current quandaries. On that point, more anon.

But here we need a brief interpolation; namely: Suppose you ground the whole thing, as McLuhan does, in a distinction between the "mechanical" wheel and an "electric age" that wholly transcends the old-fashioned era of the wheel, an era that rejects both wheel and mechanism. Then suppose that, on looking up the definition of an *electric* dynamo, you learn that this *new-age* medium is defined (italics ours) as "A *machine* for converting *mechanical* into electric energy by *rotating* coils of copper wire in a magnetic field." In brief, all these electric dynamos are *machines* that *rotate*. Yet the new "electric age" is to be presented as *antithetical* to the "mechanical" and the "rotatory" (the wheel). No matter. All you need do is say that the wheel is "obsolescent," or "in principle" obsolete.

But to the key formula, "The medium is the message." And we should keep to it, not allowing the book to dodge it, even though I heard McLuhan over the air engagingly suggest that maybe one had better change "message" to "massage." If he wants to rewrite his book by revising all his chapters in keeping with this pun, and thus showing that all media, or "extensions of man," are best understood as variations on the art of massage, I'll gladly read it. Indeed, I can even glimpse some ribald fun here, based on lewd conceits about a man's extension. But in the meantime, let's cling to the formula as given in the book now before us. The first implication of the formula is obvious enough, and McLuhan recognizes it when he summarily dismisses any and all who would approach a message in terms of "content analysis." If the *medium* is the message, obviously the important thing is not what somebody *says* in a given medium, but what medium he uses, regardless of what he says. Since this oversimplification is the very soul of *his* message, we must never let it get out of sight when considering his book. Though we all may disagree as to just what the effects of men's accumulated media are, anyone of intelligence recognizes that media must have had great effects of some kind upon our thinking, so that they have become a kind of "second nature" with us. Mc-Luhan here profits considerably by a recent increase in the ambiguity of the words "information" and "communication." If you give someone a hard blow on the head, this "happening" can now be classed as a kind of "information" that is physically "communicated" to the nervous centers of the victim's brain. Hence, whatever the difference between an electric light and a comic book, or between a chemical and the "iconic" image on a television screen, all can be classed as media in Mc-Luhan's nomenclature. And he keeps incidentally talking about "forms" in ways that would cover the same range (a point to which I shall revert when discussing Lessing's *Laocoön* —for I believe that even a mere glance at that book quickly makes clear the fatal fallacy in McLuhan's formula). And, of course, stress upon media as such fits in well with current hankerings after various kinds of "nonobjective" or "nonrepresentational" art (trends that are justifiable responses to the many new textures and materials supplied by modern technology).

The medium is the message. Hence, down with content analysis. We should at least pause en route to note that the formula lends itself readily to caricature. Primus rushes up breathlessly to his friend Secundus, shouting, "I have a drastic message for you. It's about your worst enemy. He is armed and raging and is—" Whereupon Secundus interrupts: "Please! Let's get down to business. Who cares about the contents of a message? My lad, hasn't McLuhan made it clear to you? The *medium* is the message. So quick, tell me the really crucial point. I don't care what the news is. What I want to know is: Did it come by telegraph, telephone, wireless, radio, TV, semaphore signals, or word of mouth?" The moral of my tale is simple. Though McLuhan's exotic formula serves well as a slogan, any such oversimplification is likely to show up, sooner or later, as a flat contradiction. Hence, after outlawing "content analysis" as an approach to the effects of media, toward the end of his book he comes to a terministic orgy in his enthusiasm for "information-gathering." But if the "information" that is fed into an electronic computer isn't "content," what is it? The issue always keeps turning up in the most amusing fashion when McLuhan is being questioned. For, inevitably, he is questioned about the *contents* of his position, whether these contents are being considered in his book, or in classroom discussion, or on radio or television. And it's fun to watch how he somehow manages to dodge his questioners. For he uses question periods not as opportunities to make his position more precise, but rather as challenges that he must deflect and confuse to the best of his ability (which along these lines is considerable).

Looked at most broadly, I think his terministic lineup can be seen to operate thus: Viewing technological development in terms of a *continuum,* one might note how invention has progressed pari passu with the increase of specialization. And one might conclude that the growth of specialization will continue, though modern trends (in automation and computers) might greatly modify its nature. Or one might use a terminology that introduces a principle of *discontinuity*. Thus, instead of discussing the "overall situation" in terms of technology in general, one might propose a distinction between two kinds or eras of technology. McLuhan's terms opt for this latter policy. He builds everything around a radical distinction between an earlier "mechanical" stage of technology and a presently emergent electric age." And whereas the "mechanical" stage led to extreme division of labor, he promises that in the "electric age" this tendency toward "specialism" will be reversed. The earlier "explosion" becomes an "implosion," which is somehow something quite different, despite the great *expansion* of markets for the new electric devices (and I leave it for the reader to decide whether we might compromise on simple "plosion"). By talk of the new electric age's penchant for "information-gathering" (data to be fed into computers) he uses this overall titular term to suggest that all specialization dissolves in this single common task. True, information gathered from many diverse sources can be fed into a computer; and the results will transcend the limits of any specialized pursuit (except, of course, the highly specialized pursuits that have to do with the programming and perfecting of computers). But what of the information itself? Would not chemical data require specialized knowledge of chemistry; biological data, specialists in biology; etc.? Though the computer may "process" such material in ways hitherto impossible, the treatment of the data does not at all eliminate the need for specialists to gather it. Now that any and every animate and inanimate process in all the world can be classed as a kind of "information," we must not let McLuhan use the term to suggest that merely because it can be applied to all "information-gathering," all information-gatherers would be engaged in an identical enterprise. McLuhan rightly becomes zestful in his use of the term; for high among its "subliminal" effects (if we may adapt a favorite word of his for a different purpose) is its ability to deflect the reader's attention away from the question: *Insofar as technology, under any form, produces a great diversity of media, must there not be a corresponding diversity of occupations concerned with the production, distribution, and servicing of such varied devices (whether they are in the realm of communication specifically or are to be classed as economic commodities in general)?* In sum: The highly generalized nature of his sheer *term* "information-gathering" conceals the fact that a whole army of specialists will be needed to supply the analytic material that the computers presumably will synthesize after their fashion (*and within their limits*).

Though, as with "dramatic," the book contains many passing references to language, here again it skimps, as regards the full range of the Dramatistic nomenclature. For instance, by linking perspective with "point of view" in the *literal* sense, McLuhan can persuasively advance the notion that certain new media present a kind of "mosaic" not characterized by "point of view." Hence he can treat "point of view" as obolescent, along with the kinds of individualism and specialism that marked its rise (in connection with the developments of printing). But tactics of that sort "subliminally" conceal from us the strictly terministic fact that any particular nomenclature (such as the one used in McLuhan's book) *functions* as a "perspective," or "point of view"; and to idealize a problem in its particular terms is to consider the problem *from that special angle of approach.* McLuhan's own book is, of course, a case in point —just as, similarly, while writing a monologue, he asks for the kinds of tolerance that would belong to a dialogue.

Similarly, he will talk about "repeatability" as though it were simply a matter of mass production by machines. But a more methodically *terministic* approach to his thesis would remind him that there is also a prior kind of "repeatability" intrinsic to the very nature of terministic generalization. Give me the *word* "wheel," for instance, and I thereby have a principle of repeatability much more extensive than the mass productions of any printing press or assembly line. For the word applies to every wheel-like thing that ever has been, will be, or could be—and all the more so, if you will add to the rules for McLuhan's nomenclature a "variance" whereby even reciprocating motion can be classed as "rotatory." Yet surely not a machine, but the broad relevance of such generalized terms in his nomenclature is what induces McLuhan so often to repeat the word "repeatable" when he is promising that in his "electric age" this touchstone of the "mechanical" will cease to prevail.

Since practically any artifact can be classed as a medium, and the current widened use of the term "communication" allows McLuhan to treat any such invention as a medium of *communication,* we might here propose a working distinction, for present purposes. We might speak of *directly* communicative media (such as telephones or television) and *indirectly* communicative media (in the broad sense that cars, refrigerators, foods, clothing, and guns could be called communicative). "Forms" would extend things further (as with the difference between television as a medium of communication and soap opera as a medium of communication) . Here's where we get to Lessing's *Laocoön.* I submit that had McLuhan taken that text to heart, he would have had a much better chance of arriving at a properly matured revision of his slogan "The medium is the message." Under Lessing's guidance, with regard to *directly* communicative media and their tie-in with particular forms, or artistic modes, McLuhan could have systematically asked himself *just what kind of content* is favored by the peculiar nature of a given medium. Actually, the sheer pressure of his subject matter does impose such a procedure upon Mc-Luhan at many points. For instance, in *Understanding Media* we find him concerning himself with the notion that one kind of character is a better fit for television, another kind a better fit for radio. That's the way he should have proceeded throughout, rather than merely admitting such observations without explicitly recognizing that they imply the need for the revision of his slogan (whereas the inaccuracy of that slogan served instead to keep him from recognizing exactly what all his concern with media did imply). In brief, as Lessing shows: The point is not that a given medium (in the sense of a directly communicative form) does its full work upon us *without* the element of "content." Rather, his study of the difference between painting (or sculpture) and poetry indicates how expert practitioners of a given medium may resort to the kind of contents that the given medium is best equipped to exploit. Obviously, as so approached, the issue is quite different from the blunt proposition that "the medium is the message." Yet McLuhan's muddled method does have one advantage, rhetorically. For it seems to have caught the attention in ways that Lessing's kind of treatment can no longer match.

McLuhan is prominent among current idea-men whose thought-style might be summed up as: "Down with the political, up with the apocalyptic." And there's no denying: It's much more pleasant to speculate about the possible subliminal magic of "participation in depth" when looking at the iconic image (any image) on a television screen than to suffer the burden of an explicit analysis concerned with the miseducation clearly implicit in the contents of particular programs that line people up by exploiting one set of "topics" rather than another in the concocting of their motivational recipes. Incidentally, there's a news program that I regularly follow with some confidence; yet I can't help worrying about the fact that it is sponsored by the damnedest batch of poisons and quack drugs, so I keep fearing that the show is somehow being built up for a sellout, come the strategic moment. In any case, whether you like it or not, we are here concerned with the *contents* of the programs and the ads, and not just the nature of the *medium,* in the sense of the "mosaic" screen on which they are shown, whatever its "subliminal" effects may be.

One could go on and on. But two more points should be enough for now. First, there's the problem of the "visual," and its corresponding effects in promoting a "lineal" point of view. I question whether most readers have got that matter clear. Or maybe I'm the one that has it wrong. I see it thus: One could hardly say with conviction that "lineal" thinking is essentially due to the lineal nature of phonetic writing. Other kinds of writing follow in a sequence, too, since sentences (like melody) are sequential, in contrast with a picture or piece of sculpture (which is "all there at once"). Codes of literary and musical notation allow us to approach the overall form of a work step-by-step, but the relation among the parts "just *is,*" nontemporally. On the other hand, works such as painting and sculpture first confront us in their totality, then we impart a kind of temporal order to them by letting the eye rove over them analytically, thus endowing them with many tiny "histories" as we go from one part to another, feeling the developments and the relationships among the parts. But although no work can come to life as an artistic medium unless we, by our modes of interpretation, sympathetically and "empathetically" (or "imaginatively") endow its *positions* and *motions* with the equality of *action,* there is a notable difference between paintings or sculpture on one side and notations for words or music on the other. The colors and forms of the "static" media (painting and sculpture) appeal to us directly, sensuously, as they are, right there in front of us. But codes of literary or musical notation do not thus directly appeal. Rather, they are but *instructions* for performing, whereas painting and sculpture are themselves performances, as a drama is, not when read, but when actually witnessed in a theater. In this sense, such "instructions" need not have the "tactility" of painting and sculpture. True, insofar as type is actually designed for its visual appeal, to this extent it *is* "tactile." And, ironically enough, it is the sheer data fed into computers (without either visual beauty or appeal as language and melody) that lack "tactility,"

175

though McLuhan tries to make up the difference by hailing electricity as a "biological form," and talking about the electronic "scanning finger" of a digital computer in terms of "forms" that "caress the contours of every kind of being." (The basic trick about McLuhan's "extensions" of man resides in the fact that his rhetoric induces you to forget their wholly *nonhuman* nature, albeit that humans can make their human inventions be "as though" human. To grasp this issue clearly, consider the notable difference between an "extension" of man in the sense of the wheel, and an "extension" in the sense of human offspring, or less immediately, such complexly developed artistic *forms* as drama, dance, song.) Be that as it may, this entire set of responses should be distinguished from a different kind of visuality, as when, for instance, one transforms sounds into a sheerly visual pattern. Ironically enough, many typical *electric* devices such as the cardiograph or the oscilloscope have added notably to such possibilities; yet McLuhan is probably correct when he says that writing provided a big step forward in such modes of translation (though I personally can't see why a fairly imaginative savage couldn't have picked up "lineal" thinking through the sheer problem of tracking an animal's footprints in the sand, with corresponding recognition that this sheerly *spatial* series represented a *temporal sequence,* depending on the direction in which the animal's traces showed it to be moving). But in any case, I see no reason to object if phonetic script and phonetic printing are given special credit, or blame, for such "lineality" of placement with regard to nonlineal matters, while bearing it in mind that McLuhan himself gives us a lineal theory of the steps into the mechanical age and through it into the electric age. Maybe he'd probingly concede that on this score, his own book (in being printed) is necessarily a somewhat obsolescent way of heralding the anti-Gutenberg future; or maybe not. The main point is this: Unless you are willing to worry through all those considerations I have listed, I question whether you can accurately deal with what McLuhan's quite reasonable speculations on print actually boil down to.

And the final point: There is a sense in which I have been

most unfair to our author and his in many ways admirable volumes. For though I would contend that his skimping as regards the Dramatistic perspective in its fullness greatly misrepresents the scope and center of our necessary major worries, and though I would particularly protest if such a truncated scheme is allowed to look as though it really could cover the ground, I must concede that his books (particularly as modified by the many borrowings in *The Gutenberg Galaxy* that he seems to forget in *Understanding Media*) are often incidentally incisive and delightful. Though I seriously question whether his basic slogan would ever allow you to put that puzzle together, McLuhan's admirers have already demonstrated that one can make pretty playthings of the bits.

elémire zolla*
the end and the means

Sociology, which Croce regarded as useless, given the existence of the historical disciplines, has spawned a new offspring, the so-called science of mass communication, destined, with the progress of hebetude, to absorb the ancient literary disciplines. One of its most sensational and also exquisite breeding grounds was the Centre for Culture and Technology at the University of Toronto, where Marshall McLuhan taught the new subject that perhaps someday will be imposed on innocent students, since it offers so many advantages to anyone who wants to impoverish his mind: it levels oratory, rhetoric, logic, and literature, reducing all of them to means of communication among homogeneous members of the mass. It also removes

* ELÉMIRE ZOLLA *is considered one of Italy's most brilliant social and philosophical critics. He has written a series of books on modern problems:* Eclissi dell' intellettuale (Eclipse of the Intellectual), Volgarità e dolore (Vulgarity and Pain), Storia del Fantasticare (History of Daydreaming) *and* Le Potenze dell' anima (The Powers of the Soul: a "spiritual anatomy of Man"). *He has edited an anthology of mystical writings,* I Mistici (The Mystics).

the slightest suspicion that it might be possible for one to escape the yoke of society or individual interests so as to breathe freely in an objective spiritual world, since it subordinates every impulse of the heart and mind to the development of the means of communication.

If Marxism gains strength from its unilaterality by invoking the class struggle as the decisive cause of every event, the science of mass communication elaborated at Toronto just as unilaterally enthrones the technical evolution of messages as the pre-eminent cause. This unilaterality permits an abundance of bright ideas, if not actual discoveries, just as it is true that mania increases muscular strength and blindness refines one's sense of touch. So, reading Marshall McLuhan can prove quite entertaining, if one can ignore the academic frown and take it as an ingenious, stupefying eighteenth-century causerie on the subject of mass communications, pronounced in a breathless, excited tone, with the gritted teeth that always accompany a certain brand of American political oratory in which the prolonged loud pedal seems indispensable.

Furthermore, McLuhan has several merits, such as that of quoting the 135th Psalm and leading us to meditate again on its sublime wisdom by applying it to today's follies: "They that make them [the idols] shall be like unto them" [without speech or thought]—and the idols of today are the technologies, worshiped creations of man's hand. Another benefit that he can provide is his criticism, which should prove definitive, of the platitude that affirms: "The instruments are indifferent, everything depends on the use made of them" (though mental sloth will not fail to revive this favorite son). The collective media are formative forces which shape the environment despite the intentions of he who thinks he is using them, and McLuhan recalls that John Donne praised the invention of firearms because, with their deadly effectiveness, they would shorten the duration of wars. Each time that a new technique is established people make Donne's mistake, imagining its effects as if they depended on human intentions and not on the autonomous and formative nature of the means, which bears in itself, as a forming form, certain objective and independent ends: "The effects of technology do not occur at the level of opinions or concepts, but alter sense ratios or patterns or perception steadily and without any resistance."*

When man puts himself in an objective relationship to any technology, he becomes its "servomechanism. This is why we must, to use them at all, serve these objects, these extensions of ourselves, as gods or minor religions. . . . Man becomes, as it were, the sex organs of the machine world, as the bee of the plant world, enabling it to fecundate and to evolve ever new forms. The machine world reciprocates man's love by expediting his wishes and desires, namely, in providing him with wealth."† The modern era is different from preceding eras because man is not only offered a series of extensions of the members of his body (wheels, which lengthen his legs: binoculars, which reinforce his eyes; weapons, which multiply his fists), but, thanks to cybernetic devices, an amplification of his very nervous system.

By virtue of the law of the reciprocity of effects and of the autonomy of means, one must pay a toll for this acquisition: in its turn, our private and social life becomes a process of sorting out information, precisely insofar as we have placed our nervous systems outside ourselves, in the electronic technology. . . . "The new media and technologies by which we amplify and extend ourselves constitute huge collective surgery carried out on the social body with complete disregard for antiseptics. . . . In operating on society with a new technology, it is not the incised area that is most affected. The area of impact and incision is numb. It is the entire system that is changed. The effect of radio is visual, the effect of the photo is auditory. Each new impact shifts the ratio among the senses." ‡

The new world in which one will pay this price, and for which the promissory notes have already been signed, will take over completely when the audio-visual means will have finished their work and will have reduced to systems of equations all the sciences that still avail themselves of national lan-

* Understanding Media, p. 18.
† Ibid., p. 46.
‡ Ibid., p. 64.

guages. This world will have "a general cosmic consciousness which might be very like the collective unconscious dreamt of by Bergson. The condition of 'weightlessness,' that biologists say promises a physical immortality, may be paralleled by the condition of speechlessness that could confer a perpetuity of collective harmony and peace." * So McLuhan, after an honest premise, makes a sharp swerve into Utopia, in order to be able to conclude his pages with a toast; after all, haven't we recently read an article in the magazine *Civiltà delle macchine* that urges us "to open a dialogue" with the world of the ants, whose institutions, if faithfully imitated, should cure us of the pride "of the species." Perhaps ants have the sort of collective soul exactly of the type yearned for by McLuhan for the wholly audio-visual man. Obviously the defect of such assertions lies only in the reassuring and hopeful rather than burlesque tone with which they are administered, since present-day society already in many of its aspects has the appearance of an ant heap maintained by platitudes and false problems that steer the men-ants, though they are unaware of this, along the paths of their vacuous, laborious, and up-to-date lives.

McLuhan is among the many who believe that it is necessary to place at the end of their analysis, much like the fireworks at the close of a popular festivity, a rousing *"tout ira très bien."* A public that needs such material promises proves to be so terrified that it verges on the infantile; the McLuhans (that is, almost all of today's writers) do not show any restraint in furnishing them with their modest but irritating euphoria-producing pills.

At times McLuhan, compelled by his frenzy to applaud novelties whatever they might be, becomes quite absurd and sophistical. Thus he speaks of Baudelaire's poetry as a presage of the integrated, audio-visual world, a return to a primeval carnality—almost as if the two things were not at antipodes—basing his assertions on the title Baudelaire wanted to give *Les Fleurs du mal: Limbes,* that is, limbos or mazes. The connection remains obscure until one realizes with horror that McLuhan has trusted the look of the French word, similar to the English

* *Ibid.,* p. 80.

word "limbs," and has thought that Baudelaire wished to compare his poetry to a laparotomy of Paris, or at least its carnal exploration.

The praises showered by McLuhan on the audio-visual world as the renewal of the integrated community, of the harmonic and reciprocal fullness of the senses and the intellect, which was part of man until the threshold of the modern era, are as gratuitous as his divigations on Baudelaire: the televisional limbo of bland befuddlement, of bludgeoning inorganicness, is mistaken for the living, corporeal carnality of the ancient world.

McLuhan himself is still imprisoned in the paper or Gutenbergian civilization, or at least in its shadow, deprived as he is of oratorical, musical, rhythmical gifts, contenting himself with statements that seem to be set forth like diagrams, readable only in silence, almost unpronounceable. He who announces with delight the disappearance of the Gutenbergian civilization and salutes the restoration (televisional) of the oral-auditive world, should be able to nourish us with the rich, meaty images of the itinerant street singers, caressing the ear with oratorical flights; should give us again the impetuosity of Ciceronian prose, modeled indeed on the ancient need to marry rationality and phonic enchantment. Does McLuhan, despite the fact that he has a dim, drab style, have the right to praise *plein air,* just as the puny have the right to offer eulogies to the mighty of limb? No, one must censure his slovenliness, because he has dared, precisely out of slovenliness, to confuse the oratorical plenitude of the ancients with the degradation not only of the eye but also of the ear produced by television. It will not be television that will make prose sing, rejoin dialectics and rhetoric like two severed halves, for television demands the mannered diction of someone who addresses a human mush, the simulated cordiality that can exist only in the relations mediated by the machine, the sick excitement of the sportscast or advertising spiel; something much different from the restoration of the Socratic dialogue or the ecclesiastical chorus.

McLuhan declares that the disorder of the senses started to become noxious with the Renaissance; and he sees in *King*

Lear the threnody of the harmonious world in which the five senses were attuned to each other, and the announcement of a new world in which the primacy of sight will result in both technical power and moral poverty, pragmatic rationality and madness. Machiavelli shows us what the specialized political life is; perspective shows us what sight specialized at the expense of tactile values is; *King Lear* sets before us a king who wants to segment, to delegate power in its special aspects; the evil sisters, who by now are individualized and "visual," ready to accept that rash division; and, finally, the sweet Cordelia, who does not relinquish the ancient ceremonious and impersonal loyalty. These modifications of life are owed, according to McLuhan, to the invention of the printing press, which taught people to accumulate information just as money and stocks led to further accumulation and the multiplication of money and stocks; they are the harbingers of the mechanical era which will be fully unleashed in the middle of the nineteenth century. But "now that the assembly line recedes before the new patterns of information, synchronized by electric tape, the miracles of mass-production assume entire intelligibility [while] . . . the novelties of automation, creating workless and propertyless communities, envelop us in new uncertainties." *

One of the pedagogical merits that might be attributed to the pleiad of scholars to which McLuhan belongs (together with Father Ong, Harold Innis, and others) resides in the fact that they furnish all the desirable proofs of the indistinguishability of ends from means. Nothing very new, but of great usefulness, if one still happens to hear such crudities as: The mass means in themselves are neither good nor bad, everything depends on the use that is made of them. After having considered carefully the analyses of these scholars, no one could, even while disagreeing in a thousand ways, deny that the means of communication are, like the means of exchange, forms that shape the content; for the rest, cooks already know that the form of the dish confers a special tang to the flavor, and winemakers learn that the curve of the cask is not unrelated to the aroma of the wines. McLuhan disperses the illusion that the

* *The Gutenberg Galaxy*, p. 275.

press, communications by means of waves, and so on, are successive suppliers of neutral means in favor of an abstract communication between men that supposedly would remain intangible. The introduction of money did not only accelerate barter but modified it and, along with it, the face of civilization; in the same way, the alphabet, projecting in a neutral space segmented and regimented sounds, modified the mind of man, promoting the tendency to organization and accumulation so that war received an impetus, as Harold Innis demonstrated, when he asserted that the myth of Cadmus is linked to these developments: Cadmus introduced letters into Greece and, so the myth goes, sowed the earth with dragon's teeth (alphabetical signs) from which grew warriors who sowed slaughters.

The use of the press extirpated rhetoric and eloquence from reason and promoted the new logic of the Renaissance, the logic of Ramus. Today new techniques destroy that Renaissance structure; from this Father Ong draws the conclusion that the Church will triumph over its enemy born with the Renaissance, but leaves the prophecy vague and undefined, not even toying for a moment with some detailed project of television programs exclusively based on the liturgy. McLuhan abstains from prognostications but emits some idiotic suggestions, such as reading *Finnegans Wake* aloud or looking at avant-garde paintings, though without applying the proof that *Finnegans Wake* is more pleasant than the *echolalia* that can be registered in any insane asylum; or that avant-garde painting could not be executed by those very same patients. It is true that Father Ong expatiates on the use of newspapers in certain collages of painters celebrated by the Paris art merchants as the sign of the overturning of the corresponding surface-plane in the typographical era, but first of all he has to prove that any janitor splattering coffee grounds on the surface of his newspaper does not also express every morning cosmic anguish, panic joy, the primacy of instinct, the collapse of values, and the value of art for art's sake.

In the days when this group of thinkers published a magazine, *Explorations,* in Toronto (this was just after the Second World War), they did not hesitate to tie their antitypographical doctrine to the good Canadian political emotions of the moment, singing the praises of Winston Churchill and the Russian "comrades-in-arms," both representing an oral-acoustical world of harmoniously integrated senses, as opposed to the petty, purely diagrammatic state planning enslaved by the opprobrious visibility of the printed page. It is inevitable that one becomes absurd and funny if instead of letting one's ideas grow, clarify, and mature by themselves, one immediately wants to apply them in practice. But there is also another vice that explains these comic results: those unable to limit themselves to interrogating reality in order to discern the true and the false also want to reassure us by striking optimistic, positive, constructive attitudes. The preoccupation with appropriate attitudes should be left to show-window dummies. In his *History of Florence* Machiavelli warns us that it is a human vice to desire that which is beyond reach instead of thinking to grasp that which is actually available.

anthony quinton*
cut-rate salvation

Any effort to get a clear view of Marshall McLuhan's doctrines is seriously discouraged by his explicit and repeatedly expressed scorn for old-fashioned, print-oriented, "linear" rationality. By rejecting as obsolete the humdrum business of setting out definite theses, assembling evidence in support of them, and undermining actual and possible objections, he opts out of the usual argumentative game of truth-seeking, rather in the style of a chess player who kicks over the table. In this situation ordinary criticism is enfeebled by an uncomfortable suspicion that it is missing the point.

Although he writes books plentifully sprinkled with the familiar vocabulary of linear rationality ("thus," "therefore," "it follows," "it is clear that"), there is, I think, no doubt of McLuhan's seriousness about this negative and seemingly self-destructive commitment. For although his books are recognizably books, for the most part full of moderately grammatical

* ANTHONY QUINTON *is a Fellow of New College, Oxford, and University Lecturer in Philosophy. He writes for the leading journals of literary opinion, such as* The New York Review of Books.

prose, they do deviate in various ways from standard forms of exposition. The two main works look ordinary enough at first. But the chapters of *The Gutenberg Galaxy* are mostly short, have no numbers, and have very long titles. What really enforces one's bewilderment are the not infrequent cases where the title-aphorism has only a very remote connection with the chapter beneath it. The thirty-three chapters of *Understanding Media* do have titles of a familiar, Vance-Packardy sort (*e.g.*, "Clocks: The Scent of Time" and "Television: The Timid Giant"); seven of them are about media of communication in general, the rest about twenty-six particular media (or near-media, *e.g.*, clothes). But the content, of the later chapters at any rate, is largely jottings, transferred, it would seem, from the notebook with a minimum of working-over. However dense and organized the prose may look, what it says is connected more by associative leaps than logical linkages. With *The Medium Is the Massage* a rather thin diet of prose is eked out with a great deal of typographic space-wastage and photographic interruptions, in an attempt to produce something nearer the specifications of his theory.

In varying degrees, then, his writings avoid conventional, linear logic and he instructs his readers to approach them in a non-linear way. *The Gutenberg Galaxy,* he says, is a "mosaic image" not "a series of views of fixed relationships in pictorial space." You can, in effect, start anywhere and read in any direction you like. The same spirit is revealed in McLuhan's regular tactic for dealing with objectors. He sees such linear automata as bogged down in a desperate "unawareness," so dominated by the print medium to which they are bound by habit and professional interest that they are simply not equipped to see what he is getting at.

Quite a good way of arriving at a general idea of what he is up to is provided by *McLuhan: Hot and Cool,* a collection of thirty items mostly about, but a few by, McLuhan, finished off by a thirty-six-page dialogue between McLuhan and the editor. The items about him vary from fairly devotional pieces, among which is a quite astounding architectural meditation in the McLuhan manner by an architect called John M. Johansen, through the slightly nervous display of interest by Tom Wolfe, to the somewhat predictable broadsides of reflex liberal ideology from Dwight Macdonald and Christopher Ricks. These are mostly rather short pieces, and even if the commentators had any inclination to give more than the most cursory survey of McLuhan's ideas (as Kenneth Boulding, a shrewd but amicable objector, clearly has), they have not had the space for it. An interesting feature of this collection is the extent to which people writing about McLuhan tend to be infected by his style, with its fusillade of scriptwriter's pleasantries, rather in the way that one's voice falls to a whisper when one is talking to a sufferer from laryngitis. What the collection lacks is any extended effort to elicit a reasonably definite structure of theory from McLuhan's writings. I should not make this complaint if I did not think the thing could be done. If McLuhan is desultory (as a matter of principle), he is also exceedingly repetitious; not only does the same quite large but wholly manageable body of leading themes recur time and time again in his writings, they are even presented in the same jocular words (he has a grandfatherly indulgence toward his own phrases). What I wish to maintain is that if we ignore his anti-linear instructions, we can easily discern beneath the thin camouflage of his expository idiosyncrasies an articulate theory of society and culture, with all the usual apparatus of first principles, explanatory supplements, and logically derived consequences. What is more, this entirely linear theoretical contraption is of a classic and familiar kind, having a very close formal analogy with the main doctrines of Marx. To speak just once in McLuhanese: he is an academic sheep in Tom Wolfe's clothing.

The fundamental principle of McLuhan's system is a theory of the main determinant of historical change in society, culture, and the human individual. Such changes according to this system are all ultimately caused by changes in the prevailing or predominating medium of human communication. McLuhan got this idea from the later works of the Canadian economic historian Harold A. Innis, but what the teacher used vertiginously enough, as an interpretative clue, the pupil asserts, with only the most occasional and perfunctory qualification, as the basic truth about causation in history. The main evidence for this proposition is provided in *The Gutenberg Galaxy* in which a vast array of disparate works is ransacked for quotations (they must make up half the book) describing the social and cultural effects of the invention of printing. Print, he tells us, *created* (that is his usual word in this connection) individualism, privacy, specialization, detachment, mass-production, nationalism, militarism, the dissociation of sensibility, etc., etc.

The connection between cause and effect affirmed in the fundamental principle is explained by the doctrine of "sense-ratio," which McLuhan derived, it appears, from the work of Father Walter J. Ong. McLuhan associates different historical periods or cultural situations with different balances of emphasis in the communicative and mental life of human beings as between the various senses. Tribal man, with his oral culture, was a conversational being who heard, smelt, and felt the people he was in communication with. Gutenberg man acquires information through focusing his eyes on clearly printed rows of alphabetic symbols. Tribal man brought all his senses to bear on his world in a healthy balance; Gutenberg man over-concentrates on vision and leaves his other senses numb and deprived.

The third element of McLuhan's system is a patterning or schematization of history, which is achieved by applying the fundamental principle to raw historical fact. Broadly conceived, the schema divides human history into three parts: the remote or pre-Gutenberg past, the immediate or Gutenberg past, and the immediate or electronic future. The first and longest of these eras further subdivides, on closer inspection, into a tribal epoch of oral, face-to-face communication, an ideographic epoch, and an epoch of alphabetic handwriting (*i.e.*, prehistory, the East, and Western civilization from the Greeks to the Renaissance).

The final stage of this schema, the electronic future, develops into a large-scale prophecy which also implies a diagnosis

189

of current cultural discontents. With electronic means of communication rendering printed matter more or less obsolete we are on the edge of a new type of society and a new type of man. Indeed the new men are already among us: they are our children with their sense-ratios transformed by TV-watching at an impressionable age, dedicated to "cool," participative enjoyments like the frug, and altogether alienated from the Gutenberg assumptions of traditional instructional schooling. That is why we get on with them so badly. The coming society will be appropriate to this type of human being. It will be a "global village," a unitary world of neo-tribesmen, sunk in their social roles and fraternally involved with one another in a way that excludes what their forebears would regard as individuality.

Faced by the inevitable we need some kind of strategy to meet it with. Here McLuhan recurs, with a frequency unusual even for him, to Poe's story about a sailor caught in a maelstrom who saved himself by coming to understand how it worked. As things are, ignorance about the irresistible effects of new electronic media is general and blinding. The first step, at any rate, is to understand them by directing attention away from their content to their form and its effects on sense-ratios. It is not wholly clear that there is a second step, that anything more than understanding is required.

The global village is as welcome to McLuhan as it is inevitable. In *Understanding Media* he says that the faith in which he is writing is one that "concerns the ultimate harmony of all being." Generally the social and cultural features of the Gutenberg era that we are about to lose are described in an unfavorable way, their connection with war, inequality, indifference, the mutilation of the self is emphasized. But on the other hand, from the time of *The Mechanical Bride,* McLuhan has been insisting that he is not concerned with whether the changes he is investigating are "a good thing," and strongly suggests that this is a crude and unenlightened sort of question to ask. Rudolph E. Morris in *McLuhan: Hot and Cool* is sufficiently impressed by these protestations of detachment to praise the book, quite wrongly, for its freedom from moral indignation (a fairly dense cloud of moral steam rises from McLuhan's collar on page 13 of *The Mechanical Bride,* for example). Despite his insistence on detachment there is no doubt that he strongly favors the future as he descries it.

Finally McLuhan has a special intellectual technique, both of exposition and defense. His procedure is to heap evidence up in tumultuous and disparate assemblages, with little critical appraisal of his sources—unless they deviate very grossly in some way from one of his main theses—and with only the most tenuous thread of topical relevance to connect them. To justify this shapeless and enthusiastic technique of almost random accumulation he falls back on the idea that he is producing a mosaic, not a linear argument. In fact he is producing a linear argument, but one of a very fluid and unorganized kind. Objectors are discounted for benighted visuality and obsession with print. Yet McLuhan not only writes books, he is immensely bookish, in the manner of some jackdaw of a medieval compiler or of Burton in *The Anatomy of Melancholy.*

The analogy between this system and Marx's is plain enough to be set out briefly. Each system begins with a general interpretation of history, an account of the ultimate cause of historical change. Each applies this to arrive at a schematization of the actual course of historical events. For exciting, practical purposes each schema divides history into three parts: the remote past (before print or capitalism), the immediate past (print or capitalism), and the immediate future (global village or classless society). But the remote past can be divided further, into prehistory (the oral tribe or primitive communism), the East (ideographic script or slave economy), and the early West (alphabetic script or feudalism). Both McLuhan and Marx devote their main work to the shift from the early West to the immediate past: as *The Gutenberg Galaxy* tells what print did to the scribal culture, so *Capital* describes the emergence of capitalism. Each system concludes its historical schema with a prophecy of imminent major change to a state of affairs that is nebulously described but enthusiastically welcomed. In each case the welcomed future is a reversion, in a major respect, to the initial phase of the whole historical process. McLuhan and Marx both present strategies for dealing with the inevitable. Marx calls for an activist endeavor to ease the birth-pangs of the coming order; McLuhan, less exigently, calls for an effort to understand, best pursued by reading his works. Both are strongly in favor of the future that they predict, for all its obscurity of outline. Finally both have a brisk way of disposing of hostile critics. They have a self-sealing device against any possible attempt at refutation: the theory predicts it and explains it away, what Popper calls "reinforced dogmatism." Objectors must be visual or bourgeois.

To point out this analogy is not to criticize McLuhan, except insofar as he maintains that his ideas cannot be set out in a conventionally systematic way. But it does put one on one's guard. A system of his form embodies two crucial elements about whose acceptability very general and very elaborately worked-out doubts have been raised: a schematization of history that implies the inevitability of a predicted state of affairs and a strongly positive evaluation of this none-too-clearly-described inevitable future.

There is clearly something in McLuhan's fundamental principle, just as there is in Marx's. Major changes in styles of communication do have large effects. What is wrong here is the violent exaggeration with which McLuhan blows up a truth about the causal relevance of media into a full-blooded and unqualified theory of historical change. What he usually does is to argue that some change in media of communication is a necessary condition of a certain major social or cultural change, and then to represent his discovery as an account of what *created* the major change in question. Print, he says, created the large national army of modern times. Now it may be that the large national army does make a good deal of use of printed matter for such things as training manuals and quartermaster's forms. But the railway, as indispensable for rapid mobilization of large numbers, is obviously more important. Anyway McLuhan's timing is all wrong here. The print age, for him, begins about 1500, but the type of army he has in mind first appears in the mid-nineteenth century with the American Civil War and Bismarck's wars against Austria and France, or, at the earliest, with the armies of the French Revolution and Napoleon. During the three preceding, print-dominated centuries, armies had been small bodies of mercenaries or long-service professionals.

He might, at this point, reply that the mass army of modern times was created by nationalism and that nationalism was created by print: Q.E.D. Even if we allow the questionable assumption that creation is transitive in this way, this still will not do. For how does print create nationalism? By stabilizing the vernacular? But were not Elizabethan Englishmen nationalistic even though most of them were illiterate? Or is it enough that the ruling class should be literate? Then why was eighteenth-century Italy not nationalistic?

Here, right at the foundations of McLuhan's system, a persisting vagueness of terms makes it difficult beyond a certain point to see precisely what is being said. Media, he contends, are the ultimate causal factors in history. But what is a medium? Much of the time the term is taken in a fairly ordinary way to mean a technique for the communication of ideas between human beings. It is in this sense that the concept of a medium occurs in his schematization of history. But in *Understanding Media* roads, clothes, houses, money, cars, and weapons are all included in the repertoire of media discussed, things which either do not communicate information but carry altogether heavier loads, or which communicate information only as a very minor and peripheral function (as a nun's habit says "don't ask me to have a drink with you."). In this extended sense a medium comes to be any item of technology, and the sense in which the fundamental principle is to be taken becomes very much diluted. Nevertheless, McLuhan's fundamental principle does make a point and he has certainly assembled evidence relevant to it which is impressive in its bulk and often intellectually stimulating.

This is less true of the schematization of history that he derives from its application, which simply draws old and familiar distinctions between historical periods in a new terminology.

What everyone is used to calling modern history is renamed the Gutenberg era, ancient and medieval history is renamed the era of alphabetic script, the epoch of the Oriental empires is renamed the ideographic era. This would be all right in a modest way if it served to confirm a well-known distinction and to deepen our understanding of it. But here a pedantic-looking doubt must be voiced. What does he mean when he says of some medium that it is *the* dominant medium of a given historical period? Does it mean that everyone was preoccupied with it, in which case the Gutenberg era began in Europe only a hundred years ago with a fair approximation to universal literacy? Or does it mean that *the* medium of an era is the one through which the ruling class acquires most of its information or most of its important information? In that case the beginning of the Gutenberg era is pushed back to where he wants it all right (1500 roughly), but the basis of his claim that we are on the edge of an electronic age dissolves. This serious indeterminacy is one that he generously exploits. He says that England is much less visual and print-oriented than the United States. Yet England was the first country to exhibit most of the social and cultural symptoms of Gutenbergian domination: mass-production industry, big cities, individualism, nationalism, etc. Allowing himself this degree of freedom he deprives his schematization of any definite content.

At this point his explanation of his fundamental principle by means of sense-ratios needs to be considered. Once again a very ample point seems to have been exaggerated into confident and unqualified assertions that cry out for justification. It is reasonable and enlightening to say that tribesmen do not have a detached, impersonal point of view on a visually conceived world stretching out uniformly from them in space and time. But to talk of sense-ratios suggests a kind of mathematical precision about this kind of perception which he nowhere begins to achieve. To raise a very simple question: Why does he say nothing about the blind? Plenty of blind men display all the marks of extreme visuality in his terms, are individualized, specialized, detached, and so forth. But how can this be possible for people who have been blind since birth and have had to get their information either tactually through Braille or auditorily through a reader?

This becomes highly important when he arrives at the final stage of his schematization, his prophecy about the electronic age just ahead of us, peopled with its global villagers. All the alleged products of print are declared moribund and about to disappear: the individual, privacy, specialization, detachment, militarism, nationalism, mass production, and so forth. In their place the world will become a unity of emotionally involved tribesmen, aware of everything that is happening everywhere. The real basis for this prediction is his account, in terms of sense-ratios, of the effect of TV on people accustomed to it from early life. TV, he says, is a cool medium, whereas print is hot. It involves the collaboration of its watcher in what it presents, for he has to fill out its low-definition picture with imaginative efforts of his own, while print, where everything is clear and determinate, imposes a passive receptiveness on the reader.

My limited observation of children's TV habits makes me doubt this. If the show interests them they watch it with passive absorption; if it does not they leave it buzzing on around them and get on with something on the floor. But I would not rest the case on such anecdotal material, particularly since the effect is alleged to take place at a fairly subconscious level, as inaccessible to naïve observation as it is to modification or control. It seems reasonable, however, to argue that despite its low pictorial definition. TV leaves a lot less to the supplementative imagination of its readers. But even if electronic media do decrease detachment, as they might be held to do by the very lifelikeness of their representations, why does he infer that this involvement will inevitably be fraternal and charitable? There is no necessary connection whatever between making people more emotional and excitable and making them more humane and unselfish. Words like "sensitive" and "involved" can be used to mean either sympathetically concerned with the welfare of others or, more neutrally, just concerned. No doubt young people at present are more given to global idealism than their elders, but then that is nearly always the case; having few other responsibilities they can afford this emotional expenditure.

Again it is not at all clear why the involving nature of exposure to electronic media should eliminate individuality. If print makes men passive, it should, according to McLuhan's own argument, presumably be well equipped to stereotype them. No doubt there are many forces in the world making for Riesman's other-directedness, but TV with its rapid diffusion of advertisers' ideas of fashionable life-styles is only one of them.

McLuhan's predictions often go far beyond the global village toward the imminent formation of a kind of cosmic, preverbal consciousness. Media, like all technologies, extend or externalize our faculties. In particular media extend our senses. Electronic media he goes on, extend or externalize the central nervous system. Here he has really taken off. Certainly tools can augment the power and precision of our muscular operations. In line with this, media strictly so called can be regarded as ways of improving the performance of our sense organs, though this more accurately applies to things like microscopes and telescopes. Going a little further still, we can allow that computing machines can assist and improve on the thinking work of the central nervous system. But this is not to say that computers or other media detach our faculties from us altogether, that they literally externalize the human capacities they reinforce.

Perhaps a community could enslave itself to a computer by programming it to make social decisions on the basis of its inflow of information, and by linking it up with machinery designed to put the decisions into effect. Such a community would be well advised to put the main power switch in an accessible position. But since in our entropic universe destruction is easier than construction, the descendants of people clever enough to construct such an appliance ought to be clever enough to blow it up if it gets out of hand. Moreover, whatever sort of computer it is, it will not be preverbal in McLuhan's lavish sense: its tapes may have combinations of 1s and 0s on them instead of ordinary words but it will not operate with blank tape. I have almost certainly misunderstood McLuhan on this topic, probably by taking his word "externalize" literally. If he does not mean it to be understood in that way, all he can mean is that there will be a collective consciousness—or subconsciousness—of the kind an excited patriotic crowd might have, with everybody thinking or feeling the same thing. We must try to avoid this unappetizing prospect by leaving TV-watching in its current voluntary condition and keeping more than one channel going.

McLuhan describes the electronic future in reasonably attractive ways on the whole. Not least in the phrase "global village" itself with its intimations of rusticity, friendliness, the simple life. But this neoprimitive future does seem to be without most of the things men have laboriously struggled to achieve and in virtue of which, despite everything, they still think of themselves as superior in more than brute strength to the other animal species: freedom, individuality, foresight, even detachment, the indispensable condition of rationality itself. Insofar as the outlines of the electronic future are clear they are by no means enticing, but then insofar as they are clear the arguments on which their inevitability is based are very far from persuasive. And insofar as they are not clear there is nothing to take a position for or against. But anyway taking a position about the future has little point in McLuhan's system, since it is not shown how the understanding he offers is related to any possible action. What he really offers is a kind of general relief from historical anxiety: Amazing things are going to happen but considered in themselves they are not at all bad, and the disturbance of their arrival can be brought within manageable bounds by one's being intellectually prepared for them.

Whatever else he is McLuhan is consistently interesting. His scope is unlimited and there are the added attractions of his remorseless and all-inclusive contemporaneity and his jokes. Contemporaneity is a rapidly wasting asset. *The Mechanical Bride*, which is now sixteen years old, has a largely camp interest. The jokes often seem a little automated, like those in a

Bob Hope show. His technique has a Gutenbergian repeatability. "Money," he says, "is the poor man's credit card." Why not "Gratitude is the poor man's tip" or "Changing the furniture around is the poor man's interior decoration." But there are so many of them that the strong can carry the weak. What he claims to offer is much more than this, a general scheme of individual and social salvation. Compared to all such schemes it perhaps makes the least exacting demands on those who would like to follow it. They do not have to mortify the flesh or hurl themselves against the armed lackeys of the bourgeoisie or undergo five hundred hours of analysis. All they have to do is to read a few books, a curiously Gutenbergian device. If, as I have argued, the scheme does not stand up very well if approached with the good old linear questions, "Just what does he mean?" "Is there any good reason to think that it is true?" they must remember that they were offered salvation at a bargain price.

thelma mccormack*
innocent eye on mass society

I used to think that Marshall McLuhan was an innocent who had discovered depth psychology and called it "television." Since depth psychology is as good an approach as any to the mass media, a great deal better than some, McLuhan, with all his mannerisms was working in the right direction. This impression is borne out in *Understanding Media,* where what he has to say about the mass media of communication is contrived, autodidactic, amusing, occasionally right, and occasionally dangerous. But below the surface of his comments about the media is an insight and system that bear serious attention whether one is interested in the media or not. McLuhan has now gone well beyond discovering depth psychology; he has discovered mass society.

The metaphors he draws upon are from preliterate societies. In particular, he is entranced by the group cohesion and group consciousness of an "oral" culture, a term that summarizes a closed, static, tradition-bound social structure where relation-

* THELMA MCCORMACK, *an Assistant Professor of Sociology at York University in Toronto, has published in the journals of her field.*

ships are face-to-face, where there is scarcely any individual differentiation and only a rudimentary division of labor. In urban industrialized societies consensus on such a scale is an artifact, achieved by the sacrifice of critical judgment, sustained internally by anxiety and externally by manipulation. To paraphrase McLuhan's most famous dictum: the medium is history: the message is the mass movement.

Content of the media is irrelevant, according to McLuhan. Thus, he refuses to be drawn into discussions of kitsch and popular culture that have so engaged intellectuals in recent years. By "content" he means the manifest content of any particular news story, feature article, TV documentary, etc. The real stuff of the media are not facts, opinions, concepts, but the structure of symbols that emerge cumulatively. Imagine the American constitution rewritten by Joyce and analyzed through structural linguistics and you have approximately what McLuhan regards as the substance of the media. Imagine, also, *Finnegans Wake* rewritten by Thomas Jefferson and analyzed by John Stuart Mill and you have the mistake McLuhan thinks we make.

Our mistake belongs to the age of mechanical technology that produced individualism, scientific detachment, democratic pluralism, nationalism, the sequential analysis of cause and effect, the class struggle, competition, the market mechanism, critical intelligence, a rational approach to social change, and a high degree of self-conscious awareness. All of them divisive. Electronic technology of the twentieth century is unifying, communal, demanding commitment and involvement. It submerges individual personality, obliterates social differences, and denationalizes the world, restoring the ethos of the oral society. The great modern revolution for McLuhan, seen most clearly in the mass media of communication, is the shift from divisive to unifying ways of perceiving and organizing experience, from "explosion" to "implosion."

No field of science I know of has not moved in the direction of configurational concepts, and in that sense McLuhan is a popularizer of contemporary science though he appears to be unaware of these developments. His hypothesis, however, that technology is responsible for this historical change is something else again. It is legitimate to regard technology as a causal variable, but its weight in relation to other factors, material and non-material, in the social matrix, and the precise nature of its social and psychological impact, direct and indirect, are exceedingly complex problems. For McLuhan, however, this is not a provisional hypothesis. Technology is the Prime Mover, and everything, large or small, becomes its consequences. Wherever he looks, from ladies' hairdos to weapons, he finds corroboration.

The immediate model for this is depth psychology, where all behavior awake or asleep, trivial or important, accidental or planned, expresses the motivational key; a key, moreover, which we do not, will not, cannot consciously recognize. McLuhan draws upon this model further by locating the source of technology within the individual. Technology is nothing more than the externalization of our feet, hands, eyes, brain, skin, teeth, etc. The correspondences he establishes between body and machine are cruder and more arbitrary than those of a Freudian since McLuhan is not guided by a theory of motivation, least of all by one based on conflict. For Oedipus he offers Narcissus, who, having created his own image, fails to recognize it.

The Narcissus myth eliminates the dichotomy between consumer and producer just as the modern economy eliminates the price mechanism. The "audience" of the media is not the consumer; it is the producer. We are not sold General Motors cars in McLuhan's system; we are shareholders, producers of transportation. Looked at one way, he is simply saying that audiences are not passive, that communication is a reciprocal process, and the fact that communication is now mediated, conducted through a technology, does not alter this. This is one of the cornerstones of current media research, and it is characteristic of the older media as well as the newer ones. We not only select the books we read, but read into them and read out anything that is threatening. Looked at another way, this

201

is an argument for public ownership of the media, for it is, as McLuhan says, as absurd for us to "lease" to others the media of communication as it would be to "lease" speech.

Either way, this new producer role does not solve any better than the old consumer role the problem—no problem to primitive societies—of how we control the media. Being told that we own or produce the media of communication can be as politically disingenuous as Henry Luce's concept of "the people's capitalism," as dishonest as thinking that letters to the Soviet press or, closer to home, open-line radio, where the housewife and folksy disc jockey exchange generalities, are genuine forms of participation. McLuhan does not suggest that these problems constitute another area of inquiry or that they do not properly belong in a general theory of communication. On the contrary, to raise them at all, he maintains, is to misunderstand the media. This is not arrogance on his part, for it is inherent in this theory, essentially an historical theory, that these and similar questions belong to an earlier epoch.

Much of McLuhan, including his style and his penchant for anthropology, is reminiscent of Veblen who similarly began his analysis with technology and expected that its rational logic would spread to the business class and ultimately throughout social life. Engineers were Veblen's vanguard of the revolution. Instead, we got the "managerial revolution," for Veblen, like McLuhan, underestimated our capacity to use technology without being influenced by it. Technological determinism, like all forms of determinism, is never able to cope with discrepancies and must rush in concepts like Ogburn's "cultural lag," Marx's "false consciousness," and McLuhan's psychic shock or "numbness."

Historical determinism is the mystique of all modern ideologies. However, what distinguishes the ideologies of mass society in their response to alienation, their disillusionment with the democratic "left," their idealization of provincial anti-intellectual and anti-secular values. They combine, as J. L. Talmon says, two contradictory notions: social cohesion and self-expression. McLuhan and McCarthy, vastly different in every other respect, intuitively grasped the same thing. McLuhan is not interested in restoring the values of a secular-rational cosmopolitan *Anschauung,* for it destroys the cohesion of tribal life and is as obsolete as the assembly line in an age of automation.

The more passive, alienated and uncommitted we are, the more we yearn for, the more strongly we respond to ideologies of "effectiveness," provided they make no demands on us. The most successful ideology is the most ambiguous one which we structure ourselves with our infantile and wish-fulfillment fantasies. Applying this principle to the media, McLuhan distinguishes between "hot" media, like print and radio, which are highly structured, and "cold" media, like TV, which are relatively unstructured. The latter, he claims, involve us; the former do not.

Actually, they both involve us, but in different ways, the difference being the distinction between "identification"—when you cry with the martyred Elsie who is forced to play the piano on the Sabbath—and "projection"—when you see your mother's face in the clouds. Identification is the mechanism of social learning; it is growth, strengthening and broadening the ego. Projection is regression, the absence of controls and capacity for problem-solving. When McLuhan talks about "involvement," he means projection. For the alienated with their impoverished or damaged egos, projection is the only means of involvement. It goes a long way toward explaining why changes in a party line scarcely disturb the true adherent, and why, as Lasswell pointed out many years ago, logical consistency is not the criterion of ideology. The race is to the vaguest.

McLuhan goes even further, equating projection or "participation in depth" with "maturity." As he describes "participation in depth" it is the furthest extreme from introspection, the latter being private, inner-directed, self-critical, leading to a sense of apartness, a capacity to live comfortably with relative truths, to resist group pressure, and, if necessary, to endure isolation. McLuhan's definition of "maturity" is "belief," collective belief.

All historical determinism faces the problem of leadership. According to McLuhan, the group best qualified to lead us into the Promised Land are the artists who "can show us how to 'ride with the punch.' " Taken at face value, this is a puzzling choice to make since no group has had a sorrier record in the past century for its inability to understand or accept technology than artists. The explanation lies, I think, in understanding that McLuhan is talking not so much about artists as about art. He is attempting here to develop an esthetic theory that abolishes the distinctions usually made between (1) "highbrow" and "lowbrow" art; and (2) "lowbrow" and "folk" art. In his system folk art and popular art ("lowbrow") become the same, a rationale that Marxist writers used to give years ago for going to Hollywood. In a limited sense he and they are right. Structurally, popular art and folk art are both highly simplified and repetitive. They may move us at the level of universal archetypal images. Both have a social function; in the case of folk art or religion, it is to provide the closure of ritual. But, if in mass society, there is, as Malraux says, no "folk," the closure is delusional; its function is escape or pseudo-closure, harmless enough under certain circumstances, even necessary, but disastrous as a fixation and dangerous in a period of confusion and rapid social change which calls for the highest degree of political intelligence.

The distinction between "highbrow" and "lowbrow" art is minimized by recognizing that great art, too, tells us something about the "human condition." The distinction becomes even more blurred by art styles that have no cognitive content and communicate solely by involving us. In McLuhan's system, then, there is no difference between abstract art and a television screen. "Pop art" which is, on the one hand, a parody of folk art, and, on the other hand, a parody of what we have traditionally meant by the term "creative" carries this to its logical conclusion. Esthetic theory thus becomes the science of communication. It is as if we were asked to judge art by the same criteria we would use in judging snapshots of our children, and if this sounds foolish, it is no more so than the reverse fallacy intellectuals usually make in approaching the media; that is, to judge family snapshots by the same criteria they would use for judging art.

When McLuhan turns to the specific media of communication, he runs into difficulty. First, because he is forced to deal with "content" in the same terms as anyone else does, *e.g.,* "the success theme." Second, because it is almost impossible to isolate what is unique about a medium from the policies of the people who run it. For example, the diffuseness of TV, its avoidance of controversial subjects, may have as much to do with the costs of TV and the cautiousness of TV executives as it does with the intrinsic nature of the medium. We can be sure it will become even "cooler" with color. Radio, he tells us, is a "hot" medium and so can deal with ideas, personalities (Hitler, Fred Allen), and empirical data (the weather). At the same time, since it is an electronic medium, it is intimate and tribal, or, as we are more apt to say, it is the intellectuals' ghetto, just exactly what we have been hearing from TV executives. Is it because they understand the medium and we do not? Finally, whatever distinctions may be made among the different media, the distinction between "hot" and "cold" breaks down. All of the media, taken together or separately, are nothing if not flexible; radio and print are as capable of surrealism as realism; the seven types of ambiguity are as much in poetry as they are in television.

Still, McLuhan is a Godsend to the TV producer who because he is often young wants recognition and who because he is an *arriviste* to the medium wants status. In McLuhan he can find a basis for claiming that TV is unique, different from the older media; above all, different from print. Long impatient with the psychological ineptitude of most do-good preachy broadcasting and equally frustrated by the complexities of modern thought, he finds in McLuhan a mandate to experiment without worrying too much about "content." His banner is television for television's sake.

Watching TV is a revelation. More and more public affairs programs resemble Rorschach cards, each one different but no objective content in any; each one involving us, but leaving us none the wiser as citizens. One politician differs from another in the way one piece of abstract art or one page of Joyce differs from another. Just how cynical this is is revealed by McLuhan's suggestion that had Jack Paar produced Nixon, the election results might have been different. As it was, Kennedy with his more diffuse image was better suited to the medium. In other words, McLuhan is saying that TV depersonalizes and de-intellectualizes politics. The depersonalization of politics could be the hopeful start of politics based on issues in which the elected representative is held accountable for his ideas rather than his morals or character. But a de-intellectualized politics is its antithesis. Combined, they are the politics of ideology in mass society, an ill wind that blows some good to the young eager TV producer who thinks that political theory is in the hand-held camera.

TV producers are not the only ones to welcome McLuhan. Canadians in general have become more susceptible to the charms of an intellectual exploring the cultural demimonde without the usual class biases. It is an attractive egalitarian avant-garde image for a country that has not yet had its Whitmans, Sandburgs, or Pounds; a country that has only begun to face the fact that it is urban and industrialized, its quickest and best minds straining at the leash to break away from an intellectual Establishment that has been singularly obtuse, Mandarin-minded, and peculiarly punitive. Bright young men will find in McLuhan's enthusiasm for the media a populist realism, his distrust of intellectualism a revolt against dead scholarship and the demands of specialization, his approach through technology an unsentimental toughness, his removal of the issue from a context of values a liberation from petty Philistine censors, his rejection of social criticism a long overdue break with the tiresome futile leftish politics of the Thirties. It is an ideal formula for the 1960s, and to his disciples—and they are legion—McLuhan is a prophet. From a longer perspective, he is the first, original, genuine Canadian *ideologue* of mass society, but his sense-ratios were shaped by the irrationalism, determinism, and folk romanticism of the nineteenth century.

richard kostelanetz*
a hot apostle
in a cool culture

Perhaps the most telling inadequacy of American book reviewing is its impotence before some of the major intellectual works
of our time. Whereas any reasonably decent book, floated on a
modest enough promotional budget, usually earns respectful
reviews in the bigger organs and more skeptical notices in the
smaller ones, the reviewing press, from the dailies to the quar-
terlies, has largely ignored such significant recent explorations
as Norman O. Brown's *Life Against Death* (1959), Joseph
Frank's *The Widening Gyre* (1963), Buckminster Fuller's
Seven Chains to the Moon (1963), *Education Automation*
(1962), and *Ideas and Integrities* (1963), Gershon Legman's
The Horn Book (1964), Herman Kahn's *On Thermonuclear
War* (1960), Milič Čapek's *Philosophical Impact of Contemporary Physics* (1963), John Cage's *Silence* (1961), and Marshall

* Richard Kostelanetz *is a literary and social critic whose books include*
The Theatre of Mixed Means *and* Music of Today. *He has edited a number of anthologies, such as* On Contemporary Literature *and* Young American Writers, *and has written reviews and articles for* Book Week, Kenyon
Review, Partisan Review, *and* The Village Voice.

McLuhan's *The Gutenberg Galaxy* (1962) and *Understanding Media* (1964). For instance, *The New York Times Book Review*, to my memory, covered only one of them, Kahn's book, which had more prepublication fanfare (*i.e.*, briefing sessions) than the others. *Partisan Review*, for another example, caught only Joseph Frank, perhaps because he has long been a regular contributor. *The New York Review of Books*, alive since 1962, likewise treated only one, *Understanding Media*, in a very brief and abrupt review by Frank Kermode. Even when they are discussed, these works and their authors are usually brutally mishandled; precisely because they represent a departure from current thinking, books of this kind inadvertently invite several styles of critical evasion. Sometimes a reviewer uses the publication of one as an "occasion" to take a position for or against it, to gauge its possible cultural impact and probable audience, to restate his own pet thesis for the umpteenth time, to twist the work into existing categories, or to classify the book or its author with stock images. Even years after their publication, although most of these books are recognized as pertinent and imaginative, none, to my knowledge, has received that sort of thorough scrutiny we associate with engaged criticism.

Although Marshall McLuhan's two recent books, *The Gutenberg Galaxy* and *Understanding Media*, are hardly a reviewer's delight, they are, to the true critic, an intellectual necessity; and it is nothing but scandalous that, between the few short reviews in intellectual journals and the numerous profiles in the more popular press, truly open and discriminating criticism of McLuhan's thought has been sparse. The book's sentences are generally clumsily written, except for scattered moments of high grace and true wit ("When a thing is current, it creates currency"); the paragraphs are carelessly constructed; his thoughts are so diffusely organized that the book's pages need not be read chronologically. Moreover, the ideas are so original that they often evade immediate comprehension, and McLuhan's insights at first seem arbitrary in manner and excessively dogmatic in tone. The books repell the impatient reader—a category that includes, alas, most critics—before they engage the more persistent one; and to make matters more difficult, *Understanding Media* often inspires an animus (unjustified, I believe) in people excessively committed to the culture of print. (Oral preachers in the fifteenth century, Mc-Luhan remarks, expressed similar agonies over the development of printing presses). The failure of critical intelligence is as unfortunate as the books' stylistic oddities; for both discourage a serious confrontation with works that offer not only an encompassing theory of human history but also insights into the full range of human experience, both past and present, both humanistic and scientific.

In his first work, *The Mechanical Bride* (1951), needlessly out-of-print and exorbitantly expensive on the used-book markets, McLuhan explains his "method" as adapting the analytical techniques of modern art criticism to the study of both popular culture and society itself; and like the best art criticism, his original insights are most adept at illuminating what other eyes have missed—when they literally render the invisible visible. In the opening pages of *The Mechanical Bride,* McLuhan perceives, "It is on its technical and mechanical side that the front page is linked to the techniques of modern science and art. Discontinuity is in different ways a basic concept of both quantum and relativity physics. It is the way in which a Toynbee looks at civilization, or a Margaret Mead at human cultures. Notoriously, it is the visual technique of a Picasso, the literary technique of James Joyce." In addition to being indubitably true in its individual perceptions, this passage, as it incorporates a wide range of examples, succeeds in illuminating a central overarching characteristic of the contemporary sensibility.

Similarly enlightening are these sentences from *The Gutenberg Galaxy,* perhaps McLuhan's most coherently realized book, on the impact of print on the culture of Western man: "The visual (the perceptual mode of the reader) makes for the explicit, the uniform, and the sequential in painting, in poetry, in logic, history. The non-literate modes are implicit, simultaneous, and discontinuous, whether in the primitive past or the electronic present." Here McLuhan embellishes his earlier insight by explaining why contemporary culture should find discontinuity a more congenial organizing principle than causality.

Unlike *The Mechanical Bride,* realized as just a series of explanatory glosses, the two more recent books embody significant theses about the causes of historical change and the radical character of contemporary civilization. Where other contemporary thinkers concerned with cultural development have focused upon the vicissitudes of religious faith, man's changing conception of himself, his varying control over his environment, the health of libidinal energies, the conflicts of political cultures and economic systems, the revolutions in physics and intellectual thought, McLuhan adopts a mode of explanation I can only christen, against his objections, "technological determinism." In his study of historical change, McLuhan believes that the invention of a certain, crucially relevant tool or machine initiates huge changes in the environment which, in turn, engineer transformations in both man's social relations and his perception of experience. For instance, McLuhan says that the railroad, by centralizing commerce and transportation about depots, historically shaped the structure of the cities and the particular sensibilities of city people; however, the automobile similarly shaped the suburbs where houses are accessible largely, if not entirely, through private transportation. With the crossing of the new technology with the old environment—when the automobile enters the city—the result is chaos. These perceptions I take to be true.

Following this principle of technological determinism, McLuhan develops a more specific scheme of explanation, suggesting that a radical change in the technology of communication is the prime initiating force. By weaving a mosaic of examples (which offer a theme), rather than developing an argument (which offers a thesis), he suggests in *The Gutenberg Galaxy* that the invention of movable type, which led to the printing press, radically transforming the culture of Western man, producing not only the predominantly visual orientation of the man who reads print but also symphonic structure to supersede the repetitious forms of medieval music, a kind of music abstractly divorced from the art's origins in speech, a Protestant religion made possible by the book's capacity to induce individual revelation, the psychological mode of inner-direction, the forms of sequential literature, the epistemology of causal explanations, and the mechanical technology that created man's sense of alienation from his environment. As an interpretation of cultural history, McLuhan's scheme contributes to the contemporary quarrel with traditional patterns of historiography, including the emphasis upon either politicians or "great men," upon economic factors as wholly determining, upon the mind as a stronger force than matter.

The theme of technological determinism is not McLuhan's invention, for it underpins such major and respectable scholarly works as Siegfried Giedion's *Mechanization Takes Command* (1948), a particularly brilliant study of what its author calls "anonymous history"; Lewis Mumford's *Technics and Civilization* (1934), Lynn White, Jr.'s *Medieval Technology and Social Change* (1962), and Albert Payson Usher's *A History of Mechanical Inventions* (1929, 1954). The theme of the revolutionary impact of changes in communications informs, among other works, H. J. Chaytor's *From Script to Print* (1945), Eric Havelock's *Preface to Plato* (1963), Harold A. Innis' *The Bias of Communication* (1951), and André Malraux's *The Voices of Silence* (1953); and insightful studies of the historical transformations of human perception, to which McLuhan is indebted, include Joseph Frank's *The Widening Gyre* (1963), Milič Čapek's *The Philosophical Impact of Contemporary Physics* (1963), William M. Ivins, Jr.'s *Art and Geometry: A Study in Space Intuitions* (1946), Dorothy Lee's *Freedom and Culture* (1958), Anton Ehrenzweig's *The Psychoanalysis of Artistic Vision and Hearing* (1953), E. S. Carpenter's *Eskimo* (1959), Edward T. Hall's *The Silent Language* (1959), and Siegfried Giedion's two-volume *The Eternal Present— The Beginnings of Art* (1962) and *The Beginnings of Architecture* (1964). All these are relatively recent works, for only in the twentieth century have researchers been able to discern the hidden impact of technology and the cultural variations in perceptual experience. However, what is new with McLuhan is

211

his comprehensiveness—his willingness to interpret so many aspects of experience as shaped by technologies of communication—as he weaves the diverse observations of others (extensively quoted and credited) into a moderately coherent whole.

In *Understanding Media,* very much the sequel, McLuhan's theme is that the new electronic communications technologies of the twentieth century are a root force in shaping modern culture. Telegraph, telephone, radio, television, photography have changed all experience ranging from social organization to human perception, for just as the telephone significantly speeds the flow of business, so television makes all news current. Likewise, just as the contemporary newspaper page (the product of reporting that uses electronic media) has a multiplicity of headlines whose impact is simultaneous and discontinuous, so is the structure we recognize to be distinctly "contemporary" in poetry and fiction in art (especially cubism) and music. Whereas the predominant organizing principle of print culture was linear—introduction, development, and conclusion —contemporary culture is characterized by repetition, juxtaposition, overlap, and disjunction. "Electricity," McLuhan writes, "ended sequence by making things instant; it is the new mosaic form of the TV image that has replaced the Gutenberg structural assumptions." Electronic media also downgrade the visual capacity to initiate multisensuous comprehensions, required in the movies, before the television, at a happening. "Print asked for the isolated and stripped-down visual faculty," McLuhan explains, while, in contrast, television, by demanding "the unified sensorium," produces a greater "tactility"; for feelings of touch, McLuhan believes, result from the interplay of all the senses. That is, the more senses an experience engages, the more ultimately tactile it is. In this respect he offers an explanation for what others have only observed—that, in general, young people today are more responsive than their elders to the multisensuous "cool" media (they "latch on," as Buckminster Fuller put it) and less amenable to the "hot" necessities of print.

Unlike the intellectuals, who condemn the mass media completely—the larger the mass the more vehement the condemnation—or look at them only as an occasion to condemn them again, McLuhan was among the first North American intellectuals to investigate precisely what the new media implied and how their forms could affect people; and in this respect, McLuhan's first book, *The Mechanical Bride* (1951), is a prelude to Reuel Denney's *The Astonished Muse* (1957), a less insightful work, and *Television in the Lives of Our Children* (1961), a confused and superficial study by Wilbur Schramm and his associates. (This scholarship, it should be noted, differs considerably from books that focus primarily, if not entirely, on content in the new media, such as Stuart Hall and Paddy Whannel's *The Popular Arts* [1965], in which two unimaginative literary gents give out grades, or Gilbert Seldes' *The Popular Arts* [1956] and Barry Ulanov's *The Two Worlds of American Art* [1965], both of which are more or less apologetic.) Essentially, McLuhan is the first to recognize that the new media, in the book's subtitle, represent "extensions of man": as such, they embody both opportunity and threat. First, they increase the range of man's control and impact over his environment— the telephone extends the voice and ear; all switches and dials extend the power of touch; yet they also increase the environment's possible power over him—the nightmare of 1984 in which a television's cameras and microphones trace one's every move.

Continuing his probing toward *Understanding Media*, McLuhan examines each major electronic medium—television, radio, telephone, newspaper, phonograph—to define its individual character—its limitations and possibilities, as well as the ways it characteristically handles experience. Here the techniques of art criticism are crucially useful; for to define, first, the nature of the medium's expression and, second, the interaction of a medium with human attention, McLuhan posits the descriptive terms of "hot" and "cool." The former word identifies media (or experiences or people) with highly defined contents—a considerable amount of detailed information—as a movie screen or a page of print. Low-definition or "cool" media offer only outlines; examples include cartoons and television. Secondly, where a hot medium fosters detachment and skepticism, a cool medium requires that its audience mentally participate to complete the communication. Watching television, for instance, requires more concentration than mere looking, because the dots of the screen offer only outlines of figures; thus, our brain literally learns to flesh out the characters on the screen. Similarly, conversation has a low definition—it is "cool"; a lecture is definitely hot. Although most hot media create hot responses, a hot medium can be used to simulate the cool, participational quality of television, and vice versa. For examples, Alain Resnais' *Last Year at Marienbad* (1961) offers a cool experience in a hot medium; a play presented on radio has a cooler impact on radio than it would in a theatrical performance; an in-person argument creates a hot experience in the essentially cool medium of human talk. McLuhan's associate, the museum designer Harley W. Parker, succinctly demonstrates the difference between hot and cool impact by flashing a slide of his own painting in a screen. The picture portrays a number of distinctly drawn people escaping from a fire; it attains a high definition, a singular appearance. By twisting the projector's lens, Parker blurs his picture slightly until it resembles seas of color; it attains a low definition. Parker suspects, correctly I believe, that younger people, whose sensibilities were honed on television, would find this blurred image more appealing than the original.

Applying this distinction, McLuhan illuminates phenomena that others perceive but cannot explain, such as why the content and effect of television are so different from that of radio. Whereas radio requires a performance of high-definition—announcers attempt to develop a distinctive voice and tend to speak loudly—television favors people of a definition so low they appear almost bland, like Jack Paar and Ed Sullivan in America. In *Media*, McLuhan uses this distinction to explain why John F. Kennedy should have been more attractive than Richard Nixon on televison (and Nixon the dominant figure on radio) and, by implication, why Harold Wilson seemed more appealing than Sir Alec Douglas-Home. One McLuhan hypothesis I find profoundly fascinating is that television engineers the fall of high-definition politicians: "It is no accident that Senator McCarthy lasted such a very short time when he switched to TV. Soon the press decided, 'He isn't news any more.' Neither McCarthy nor the press ever knew what happened. TV is a cool medium. It rejects hot figures and hot issues and people from the hot press media. Fred Allen was a casualty of TV. Was Marilyn Monroe? Had TV occurred on a large scale during Hitler's reign he would have vanished quickly. Had TV come first there would have been no Hitler at all." At first, these assertions, with their faith in the all-pervading dominance of the media, appear absolutely preposterous, particularly because of their complete neglect of socio-political factors; but precisely because McLuhan thinks where few other minds will go, he offers ideas that, at minimum, complement our understanding.

Indeed, perhaps the most extraordinary quality of McLuhan's mind is that it discerns significances where others see only data or nothing. "What Parkinson hides from himself and his readers is simply the fact that [clerical staff always increases because] the main 'work to be done' is actually the movement of information. 'Mass media,' 'mass entertainment' [are] useless phrases obscuring the fact that English itself is a mass medium." Many of his most original insights stem from his considering how differences in the sensory ratios are related to cultural materials. One can imagine a Ph. D. thesis (if not several) slogged out of the following offhand remark: "In [contemporary] literature only people from backward oral areas had any resonance to inject into the language—the Yeatses, the Synges, the Joyces, Faulkners and Dylan Thomases." (What about the Nigerian Amos Tutuola or the Negro-American Ralph Ellison?) "The printed book will naturally tend to become a work of reference rather than a speaking Wisdom." Conversely, the advertising jingle contributes to the return to oral (and aural) guidance, "The unique character of our alphabet [unlike ideograms or hieroglyphs is that it] separates all meaning from the sounds of letters." These remarks resemble McLuhan's books; both are more valuable for their stimulating insights than for any final definitions.

Much of his books' persuasiveness stems from McLuhan's

ability to incorporate other generalizations of contemporary experience into his own scheme. For instance, he transcends David Riesman's thesis that "other-direction" is becoming the dominant psychological orientation of contemporary man by tracing its underpinnings to the shift from print to electronic media. Whereas Riesman himself, in an essay reprinted in *Abundance for What?* (1964), rather tentatively posited a connection between "inner-direction" and the experience of reading print, McLuhan says precisely that "inner-direction" is the psychological mode of literate man, while the increase in "other-direction" is a direct result of the media. As contemporary man experiences more in groups—TV and movies are more sociable than books—and his culture is encouraging participational experiences, contemporary man is undergoing what McLuhan calls a "retribalization." Riesman, as an inner-directed print-type himself, expressed ambivalent feelings toward this change; however, McLuhan is more positive, believing that it would well initiate the end of man's feelings of alienation from his community. Similarly, McLuhan transcends Joseph Frank's famous thesis about the "spatial"—non-linear—form of modern literature; for whereas Frank attributed this shift away from linear form to man's sense of his decreasing control of his environment, McLuhan argues, particularly in uncollected essays on James Joyce, John Dos Passos and William Burroughs, that the most modernist of contemporary literature imitates the formal structures of the new media. Similarly, McLuhan's ideas offer a historico-aesthetic rationale for some strains of avant-garde art, from John Cages's aleatoric experiments to Stan VanDerBeek's "multiprojection" to the intermedia arts of "happenings" and "action theater." Similarly, to the impact of the new media McLuhan traces both the revolution in consciousness implicit in the use of hallucinogenic or psychedelic drugs and the shift away from presentational theater to participational, such as Brecht's works, *The Brig*, happenings, which all decrease the distance between audience and actor.

McLuhan's ideas also have much in common with other radical tendencies in contemporary American thought. Like

Buckminster Fuller and Herbert Marcuse, McLuhan recognizes that cybernation (the automation of work processes), as it eliminates work and increases leisure, gives nearly every man the opportunity to devote all his energies to the cultivation of his powers; and not only does McLuhan favor a guaranteed income (in Robert Theobald's anthology of that title), but he also envisages that continuous education will become the prime business for future society. Also, like Paul Goodman and Edgar Z. Friedenberg, McLuhan argues that conventional education hardly engages the interest of young people and insufficiently equips them for coping with the actualities of their environment. Like Herman Kahn and Norman O. Brown, McLuhan believes in thinking which is exploratory and speculative, rather than substantive and definitive; and the books of all three are products of men who do not necessarily believe in their thoughts. Just as Norman O. Brown insists in *Life Against Death* that he tries "merely to introduce some new possibilities and new problems into the public consciousness," offering, so to speak, his free-associated speculations, so Herman Kahn imagines "scenarios" to conjecture about future possibilities; and so McLuhan speculates about the impact of media. Finally, all three men are similar in that they offer not theses but themes.

Particularly in their grasp of the development of civilization, McLuhan and Brown are implicitly closest to each other. In *Life Against Death*, Brown reinterprets the later thought of Sigmund Freud to suggest not only that the repressiveness of civilized society is the prime cause of neurosis but also that mankind, in the course of human history, is slowly eliminating instinctual repressions for a more fully libidinal existence. McLuhan parallels Brown by arguing that while mechanized technology, derived in principle from print, alienates man from his environment, electronic media ushers the end of alienation, first, by extending man's senses into his surroundings; secondly, by favoring more participational, low-definition experiences; and thirdly, by recreating that oral bond that tied primitive society together. In short, by locating the prime source of mental distress not in man but in his environment,

both men predict that as changing society becomes more sympa-
thetic to the human essence, most anxiety and neurosis will
disappear.

Similarly, both thinkers predict the end of man's slavery to
segmented time; for future man will have less awareness of
past and future. "Both time (as measured visually and segmen-
tally) and space (as uniform, pictorial, and enclosed) disappear in the electronic age of instant information," McLuhan
writes; and Brown identifies the connection between timed existence and civilization's repression: "Only repressed life is in
time, and unrepressed life would be timeless or in eternity." It
follows that as man loses his sense of quantified time (and,
thus, his conception of life as a series of stages), he develops a
different attitude toward death. "Eternity," Brown writes, "is
therefore a way of envisaging mankind's liberation from the
neurotic obsession with the past and the future." McLuhan
conjectures that the electronic media will return man to the
preprint perspective that views death as not a termination of
existence but an extension of life into a different realm—literally, a life after life. (Indicatively, only non-print cultures can
accept the idea of reincarnation).

Most conspicuously absent from *Media* is any discussion of
the future of sexual activity; but on this subject, I believe, Mc-
Luhan's implications correspond with Brown's ideas. The latter thinker envisages the decline of sexuality focused upon
genital contact and a return to the "polymorphously perverse,"
unfocused, purely libidinal pleasure characteristic of the baby;
McLuhan's thoughts suggest, by extension, that the focus upon
genital pleasure, particularly upon the genital orgasm, is related to print; for not only does genital sexuality resemble
reading in requiring a concentration of attention, but also its
conception of pleasure is analogous to the reading of a traditional novel—a progressive heightening of tension to a total
release. In contrast, polymorphous, omniattentive sensuality is
analogous to the constant pleasures afforded by the electronic
media, with their diffusion of attention and absence of climax;
and just as the child's sexuality is "cool" and unfocused until
society teaches him a "hot" genital orientation, so a baby's at-

tention is unfocused until he learns to read print. Indicatively, the sexual manuals of preprint cultures, such as the *Kama Sutra,* espouse a notion of sexual pleasure considerably different from the predominantly genital (and orgasmic) preoccupations of Alfred Kinsey and Wilhelm Reich. Sex in the future, both Brown and McLuhan suggest, will be more continuous or constant in time and more diffuse in its multiply erotogenic range. In these respects—the proliferation of pleasure, the disintegration of linear time, the increase in diverse libidinal pleasure—both Brown and McLuhan imagine a future similar to, as its participants describe it (see *The Psychedelic Reader* [1965]), the hallucinogen experience on a grand scale; and all together, these radical thinkers and actors suggest a future utopia on earth not unlike our traditional conceptions of heaven.

Not everything in McLuhan's books is true or perceptive; for McLuhan's methods for achieving insights frequently inspire incredible, if not inscrutable, leaps from reality. Some problems stem from his major theme that, "The medium is the message," which is to say several things: first, the ultimate content of the medium is the medium itself; that is, people watch movies primarily for the pleasures of the kinetic screen accompanied by relevant sound, just as people like reading for the joy of watching print pass before their eyes. Second, "It is the medium that shapes and controls the scale and form of human association and action"; that is, communications media are the primary force in shaping a society. Third, the "message" of a medium is its impact upon society; that is, "The message of the movie medium is that of transition from lineal connection to configuration."

In the first sense, I believe that McLuhan is only partially right, which is to say he is largely wrong; for he completely discounts the question of what appears on the screen and speaker. As anyone who has ever watched movies knows, some of them are more interesting—more engaging and stimulating —than others (just as some are more soporific); and much of the difference depends upon the quality of what we traditionally call the program's "content." Similarly, to refer to a recent

219

American example, the fifth rerun of *I Love Lucy* is a considerably different TV experience from a presentation of George F. Kennan addressing the Committee on Foreign Relations on the War in Vietnam; and I doubt if many people watching Kennan stayed with that channel when Lucy appeared in his stead. Even on the medium which has perhaps the narrowest range of quality, content does count.

The second corollary of "The medium is the message" has considerably more truth. What McLuhan is saying here is that the medium determines what kind of experience and information can best be presented on it and thus what kinds of impact it can have. For philosophical exposition, for instance, the book is quite obviously the most viable form; for it allows each reader to peruse the thought at his own pace, as well as permitting rereading. (McLuhan predicts, however, that soon individuals will be able to borrow TV lectures from a library and run and reverse them at speeds to suit their taste. This technological advance, of course, would make TV a more suitable medium for a lecture on philosophy than a classroom.) Moreover, the second corollary says that as media shape the modes and situations of response (by oneself, or in a group; continuity or discontinuity), they influence ("shape" more than "control") human social life (thus, TV and movies will initiate retribalization). In short, then, where McLuhan's thesis of the medium and the message runs false is precisely in its exclusionary determinism. *The medium is not the entire message, just as it does not totally control the message.* What McLuhan does, here and elsewhere, is escalate an insight into an iron-clad generalization; so that only if one takes these grandiose statements with skepticism will he grasp the real truths they have to offer.

McLuhan's mind is, to his credit, more admissive than exclusionary; not only is it open to experience that other intellectuals either dismiss or neglect, but he also exhibits the tendency to admit all his own thoughts to print. Just as some of them are more comprehensible than others, so some are considerably more perceptive. What I fear is that many people impressed with the brilliance of so much will suspect that everything McLuhan says is true—even worse, true in precisely the way he says it. However, as even the author regards his insights as "exploratory probes," the reader must, of necessity, subject these perceptions to the most rigorous critical scrutiny. McLuhan is deeply indebted to James Joyce—indeed, floating around in *Media* is the nucleus of a brilliant critical book on Joyce's work—and McLuhan has said, "Much of what I talk about is in *Finnegans Wake*." The trouble is that in taking his love of punning from Joyce, McLuhan also adopts Joyce's most indulgent habits of thought. The organizing principle of the *Wake*, one remembers, is that one story is all stories—to put it differently, at the base of the novel's major actions is the tale of familial conflict. Thus, on the same page, Joyce writes about a range of filial relationships—England and Ireland, Eliot and Yeats, Romulus and Remus, Mutt and Jeff, Shem and Shaun, Greece and Rome. What Joyce did, then, was transcend the metaphoric relation—that one story is like another—for associations that eliminate the metaphoric dimensions completely. McLuhan performs similar leaps, writing in *Media,* for instance, that, "The electric light is pure information." By this gnomic sentence, he intends a metaphoric meaning—that the electronic light resembles an information medium in that it tells us about something else; without the light, we would not recognize the content it illuminates. However, such elliptical statements obfuscate meaning, and such an inclusive intelligence loses its sense of discrimination—if they are so like each other, then there is no discernible difference between them. Indeed, this process of converting analogies into identities accomplishes, metaphorically, a transubstantiation, a doctrine that separates the postprint Protestant intelligence from the preprint Catholic; where the former says that bread *represents* the body of Christ, the latter rules that, at a certain point in the Mass, it *is* the body of Christ.

What may rationalize McLuhan's inclusive logic, perhaps, is his notion that differentiation and classification are modes for the age of print; for example, he notes that the notion of "childhood" as a distinct stage did not arise until the seventeenth century. In contrast, the contemporary modes are inclusion and unification; and just as the avant garde in each modern art overlaps into another—theater into dance with *The Brig* and Happenings and music into theater with John Cage—so newspapers and magazines deny traditional differences by homogenizing all experience. Similarly, where uniformity in grammar and definitions is a product of print, the new writing, like the new art (and McLuhan's new scholarship), is less committed to traditional precision; and McLuhan's use of abstract words such as "myth" and "archetype" is highly idiosyncratic—perhaps more metaphoric than accurate. ("Printed grammars since the 18th century," McLuhan writes, "created a fog based on the concept of correctness.") The major troubles with such transformations of analogies into identities are, first, that they betray the experience we know—the light bulb is simply not an informational medium the way television is—and, second, that such statements, as they defy precise analysis, corrupt the language of explanation. Until man ceases to recognize such crucial differences, perhaps an inevitable concomitant of the electronic revolution, McLuhan errs in neglecting them. "You can prove nothing by analogy," says Ezra Pound in *ABC of Reading*, incidentally one of McLuhan's favorite books. "The analogy is either range-finding or fumble. Written down as a lurch toward proof . . . it leads mainly to useless argument." Alas, Pound too exaggerates his perception.

Likewise Joycean is the circular structure of all McLuhan's books; for the principle he suggests in *The Mechanical Bride* —"No need for it to be read in any special order"—is more or less applicable to his other books. McLuhan's rationale for such a procedure is buried in an extraordinary passage on page 26 of *Media*: "The Hebrew and Eastern mode of thought tackles problem and resolution, at the outset of a discussion, in a way typical of oral societies in general. The entire message is then traced and retraced, again and again, on the rounds of a concentric spiral with seeming redundancy. One can stop anywhere after the first few sentences and have the full message, if one is prepared to 'dig' it. [This] redundant form [is] inevitable to the electric age, in which the concentric pattern is imposed by the instant quality, and overlay in depth, of electric speed. But the concentric with its endless intersection of planes is necessary for insight. In fact, it is the technique of insight, and as such is necessary for media study, since no medium has its meaning or existence alone, but only in constant interplay with other media." This I consider among McLuhan's most disturbing ideas; and although I see that presentation and argument are rhetorically tied to the linear form, I am not sure, as McLuhan is, that insight is necessarily instantaneous. A full understanding of any process, whether of complicated mechanisms or complex ideas, requires some form of successive thought; and if the process is to be effectively communicated, the writer (or speaker) should use developmental syntax. Indeed, while the densely insightful character of McLuhan's own prose can perhaps be traced to his compositional method of dictation, his disordered exposition is largely responsible for the failure of so many readers to grasp the range and complexity of the revolutions he describes.

My own central criticism of McLuhan's interpretations is his rampaging tendency to overexplain. Not only are his ideas overly deterministic, not only does he facilely transform analogies into identities, not only does he tend to encompass all other schemes within his own (rather than arguing against them), but he ties up his materials into a package too neat for their realities. In one sense, McLuhan admits this, insisting that his ideas are just explorations; he feels no need to defend them as scrupulously as a Ph.D. candidate would his thesis. On the other hand, as his dogmatic style and messianic tone subvert his more modest intentions, his lack of rigor makes him an easy target for the eager debunkers.

Too often McLuhan becomes the victim of his own schemes, foisting his interpretations upon resistant evidence. Much of his prophecy stems from the speculation that as man overcomes his slavery to literacy, he will attain a sensibility similar to that of primitive man; thus, McLuhan continually refers to preprint experience for his images of the present and future. He notes in *The Gutenberg Galaxy* that soon after the impact of print, music became divorced from its origins in song (and speech); therefore he expects that all contemporary music will complete the circle, asserting that not only does jazz have its origins in speech but also that, "Schoenberg and Stravinsky and Carl Orff and Bartók, far from being advanced seekers of esoteric effects, seem to have brought music very close to the conditions of ordinary human speech." This may be true for Orff, it might be somewhat true for Bartók; but as for Schoenberg, the remark has nothing to do with his central contribution to contemporary musical thought. Serial music is so abstract, so divorced from speech, that an accurate description of its methods forbids extrinsic analogies. At another point, McLuhan suggests that since preprint art was corporate and anonymous in authorship, so will be postprint art. However, TV is corporate less because of the nature of the medium than the existing practices for making programs; and the greatest films, except perhaps the Marx Brothers, reveal the touch of an individual director. The point is that once a society develops a certain mode of conceptual awareness, it will not necessarily disappear when that society or its communications technology changes. Historical memory will survive new situations.

McLuhan commits a similar error in *Media* when he writes, "Every kind of entertainment in the TV age favors the same kind of personal involvement," adding, a few lines later, "Therefore the highbrow paperback, because of its depth character, may appeal to youngsters who spurn ordinary narrative offerings." However, it is difficult to envisage how something as hot, extrinsically and intrinsically, should have any resemblence to the coolness of television; in fact, the reasons for the quality paperback's success are predominantly economic—it is a cheaper form of a traditional item, arriving at the same time when people have more money for luxuries—and educationally the expansion of university enrollments. Here and elsewhere, McLuhan uses examples that do not confirm his points; and sometimes his use of evidence appears more opportunistic than scrupulous.

The point is that other forces besides media shape experience, both contemporary and historical. The drive for money, for instance, is a universal quality, doled out in unequal measure; and McLuhan's ideas are unable to explain why this should be so. His chapter on money, almost the foggiest in

Media, makes the obvious prediction that the credit card will replace printed money as the "currency" in the new age. However, these remarks do not really cope with the importance of money in media; after all, as Harry J. Skornia shows in *Television and Society* (1965), a book McLuhan blurbed, the major inspiration behind American television today is the possibilities of enormous profits, not the potentialities of the medium; and as McLuhan's commentary hardly approaches the crucial question of media ownership, they cannot explain the truly vast difference between British radio and television and American.

Similarly, McLuhan, in his complete emancipation from Sigmund Freud, hardly mentions sexual desire, except to say at one point that it represents the ultimate form of tactile activity. When he tells us that mesh stockings are more appealing to male eyes than slick-surfaced, because in their dotted surface they resemble a television screen (and thus encourage participatory viewing), he makes an insightful comment; but surely McLuhan does not believe that men look at female legs to observe the dots of the stockings. A bare leg is, after all, more enticing than a stockinged one, mesh or no mesh. Thirdly, as McLuhan attempts to downgrade the power of politicians and political structures, he has little awareness of how they can, in fact, shape a considerable portion of our existence, even our relationship to the media. People cannot have television unless their state permits it; and governmental policies, as we noted, often influence, if not control, the content of programs, usually with scant awareness of the nature of the medium. Absent from *Media* is any elaboration of Harold A. Innis' version of "The medium is the message"—that each new form of communication initiates a shift in political power. Furthermore, it is simply preposterous to say "The Cold War is largely a conflict between cultures where different sense-priorities prevail. The U.S. is eye-oriented. The Soviet Union, with its limited traditions of literacy, is ear-oriented." Similarly naïve is McLuhan's prediction that, "If the 'Voice of America' suddenly switched to jazz, the Kremlin would have reason to crumble." In the end, McLuhan's insights into experience are more acceptable as a complement to, rather than a replacement for, other interpretations. He is innocent to omit economic activity, sexual desire, and political forces from his explanatory schemes; for as they remain potent factors in modern society, mere forgetting them will not make them go away.

McLuhan's images of life in the future are contradictory on two major issues—specialization vs. generalism; freedom vs. social control. First, he insists that technology will make man more of a generalist (for machines will handle all the specialized work); however, he fails to consider the intermediate stage in the immediate future—the antithesis, so to speak—where automation requires the most specialized tasks. (Here, perhaps, he is seduced by his theme that life in the future will resemble life before print, if not before script.) Secondly, Mc-Luhan insists, on one hand, that the media, as extensions of the senses, give each man a greater control over his own environment; on the other hand, he admits that, "Leasing our eyes and ears and nerves to commercial interests is like handing over the common speech to a commercial corporation." Moreover, a politician who masters the television medium, as Mc-Luhan points out in his perceptive remarks on Fidel Castro, can stifle (cool) dissident activity. Then too, behind the notion of retribalization before the TV screen, controlled by either despots or media moguls, lies a totalitarian image; and McLuhan does not reassure when he says, "The computer, in short, promises by technology a Pentecostal condition of universal understanding and unity." McLuhan fails to separate dimensions of experience which will have increased freedom from those with greater constrictions; thus, he leaves the issue of future freedom unresolved.

In this last respect, McLuhan avows that the central purpose of his writing is the increase of perceptive knowledge; for only by knowing how the media really effect experience (by making the invisible visible) can we transcend their determining influence upon us. Through knowledge, man attains freedom—this is a decent Benthamite principle; and no McLuhan prescription is more urgently true than the need for education in school, on all levels, for truly discriminating use of the new media. However, as each new medium is a ditto machine for its predecessor—as cinema was for theater, so Telstar is for television—and each has a progressively larger power to standardize knowledge and opinion, so the need for effective antidotes becomes even greater. What McLuhan's observations suggest, then, is that at the same time that we must understand the new media, so must we also cultivate print, especially for those tasks that print does best, if only to preserve the possibilities of privacy and individual contemplation in a future characterized by increasing mass response. Moreover, "cinema and television," as Paul Goodman once wrote, "have so far produced pathetically inferior works that cannot pretend to compare with the masterpieces of book and stage over 2,500 years."

Although McLuhan posits no political directives in any of his books, *Understanding Media* strikes me as a most persuasive polemic for the necessity of communitarian anarchism. McLuhan continually predicts that the electronic media will produce the decentralization of society (perhaps because it fits into his historical scheme); however, he never quite explains how, in the age of networks, this "uniqueness and diversity" will occur. Indeed, by implication, particularly in their images of a possible future, his books suggest that the only way to overcome the incipient nightmare of 1984 is through the dismantling of society to its natural boundaries of existing communities—the political separation of cities from their suburbias and both from the rural areas—and the creation of wholly autonomous communications media within each of these enclaves. McLuhan implies this when he writes, "Restraints of electric absolutist power can be achieved not by the separation of powers, but by a pluralism of centres." Such action, it seems to me, is not only a desirable political solution to this age of superpowers but also a spiritual necessity in an era of possible global conformity; and McLuhan confirms this prognostication by suggesting that rebellion will not attract sympathy unless it is instigated by a group, for the sake of a *community* opposed to unjust authority. To put it differently, individual heroism is passé—one can hardly remember the names of the astronauts; instead, the contemporary heroes, from Mario Savio through

Robert Parris-Moses to Jeffrey St. John, are spokesmen for groups; and most of these heroes espouse the decentralization of social authority.

As intellectual endeavors, McLuhan's books merit nothing but highest praise; despite their intrinsically high-definitional quality, they invite participation in their thought processes, initiating not only dialogues between the reader and the book but between one reader and another. They are among the most richly insightful books of our time; and I doubt if any intelligent person can read them without being enlightened, if not influenced, in some way by McLuhan's perceptions—educated to cope better with his present environment. Amidst all the chaff, they contain much truth; more important, to many of us, they initiate an education—an awareness of dimensions previously hidden to us. Like other great American thinkers, McLuhan embodies that particularly, if not peculiarly, North American capacity to push ideas, often derived from others, beyond conventional bounds to the wildest conclusions—literally levels beyond other minds in the same field—creating a book in which enormous good-sense and outright nonsense are so closely entwined; and in our post-Marxist, post-existentialist, post-Christian age, such exploratory thought is more necessary and valuable to our culture than another serving of timeworn ideologies.

anthony burgess*
the modicum is the messuage

I make no apology for that title, especially as Professor McLuhan will, if he goes on as he is going on, be forced to use it himself sooner or later. A messuage is legally defined as a house with outbuildings and garden. Professor McLuhan has created a very commodious messuage, productive of most satisfactory rent, with a modicum of raw material. Good luck to him.

There are various approaches to Professor McLuhan and, during the recent McLuhan season marked by the publication and reissue of four of his books, most of them have been tried. I diffidently suggest a new one. McLuhan started his academic career as an engineering student at the University of Manitoba, but then changed to English. This is an interesting example of the influence of a hot medium, linear alphabetical arrangement leading McLuhan ineluctably from *Engi* to *Engl*. He went to Cambridge, where he came under the influence of

* ANTHONY BURGESS *is the prolific English novelist and literary critic whose books range from a study of James Joyce,* Re Joyce, *to a novel about Shakespeare and Elizabethan England,* Nothing But the Sun. *He has recently edited a shortened version of Joyce's dream book* Finnegans Wake.

I. A. Richards and, one presumes, must have at least been touched by the terrible magic of F. R. Leavis and *Scrutiny*. In 1939 he wrote a thesis on Thomas Nashe, an Elizabethan notable for high auditory prose and an appeal to the entire sensorium. It may or may not be relevant to add that in 1937 he was converted to Catholicism and was thus enabled to leave teleological matters in hands other than his own. No need to speculate about the purpose of life: from now on the epistemological would be enough.

The important thing, though, is the Cambridge esthetic. *Scrutiny* taught that, in an acceptable work of literature, it was not possible to separate content from form. You couldn't talk about the *meaning* of a poem: to explain it in terms of a prose paraphrase was not merely heretical but destructive of a highly wrought artifact. In a work of art the form is the content, the medium is the message. But *message* implies intellection—the reading eye of the mind. And so, through a pun that Thomas Nashe would have approved, suggest through *massage* the laying on of pummeling hands, the beneficent attack on the skin and the nerve endings. It was all there in Eliot, a *Scrutiny* darling, who complained about the dissociation of sensibility in the (hot medium) Romantics, and not only taught but demonstrated the need for modern poets to submit to the massage of (the Twenties man's mechanical bride) the internal combustion engine.

McLuhan's gimmick has been to push an esthetic doctrine to the limit. Nobody denies that a piece of music represents the condition to which all works of art must tend—a condition of unparaphrasability, total identification of form and content. Painting and sculpture became non-representational; literature became symbolist or surrealist: they were trying to be like music. But what makes one art different from another is, of course, the medium. The painter loves squelchy pigment, the sculptor loves intractable stone. The old baroque way was to ignore the character of the medium, so that stone became ridiculously plastic, losing its stoniness, and orchestral instruments were made to behave like each other and like the human voice. The medium must be allowed to have its own way: the artist resists its tyranny at his peril.

But McLuhan is concerned with society more than art (though art, being something that just "happens," has no hieratic status in social patterns). Applying the Cambridge esthetic to all the communication media, he is led to distort it in a very interesting way. He deliberately refuses to distinguish between a medium as the determinant of an art form and a medium as a transmissive device. I watch, on television, a film of a man reading a poem. Now obviously there are separables here—three media of communication concentrically set about the thing that is being communicated. But, to McLuhan, there are really four things of the same order. A medium has to have a content, but the content is always itself a medium. Nor is any medium transparent: it modifies our perception of the medium which is the content. Thus, an old film seen on a TV late late show is a different experience, and hence a different art form, from the original performance in a cinema.

McLuhan is absolved from the need to get to the core of a communication process by his deliberate identification of the artistic "message" with the purely informative or didactic one. Ends are not his concern; indeed, they may not really exist. It seems to me that his doctrines have progressed from (as in *Understanding Media*) an insistence on our accepting the importance of knowing what the massage is doing to us, to an elevation of the massage-machine to the rank of demiurge. His adoration of the Beatles (always, to me, an index of intellectual unsoundness) is based presumably on their having become priests of electronics. That they have to refuse a million dollars for a live concert in the United States (their new electronic medium being unable to accommodate the protoelectronic one) must be, to McLuhan, a sign of ultimate grace.

But he is very good and suggestive when he tells us of, say, the influence of the typewriter on the art, not just the craft, of authorship. Henry James became a new kind of writer when he began to dictate to a stenographer. The *vers libre* and typographical tropes of e. e. cummings owe, thinks McLuhan,

231

everything to the machine (how much more this applies to the admirable work of Don Marquis). I myself, humbler but still an author, know that my prose, such as it is, has been determined by a lifelong devotion to the typewriter: coming to the end of a line, unwilling to split a word with a hyphen, I will often use a shorter word than the one I intended. This is utter slavery to the machine. And McLuhan is right to insist on the *worthiness* of such commercial media as the advertisement. A special edition of an American magazine, compressed for airmail transmission by the elimination of advertisements, was promptly rejected by its GI recipients: it was the advertisements that they primarily wanted. They wanted them, says McLuhan, because advertisements are always by far the best devised feature of a periodical. (True, and because of the urgency of their aim, which McLuhan does not mention—to sell goods.)

McLuhan is at his most Cambridge when he preaches the repressive and limiting force of our Western visual culture and our failure to maintain the richer auditory and synesthetic traditions of tribal societies. Alphabetic writing he calls a "hot" medium: it is explicit and authoritative and it doesn't invite participation; it imposes a linear way of looking at the universe; it attacks one sense only. Ideograms and syllabaries he regards as functioning quite differently. Thus, the ideogram of Chinese writing does not impose meaning with the explicit brutality of a quasi-phonetic script: it is "cool," the meaning is suspended airily between you and it. All this strikes me as a lot of nonsense. To read Chinese and a Western language involves much the same process of instant recognition: we take in a word whole, as a Chinese takes in an ideogram. To present the traditional East-West difference in terms of irreconcilable modes of writing will not do. Islam is as alphabetic as Christendom, and Islam's history went, for centuries, in an opposed direction to that of the West. It is ideas, not scripts, that change cultures. Ultimately, all scripts function in the same way. We do not take in the word *not* as a collocation of three sounds; the Chinese do not take in *pu* (which means *not*) as a graphic representation of a little plant prevented from growing (a metaphor of notness): the semantic signal flashes in a split second. And yet on the factitious notion of radical differences of function McLuhan erects a whole historiography.

Perhaps he is right—though I'm not at all sure—when he says that the West is being dragged by the new electronic media out of the Gutenberg or Caxton age. Children, he says, brought up on the cool medium of television (a medium that invites participation) find difficulty even in the visual adjustment required when reading is forced on them. The straight-line chronology symbolized by a book belongs to the pre-Einsteinian era. Television is a norm we have to accept, not an upstart deviant that hypnotizes the young. There is nothing sacrosanct about a medium that hasn't changed since the fifteenth century, despite the halo that all books, however bad, borrow from the good one. But in refusing to accept that ideas are stronger than media, that the influence of media is (appropriately: I'm thinking of my typewriter prose again) marginal, McLuhan is perhaps guilty of a heresy worse than the esthetic one that thought the message was all. I say "perhaps": I'm not sure. That McLuhan should shake our minds up and make us powerfully aware of the pressure of media is probably enough. But he wants more than that.

arthur a. cohen*
doomsday in dogpatch:
the mcluhan thesis examined†

Imagine if you will the family of Yokums, big-boned, with
oversized shoes, ill-fitting, patched clothing, smoking corncobs
and swilling moonshine, arrayed about the potbelly stove—
not, however, engaged in that wry conversation that devastated
a generation of Americans not too long ago, obliging them, despite their ostensible squareness and conservatism, to find Senator McCarthy ridiculous, war-making folly, race hatred a concession to ignorance, but rather—or shall we say instead?—
displayed in readiness to beat one another in some madcap
exhibition of sadomasochism. Imagine Pappy Yokum, bearing
whip, about to excoriate the flesh of Mammy Yokum, or Li'l
Abner chuckling with cruelty as he places Daisy Mae upon the
rack, applying thumbscrews, inserting needles beneath her fin-

* ARTHUR A. COHEN *is editorial consultant for E. P. Dutton and has writ-
ten many books on theology and history, notably* The Natural and the
Supernatural Jew. *His essays have appeared in* Harper's, Commonweal,
Commentary, *and* Partisan Review.

† Adapted and expanded from an address delivered at the Fifty Books
Show Dinner of the American Institute of Graphic Arts at the Waldorf
Astoria, April 18, 1966.

gernails. Would it be believed? Would the vigilantes of our culture take Al Capp to court, accusing him of debasing the currency of his own realm, resorting to sadism and erotic violence to ballast the collapsing balloon of his imagination? Would he be charged with obscenity, with purveying pornography, with appealing to prurient interest? I think no. It would be understood that, despite a regrettable lapse of good taste, Li'l Abner could never be mistaken for Gilles de Rais. The Yokums could not be taken seriously in their roles as flagellants and torturers.

The comic strip is just that—the comic *strip,* a succession of frames, wildly colored, vulgarly drawn, excessive, loud, unfit for the kind of subtlety that depends upon indirection, afterthought, reflection, the various sideshows of the intellect which enable a point of view to acquire accretive, slowly forming power, the undertow of impact by which tension (adumbrated and then reinforced) becomes ultimately overwhelming. The comic strip is working upon presentiments that pin the meaning to the medium, and the medium, in this case, transports such a direct and uncompromising message that for it to carry another message is to require another medium. The comic strip is a device of propaganda. It has a single message unit: to speak bluntly, to bonk on the head, to crush sensibility into submission. It succeeds.

The comic strip is not a modern medium, although Marshall McLuhan has dated its origin in 1935. The comic comic strip is perhaps of recent origin, but not the cartoon strip, for cartoons, as McLuhan might have known, are as early as print, having been introduced early in the sixteenth century as a didactic device, imprinting moral virtues and exhibiting moral depravities. One thinks of the Renaissance and Reformation etcher and lithographer—Dürer and Cranach, for example—as humane moralists, in the traditions of humanism, employing the simplicities of the uncolored line, to which, very often, an exhortation is attached. These single-frame cartoons were expanded, particularly in the baleful atmosphere of post-Reformation Germany, into drawn-out warnings against the snares and deceptions of the Devil, the devices by which he

235

tempts and woos to the wild regions of hell and damnation. A kind of prototypic black humor, this. Very modern propaganda. All forceful; all simple; pure ideology, uncompromised. These cartoons were rather unfunny. They were a visual medium, a medium controlled by lineal succession of images, the cumulative effect of flashcard repetition, characteristic of a verbal, typographic culture—medieval McLuhanism.

But to return to our first image: What would happen to those perverse Yokums, now epigones of the Marquis de Sade, were they to be rendered in their flagellation postures, lacking, however, the telltale marks of rural, hillbilly folk, drawn straight, that is, without the exaggerating tipoffs that characterize the comic strip, drawn with even greater realism than the redoubtable Barbarella, but still called Yokums—Pappy, Mammy, Li'l Abner, Daisy Mae? What if these same four, speaking the same lines, were drawn now like Steve Canyon (a more realistic, clean-cut, all-American confection)? Undoubtedly the censors would become nervous; the visual statement would have begun to assault a traditional retina, a retina so well formed and anesthetized that, despite the continuance of hillbilly speech, the visual recognition, the congruity between the body of fantasy and the body of actuality, the whip imagined and the whip employed, the dreamed pain and ecstasy and the real pain and ecstasy would begin to connect.

Only the obvious displacement wrought by language, the inability of Li'l Abner to speak like the Marquis de Sade, would prevent the illusion from being complete. Disbelief would triumph. The medium, even realistically employed, defies the literalism the imagination requires for the consummation of the pornographic suggestion.

Pornography, like anything else, depends upon a tradition of conventionalized images (it is for this reason, if for none other, that there can be nothing new in pornography and hence no real danger), and as long as the conventional medium of pornography is not employed, the visual realism in itself cannot function.

Note well that even in works of explicit pornography the use of pictures is intended to interrupt the suggestiveness of language with the penultimate stage of erotic suggestion. The picture can never show the orgasm, for the orgasm is post-erotic and never pornographic. As Lessing observed in his essay on the classic sculpture of Laocoön in his death agony, the high moment of art is the moment before the ecstasy, whether of joy or of death, and that moment cannot be stated in art, for it is the experience beyond statement. Otherwise said, it is the moment for which the whole sensorium of the body is appropriate, the whole integrated welter of the senses, and there is no single medium able to transmit meaning to the whole sensorium; all media are partial and partitive, and no medium makes a comprehensive address. Consequently it is the moment before the end that is interpreted by art.

Pornography is a mixed genre and relies upon two media—the picture and the text—alternating, balancing irony with explication, suggestion with elucidation, description with moralism. Pornography, quite obviously, is a bastard form. It should be censored only because humanity is stupefied by literalism, is, in fact, stupid, and cannot be relied upon to know when to laugh.

Such a case for censorship, grounded upon the notion that we must punish mankind for its stupidity, is invidious, not seriously intended; however, the judgment *is* rendered seriously. Can mankind be blamed for visual idiocy? Surely not, for the sensorium is a conditioned mechanism and the conditioning of the last two thousand years has been that of the written and the printed word.

The cultural metaphor that Marshall McLuhan has identified as the culprit of these millennia—the culprit whose culpability includes the radical individualism of post-Renaissance man to which is ascribed man's isolation, incommunicateness, emotional desiccation, and desensitization (and McLuhan, unlike aristocratic intellectuals among whom I count myself, cares more for the loss of man's sensibility than man's mind)—is that the primary and dominant instrument of human instruction has been the written and printed word.

The word comes off the page, not as an ideogram, a picture that points to sights seen and remembered, textures felt, charges and muscular displacements undergone, but as single words, whose significance must be learned, stored, and recollected in order for meaning to be obtained. Words move serially, one stepping after the other, and the eye is trained to move serially, breaking up the universe of experience (given us by nature as a whole) into pieces, fragments of partial meaning. The whole mechanism of man—his vital organs, his passions, his divine *equipage*—atrophies, for it goes unused.

Instead, relying upon the dubious connection between the word, the memory, and the intelligence, what is known by art as unity is broken up by typographic-verbal man into separate and disconnected parcels of information. The result is that since man is never properly educated, the artificial mechanics that has been imposed by the medium of print upon the sense system—the sensorium of man—produces distortion. The distortions—those calamities of bad education—prejudice, unreason, fanaticism, narrow-mindedness, temper, and violence—what are these but simple markers of the breakdown of the ill-adapted human mechanism? The mechanism, truncated by print, to accept a linear, consecutive, orderly, time-sequential, cause-effect-dominated metaphysic, cannot function except by lapse and omission.

Since man has an insufficiently trained imagination, he does not know how to correct what he reads, how to improve upon word-ingesting sight, how to perfect the inadequacy of print. He tries, of course, by embellishing type, designing it for the eye, laying it out in order to direct the eye more pleasantly, but only rarely and by extraordinary feats can type be laid out as more than type.

The graphic designer is a prisoner of the traditional retina and sequential logic. Only when he elects to destroy language, to create simultaneities and instantaneous assaults which go beyond accepted meaning, does he attack the traditional assumptions of the eye. In that case he manages, as did Apollinaire, Marinetti, the Dadaists, Duchamp, to concatenate the verbal-visual with displacements of typographic energy that resemble architecture, that force the muscles of the body to work, that demand total kinesthetic responses.

The effort to take the media McLuhan calls "hot" media, those that force information upon us, and convert them into "cool" media, those that are passive before the action of the participant public, is a nice challenge, but not a challenge at all. There is nothing to be done, but to understand what is done to us. That is, perhaps, the secret of McLuhan's optimism. It is a kind of Stoic optimism—the optimism of the Stoic before he drew his sword and cut himself open. The Stoics called this virtue *ataraxia,* the calm dispassion of wisdom which understands the mechanism of fatality. The optimism of McLuhan is the optimism of a healthy-minded fanatic with a curative doctrine, a doctrine which will make all the horror of the twentieth century bearable, precisely because it is the death knell of an age, an age coming to an end, from which a better age will be born. McLuhan does not despair. McLuhan knows and informs us of his knowledge and does not despair to die. No less Marcus Aurelius.

Of what do we learn? The fact that in this doubtfully Great Society everyone is to be educated, absolutely educated, makes it reasonable to assume that education is coming to an end, that no one will be educated, that the overworked eyeball will at some point riot against the hopelessly impossible odds against which it struggles. Who can possibly learn enough now in this age when information is computerized and banked? When there has been a greater accumulation of valuable information in the past two decades of science alone than in the previous two thousand years of scientific inquiry, how is anyone to be educated? No one will be educated, although there will be more specialists and technocrats than ever before, more people with little packets of disconnected and unhuman knowledge than ever before.

It is not McLuhan's trust, but it is my hope, that the whole thing will collapse, topheavy and overloaded, like the biblical Tower of Babel, a crash of language and communication, a crossing of all the wires of every computer storehouse in the world, and that out of this people will rediscover the relevance of telling stories to one another, passing legends by word of mouth, perhaps beginning once more to sing, to make unplanned noise, to dance, moving untried muscles, rediscovering the body and the mind as an integer, a wholeness that unifies the world, rather than bringing it ever more close to the abyss where hopelessness confronts ignorance and courts disaster.

My apocalypticism, unlike McLuhan's, has a sturdy simplicity. One may accept all of McLuhan's strictures and postulations, his descriptions of environments and antienvironments, transformations of energy from mechanical to electronic cultures, calls to program the sensory thresholds of underdeveloped societies in Southeast Asia and overdeveloped, overexposed societies like our own, but in the reckoning of his vision one wonders what becomes of Man. It is not enough to vocalize what I often feel of his intellection, that his is a mind riding the coattails of a few ideas. Such an abuse, like all abuse in rhetoric, is a half-truth and hence not a truth at all. But there is a kind of frenzy in his writing, in the transcription of his lectures and obiter dicta, which suggest something of a demonic urgency to try to connect everything, to produce, not simply a description of the cultural situation (which is the indispensable preliminary to any diagnosis and descriptive assessment), but a new synthesis, a new holism, a modern architectonic system that will make McLuhan to our age what Herbert Spencer or Auguste Comte were to the steam engine culture of the past century. Such will not do—not only because the problems are more vast (I don't believe they are) nor for the reason given by the University of Chicago physicist, whom McLuhan has quoted approvingly, that the world is now so dangerous that nothing but Utopia will do—but rather for the fact that throughout all of McLuhan's writing there is hardly any consideration of Man as such. Man has become in McLuhan's thought an artificial construct, an analogue to the computer, a model to a mass scientific experiment with sensory levels and potencies. He has it upside-down, even though the elements he has reversed may be the right elements for scrutiny. It may well be true that we are all standing on our heads, or looking through mirrors at Medusa, but the fact remains that it is for Man that the enterprise is undertaken and it is for Man that the inquiry goes on. I would not accuse McLuhan of a totalitarian humanism were it not my conviction that his honor and awe of technocratic intelligence and technology as such has dulled his own sensorium, caused him to neglect—as all well-heard prophets tend to neglect—the only ultimate, un-winnowed, irreducible question: What is Man? His is no voice crying in the wilderness. Quite the contrary. It is one of the best-heard voices of our time and it is becoming shrill, strident, reedy, forced as it is—human instrument that it is—to make itself heard over the hum and buzz of all the connectors and circuitry which routinize and level our humanity.

john m. culkin, s. j.*
a schoolman's guide
to marshall mcluhan

Education, a seven-year-old assures me, is "how kids learn
stuff." Few definitions are as satisfying. It includes all that is
essential—a who, a what, and a process. It excludes all the people, places, and things which are only sometimes involved in
learning. The economy and accuracy of the definition, however, are more useful in locating the problem than in solving
it. We know little enough about *kids,* less about *learning,* and
considerably more than we would like to know about *stuff.*

In addition, the whole process of formal schooling is now
wrapped inside an environment of speeded-up technological
change that is constantly influencing kids and learning and
stuff. The jet-speed of this technological revolution, especially
in the area of communications, has left us with more reactions
to it than reflections about it. Meanwhile back at the school,
the student, whose psyche is being programmed for tempo, information, and relevance by his electronic environment, is still

* JOHN M. CULKIN, S.J., *is Director of the Center for Communications
at Fordham University, at which Marshall McLuhan is presently conduct-
ing a course in mass communications.*

being processed in classrooms operating on the postulates of another day. The cold war existing between these two worlds is upsetting for both the student and the schools. One thing is certain: It is hardly a time for educators to plan with nostalgia, timidity, or old formulas. Enter Marshall McLuhan.

He enters from the North, from the University of Toronto, where he teaches English and is Director of the Center for Culture and Technology. He enters with the reputation as "the oracle of the electric age" and as "the most provocative and controversial writer of this generation." More importantly for the schools, he enters as a man with fresh eyes, with new ways of looking at old problems. He is a man who gets his ideas first and judges them later. Most of these ideas are summed up in his book, *Understanding Media.* His critics tried him for not delivering these insights in their most lucid and practical form. It isn't always cricket, however, to ask the same man to crush the grapes and serve the wine. Not all of McLu is nu or tru, but then again neither is *all* of anybody else. This article is an attempt to select and order those elements of McLuhanism which are most relevant to the schools and to provide the schoolman with some new ways of thinking about the schools.

McLuhan's promise is modest enough: "All I have to offer is an enterprise of investigation into a world that's quite unusual and quite unlike any previous world and for which no models of perception will serve." This unexplored world happens to be the present. McLuhan feels that very few men look at the present with a present eye, that they tend to miss the present by translating it into the past, seeing it through a rearview mirror. The unnoticed fact of our present is the electronic environment created by the new communications media. It is as pervasive as the air we breathe (and some would add that it is just as polluted), yet its full import eludes the judgments of common-sense or content-oriented perception. The environments set up by different media are not just containers for people; they are processes that shape people. Such influence is deterministic only if ignored. There is no inevitability as long as there is a willingness to contemplate what is happening.

Theorists can keep reality at arm's length for long periods of time. Teachers and administrators can't. They are closeted with reality all day long. In many instances they are co-prisoners with electronic-age students in the old pencil-box cell. And it is the best teachers and the best students who are in the most trouble because they are challenging the system constantly. It is the system that has to come under scrutiny. Teachers and students can say, in the words of the Late Late Show, "Baby, this thing is bigger than both of us." It won't be ameliorated by a few dashes of good will or a little more hard work. It is a question of understanding these new kids and these new media and of getting the schools to deal with the new electronic environment. It's not easy. And the defenders of the old may prove to be the ones least able to defend and preserve the values of the old.

For some people, analysis of these newer technologies automatically implies approbation of them. Their world is so full of *shoulds* that it is hard to squeeze in an *is*. McLuhan suggests a more positive line of exploration:

At the moment it is important that we understand cause and process. The aim is to develop an awareness about print and the newer technologies of communication so that we can orchestrate them, minimize their mutual frustrations and clashes, and get the best out of each in the educational process. The present conflict leads to elimination of the motive to learn and to diminution of interest in all previous achievement: It leads to loss of the sense of relevance. Without an understanding of media grammars, we cannot hope to achieve a contemporary awareness of the world in which we live.

We have been told that it is the property of true genius to disturb all settled ideas. McLuhan is disturbing in both his medium and his message. His ideas challenge the normal way in which people perceive reality. They can create a very deep and personal threat since they touch on everything in a person's experience. They are just as threatening to the Establishment whose way of life is predicated on the postulates he is questioning. The Establishment has no history of organizing parades to greet its disturbers.

His medium is perhaps more disturbing than his message.

From his earliest work he has described his enterprise as "explorations in communication." The word he uses most frequently today is "probe." His books demand a high degree of involvement from the reader. They are poetic and intuitive rather than logical and analytic. Structurally, his unit is the sentence. Most of them are topic sentences—which are left undeveloped. The style is oral and breathless and frequently obscure. It's a different kind of medium.

"The medium is the message," announced McLuhan a dozen years ago in a cryptic and uncompromising aphorism whose meaning is still being explored. The title of his latest book, an illustrated popular paperback treatment of his theories, playfully proclaims that *The Medium Is the Massage*—a title calculated to drive typesetters and critics to hashish and beyond. The original dictum can be looked at in four ways, the third of which includes a massage of importance.

The first meaning would be better communicated orally—"the *medium* is the message." The *medium* is the thing you're missing. Everybody's hooked on content; pay attention to form, structure, framework, *medium*. The play's the thing. The medium's the thing. McLuhan makes the truth stand on its head to attract attention. Why the medium is worthy of attention derives from its other three meanings.

Meaning number two stresses the relation of the medium to the content. The form of communication not only alters the content, but each form also has preferences for certain kinds of messages. Content always exists in some form and is, therefore, to some degree governed by the dynamics of that form. If you don't know the medium, you don't know the message. The insight is neatly summed up by Dr. Edmund Carpenter: "English is a mass medium. All languages are mass media. The new mass media—film, radio, TV—are new languages, their grammars as yet unknown. Each codifies reality differently; each conceals a unique metaphysics. Linguists tell us it's possible to say anything in any language if you use enough words or images, but there's rarely time; the natural course is for a culture to exploit its media biases. . . ."

It is always content-in-form that is mediated. In this sense, the medium is co-message. The third meaning for the M-M formula emphasizes the relation of the medium to the individual psyche. The medium alters the perceptual habits of its users. Independent of the content, the medium itself gets through. Preliterate, literate, and postliterate cultures see the world through different-colored glasses. In the process of delivering content the medium also works over the sensorium of the consumer. To get this subtle insight across, McLuhan punned on message and came up with massage. The switch is intended to draw attention to the fact that a medium is not something neutral—it does something to people. It takes hold of them, it jostles them, it bumps them around, it massages them. It opens and closes windows in their sensorium. Proof? Look out the window at the TV generation. They are rediscovering texture, movement, color, and sound as they retribalize the race. TV is a real grabber; it really massages those lazy, unused senses.

The fourth meaning underscores the relation of the medium to society. Whitehead said, "The major advances in civilization are processes that all but wreck the societies in which they occur." The media massage the society as well as the individual. The results pass unnoticed for long periods of time because people tend to view the new as just a little bit more of the old. Whitehead again: "The greatest invention of the nineteenth century was the invention of the method of invention. A new method entered into life. In order to understand our epoch, we can neglect all details of change, such as railways, telegraphs, radios, spinning machines, synthetic dyes. We must concentrate on the method in itself: That is the real novelty which has broken up the foundations of the old civilization." Understanding the medium or process involved is the key to control.

The media shape both content and consumer and do so practically undetected. We recall the story of the Russian worker whose wheelbarrow was searched every day as he left the factory grounds. He was, of course, stealing wheelbarrows. When your medium is your message and they're only investigating content, you can get away with a lot of things—like wheelbarrows, for instance. It's not the picture but the frame. Not the contents but the box. The blank page is not neutral; nor is the classroom.

McLuhan's writings abound with aphorisms, insights, for-instances, and irrelevancies which float loosely around recurring themes. They provide the raw materials of a do-it-yourself kit for tidier types who prefer to do their exploring with clearer charts. What follows is one man's McLuhan served up in barbarously brief form. Five postulates, spanning nearly four thousand years, will serve as the fingers in this endeavor to grasp McLuhan:

(1) 1967 B.C.—*All the senses get into the act.* A conveniently symmetrical year for a thesis that is partially cyclic. It gets us back to man before the Phoenician alphabet. We know from our contemporary ancestors in the jungles of New Guinea and the wastes of the Arctic that preliterate man lives in an all-at-once sense world. The reality that bombards him from all directions is picked up with the omnidirectional antennae of sight, hearing, touch, smell, and taste. Films such as *The Hunters* and *Nanook of the North* depict primitive men tracking game with an across-the-board sensitivity that mystifies Western, literate man. We mystify them too. And it is this cross-mystification that makes inter-cultural abrasions so worthwhile.

Most people presume that their way of perceiving the world is *the* way of perceiving the world. If they hang around with people like themselves, their mode of perception may never be challenged. It is at the poles (literally and figuratively) that the violent contrasts illumine our own unarticulated perceptual prejudices. Toward the North Pole, for example, live Eskimos. A typical Eskimo family consists of a father, a mother, two children, and an anthropologist. When the anthropologist goes into the igloo to study Eskimos, he learns a lot about himself. Eskimos see pictures and maps equally well from all angles. They can draw equally well on top of a table or underneath it. They have phenomenal memories. They travel without visual bearings in their white-on-white world and can sketch cartographically accurate maps of shifting shorelines. They have forty or fifty words for what we call "snow." They live in a world without linearity, a world of acoustic space. They are Eskimos. Their natural way of perceiving the world is different from our natural way of perceiving the world.

Each culture develops its own balance of the senses in response to the demands of its environment. The most generalized formulation of the theory would maintain that the individual's modes of cognition and perception are influenced by the culture he is in, the language he speaks, and the media to which he is exposed. Each culture, as it were, provides its constituents with a custom-made set of goggles. The differences in perception are a question of degree. Some cultures are close enough to each other in perceptual patterns so that the differences pass unnoticed. Other cultural groups, such as the Eskimo and the American teen-ager, are far enough away from us to provide esthetic distance.

(2) *Art imitates life.* In *The Silent Language* Edward T. Hall offers the thesis that all art and technology is an extension of some physical or psychic element of man. Today man has developed extensions for practically everything he used to do with his body: stone axe for hand, wheel for foot, glasses for eyes, radio for voice and ears. Money is a way of storing energy. This externalizing of individual, specialized functions is now, by definition, at its most advanced stage. Through the electronic media of telegraph, telephone, radio, and television, man has now equipped his world with a nervous system similar to the one within his own body. President Kennedy is shot and the world instantaneously reels from the impact of the bullets. Space and time dissolve under electronic conditions. Current concern for the United Nations, the Common Market, ecumenism, reflects this organic thrust toward the new convergence and unity which is "blowing in the wind." Now in the electric age, our extended faculties and senses constitute a single instantaneous and coexistent field of experience. It's all-at-once. It's shared-by-all. McLuhan calls the world "a global village."

(3) *Life imitates art.* We shape our tools and thereafter they shape us. These extensions of our senses begin to interact with our senses. These media become a massage. The new change in the environment creates a new balance among the senses. No

sense operates in isolation. The full sensorium seeks fulfillment in almost every sense experience. And since there is a limited quantum of energy available for any sensory experience, the sense-ratio will differ for different media.

The nature of the sensory effect will be determined by the medium used. McLuhan divides the media according to the quality or definition of their physical signal. The content is not relevant in this kind of analysis. The same picture from the same camera can appear as a glossy photograph or as a newspaper wirephoto. The photograph is well-defined, of excellent pictorial quality, hi-fi within its own medium. McLuhan calls this kind of medium "hot." The newspaper photo is grainy, made up of little dots, low definition. McLuhan calls this kind of medium "cool." Film is hot; television is cool. Radio is hot; telephone is cool. The cool medium or person invites participation and involvement. It leaves room for the response of the consumer. A lecture is hot; all the work is done. A seminar is cool; it gets everyone into the game. Whether all the connections are causal may be debated, but it's interesting that the kids of the cool TV generation want to be so involved and so much a part of what's happening.

(4) *We shaped the alphabet and it shaped us.* In keeping with the McLuhan postulate that "the medium is the message," a literate culture should be more than mildly eager to know what books do to people. Everyone is familiar enough with all the enrichment to living mediated through fine books to allow us to pass on to the subtler effects which might be attributed to the print medium, independent of the content involved. Whether one uses the medium to say that *God is dead* or that *God is love* (--- -- ----), the structure of the medium itself remains unchanged. Nine little black marks with no intrinsic meaning of their own are strung along a line with spaces left after the third and fifth marks. It is this stripping away of meaning that allows us to X-ray the form itself.

As an example, while lecturing to a large audience in a modern hotel in Chicago, a distinguished professor is bitten in the leg by a cobra. The whole experience takes three seconds. He is affected through the touch of the reptile, the gasp of the crowd, the swimming sights before his eyes. His memory, imagination, and emotions come into emergency action. A lot of things happen in three seconds. Two weeks later he is fully recovered and wants to write up the experience in a letter to a colleague. To communicate this experience through print means that it must first be broken down into parts and then mediated, eyedropper fashion, one thing at a time, in an abstract, linear, fragmented, sequential way. That is the essential structure of print. And once a culture uses such a medium for a few centuries, it begins to perceive the world in a one-thing-at-a-time, abstract, linear, fragmented, sequential way. And it shapes its organizations and schools according to the same premises. The form of print has become the form of thought. The medium has become the message.

For centuries now, according to McLuhan, the straight line has been the hidden metaphor of literate man. It was unconsciously but inexorably used as the measure of things. It went unnoticed, unquestioned. It was presumed as natural and universal. It is neither. Like everything else, it is good for the things it is good for. To say that it is not everything is not to say that it is nothing. The electronic media have broken the monopoly of print; they have altered our sensory profiles by heightening our awareness of aural, tactile, and kinetic values.

(5) A.D. 1967—*All the senses want to get into the act.* Print repressed most sense-life in favor of the visual. The end of print's monopoly also marks the end of a visual monopoly. As the early warning system of art and popular culture indicates, all the senses want to get into the act. Some of the excesses in the current excursions into aural, oral, tactile, and kinetic experience may in fact be directly responsive to the sensory deprivation of the print culture. Nature abhors a vacuum. No one glories in the sight of kids totally out of control in reaction to the Beatles. Some say, "What are the Beatles doing to these kids?" Others say, "What have we done to these kids?" All the data aren't in on what it means to be a balanced human being.

Kids are what the game is all about. Given an honest game with enough equipment to go around, it is the mental, emotional, and volitional capacity of the student that most determines the outcome. The whole complicated system of formal education is in business to get through to kids, to motivate kids, to help kids learn stuff. Schools are not in business to label kids, to grade them for the job market or to babysit. They are there to communicate with them.

Communication is a funny business. There isn't as much of it going on as most people think. Many feel that it consists in saying things in the presence of others. Not so. It consists not in saying things but in having things heard. Beautiful English speeches delivered to monolingual Arabs are not beautiful speeches. You have to speak the language of the audience—of the *whom* in the "who-says-what-to-whom" communications diagram. Sometimes the language is lexical (Chinese, Japanese, Portuguese), sometimes it is regional or personal (125th Streetese, Holden Caulfieldese, anybodyese). It has little to do with words and much to do with understanding the audience. The word for good communication is "Whomese"—the language of the audience, of the "whom."

All good communicaters use Whomese. The best writers, film-makers, advertising men, lovers, preachers, and teachers all have the knack for thinking about the hopes, fears, and capacity of the other person and of being able to translate their communication into terms which are *relevant* for that person. Whitehead called "inert ideas" the bane of education. Relevance, however, is one of those subjective words. It doesn't pertain to the object in itself but to the object as perceived by someone. The school may decide that history is *important for* the student, but the role of the teacher is to make history *relevant to* the student.

If *what* has to be tailored to the *whom*, the teacher has to be constantly engaged in audience research. It's not a question of keeping up with the latest slang or of selling out to the current mores of the kids. Neither of these tactics helps either learning or kids. But it is a question of knowing what values are strong in their world, of understanding the obstacles to communication, of sensing their style of life. Communication doesn't have to end there, but it can start nowhere else. If they are tuned in to FM and you are broadcasting on AM, there's no communication. Communication forces you to pay a lot of attention to other people.

McLuhan has been paying a great deal of attention to modern kids. Of necessity they live in the present since they have no theories to diffract or reflect what is happening. They are also the first generation to be born into a world in which there was always television. McLuhan finds them a great deal different from their counterparts at the turn of the century when the electric age was just getting up steam.

A lot of things have happened since 1900 and most of them plug into walls. Today's six-year-old has already learned a lot of stuff by the time he shows up for the first day of school. Soon after his umbilical cord was cut he was planted in front of a TV set "to keep him quiet." He liked it enough there to stay for some 3,000 to 4,000 hours before he started the first grade. By the time he graduates from high school he has clocked 15,000 hours of TV time and 10,800 hours of school time. He lives in a world that bombards him from all sides with information from radios, films, telephones, magazines, recordings, and people. He learns more things from the windows of cars, trains, and even planes. Through travel and communications he has experienced the war in Vietnam, the wide world of sports, the civil rights movement, the death of a President, thousands of commercials, a walk in space, a thousand innocuous shows, and, one may hope, plenty of Captain Kangaroo.

This is all merely descriptive, an effort to lay out what *is*, not what should be. Today's student can hardly be described by any of the old educational analogies comparing him to an empty bucket or a blank page. He comes to the information machine called school and he is already brimming over with information. As he grows his standards for relevance are determined more by what he receives outside the school than what he receives inside. A recent Canadian film tells the story of a bright, articulate middle-class teen-ager who leaves school because there's "no reason to stay." He daydreams about Vietnam while his teacher drones on about the four reasons for the spread of Christianity and the five points such information is worth on the exam. Only the need for a diploma was holding him in school; learning wasn't, and he left. He decided the union ticket wasn't worth the gaff. He left. Some call him a dropout. Some call him a pushout.

The kids have one foot on the dock and one foot on the ferry boat. Living in two centuries makes for that kind of tension. The gap between the classroom and the outside world and the gap between the generations is wider than it has ever been. Those tedious people who quote Socrates on the conduct of the young are trying vainly to reassure themselves that this is just the perennial problem of communication between generations. 'Tain't so. "Today's child is growing up absurd, because he lives in two worlds, and neither of them inclines him to grow up." Says McLuhan in *The Medium Is the Massage,* "Growing up—that is our new work, and it is *total*. Mere instruction will not suffice."

Learning is something that people do for themselves. People, places, and things can facilitate or impede learning; they can't make it happen without some cooperation from the learner. The learner these days comes to school with a vast reservoir of vicarious experiences and loosely related facts; he wants to use all his senses in his learning as an active agent in the process of discovery; he knows that all the answers aren't in. The new learner is the result of the new media, says McLuhan. And a new learner calls for a new kind of learning.

Leo Irrera said, "If God had anticipated the eventual structure of the school system, surely he would have shaped man differently." Kids are being tailored to fit the Procrustean forms of schedules, classrooms, memorizing, testing, etc., which are frequently relics from an obsolete approach to learning. It is the total environment that contains the philosophy of education, not the title page in the school catalogue. And it is the total environment that is invincible because it is invisible to most people. They tend to move things around within the old boxes or to build new and cleaner boxes. They should be asking whether or not there should be a box in the first place.

The new learner, who is the product of the all-at-once electronic environment, often feels out of it in a linear, one-thing-at-a-time school environment. The total environment is now the great teacher; the student has competence models against which to measure the effectiveness of his teachers. Nuclear students in linear schools make for some tense times in education. Students with well-developed interests in science, the arts and humanities, or current events need assistance to suit their pace, not that of the state syllabus. The straight-line theory of development and the uniformity of performance it so frequently encourages just don't fit many needs of the new learner. Interestingly, the one thing most of the current educational innovations share is their break with linear or print-oriented patterns: team teaching, nongraded schools, audio-lingual language training, multimedia learning situations, seminars, student research at all levels of education, individualized learning, and the whole shift of responsibility for learning from the teacher to the student. Needless to say, these are not as widespread as they should be, nor were they brought about through any conscious attention to the premises put forward by McLuhan. Like the print-oriented and linear mentality they now modify, these premises were plagiarized from the atmosphere. McLuhan's value is in the power he gives us to predict and control these changes.

There is too much stuff to learn today. McLuhan calls it an age of "information overload." And the information levels outside the classroom are now higher than those in the classroom. Schools used to have a virtual monopoly on information; now they are part-time competitors in the electronic informational surround. And all human knowledge is expanding at computer speed.

Every choice involves a rejection. If we can't do everything, what priorities will govern our educational policies? "The medium is the message" may not be bad for openers. We can no longer teach kids all about a subject; we can teach them what a subject is all about. We have to introduce them to the form, structure, *Gestalt*, grammar, and process of the knowledge involved. What does a math man do when a math man does do math? This approach to the formal element of a discipline can provide a channel of communication between specialists. Its focus is not on content or detail but on the postulates, ground rules, frames of reference, and premises of each discipline. It stresses the modes of cognition and perception proper to each field. Most failures in communication are based on disagreement about items which are only corollaries of a larger thesis. It happens between disciplines, individuals, media, and cultures.

The arts play a new role in education because they are explorations in perception. Formerly conceived as a curricular luxury item, they now become a dynamic way of tuning up the sensorium and of providing fresh ways of looking at familiar things. When exploration and discovery become the themes, the old lines between art and science begin to fade. We have to guide students to becoming their own data processors to operate through pattern recognition. The media themselves serve as both aids to learning and as proper objects of study in this search for an all-media literacy. Current interest in film criticism will expand to include all art and communication forms.

And since the knowledge explosion has blown out the walls between subjects, there will be a continued move toward interdisciplinary swapping and understanding. Many of the categorical walls between things are artifacts left over from the packaging days of print. The specialist's life will be even lonelier as we move further from the Gutenberg era. The trends are all toward wholeness and convergence.

These things aren't true just because Marshall McLuhan says they are. They work. They explain problems in education that nobody else is laying a glove on. When presented clearly and with all the necessary examples and footnotes added, they have proven to be a liberating force for hundreds of teachers who were living through the tension of this cultural fission without realizing that the causes for the tension lay outside themselves. McLuhan's relevance for education demands the work of teams of simultaneous translators and researchers who can both shape and substantiate the insights which are

JOHN M. CULKIN, S.J.

scattered through his work. McLuhan didn't invent electricity or put kids in front of TV sets; he is merely trying to describe what's happening out there so that it can be dealt with intelligently. When someone warns you of an oncoming truck, it's frightfully impolite to accuse him of driving the thing. McLuhan can help kids to learn stuff better.

theodore roszak*
the summa popologica
of marshall mcluhan

Once when I was teaching an undergraduate survey in European history, a student came to me complaining after class that he couldn't see why I wasted his time asking him to read Cardinal Bossuet. I had to admit it was a pretty dismal assignment, wholly lacking in intellectual substance. "But," I explained, "doesn't it tell us a great deal about French society that such a mediocrity could rise to such a position of intellectual prominence? Isn't it worth knowing that the *Grand Siècle* wasn't all Molière and Pascal?"

There are people whose fate it is to be read in this spirit: not because of what they have to say, which is meager or foolish, but because of the bleaker measure they provide of their society's quality of mind and conscience. And it is in this spirit that Marshall McLuhan must be approached: as one who has little that is substantial to say, but who reveals a very great deal about the cultural permissiveness of mid-century America.

* THEODORE ROSZAK *is Chairman of the History of Western Culture Program at California State College, Hayward, and is editor of and contributor to the forthcoming book* The Dissenting Academy.

For what McLuhan has discovered is the ease with which pretensious nonsense can be parleyed into a marvelously lucrative, but at the same time academically prestigious career. And, at least up to this point, he has turned the trick more neatly than anybody else on the scene.

The strategy seems to be something like this. On the one hand, one has to be just catchy and cute and simplistic enough to draw the attention and affection of the mass-cultural apparatus: *Time, Life, Fortune,* ABC, CBS, NBC. Ingratiate yourself to the publicity makers and, presto! you get publicity. But, on the other hand, if one is to avoid degenerating into another Norman Vincent Peale, one must be able to flourish some cultural savvy. Thus, McLuhan's introduction to *Understanding Media* hops, skips and jumps over Fellini, Zen, Plato, Hesiod, Burckhardt, Sartre, Beckett, Pound. . . . In this way, you keep one foot in the intellectual camp. Or more correctly, you keep your footing among the camp intellectuals. And in this respect, McLuhan's timing has been beautifully shrewd. For he has caught a fair-sized segment of the intellectual community just as it was weakening, playfully, in the direction of camp and pop. Up go posters of Batman and Bogart on living-room walls all over America, and onto the bookshelf goes McLuhan. The Campbell's soup can becomes an object of art and the Jack Paar show a subject of deep philosophical analysis. If we are to have pop art, why not pop metaphysics too?

And that is precisely what McLuhan has given us: an almost Thomistic systematization of our society's funk culture, a veritable *Weltanschauung* for the fastidious connoisseur of Smilin' Jack and Mae West. Surely the effort deserves to survive. We would want posterity to know, would we not, that America of the mid-Sixties had its lighter side, that the year which produced the Johnson Administration and the Vietnam war also brought us *Understanding Media,* the *Summa Popologica.* Is it prudish to become severe about such larks? Perhaps it is. If the cultural millions American society can now afford to lay out on "exploding plastic inevitables" didn't go to the entertainments provided by the Andy Warhols and Marshall Mc-

Luhans, perhaps they would go for worse. But it *is* distressing to see so many decent minds and talents taking these oppy-poppy flirtations quite as seriously as they do. It is especially unfortunate to see so many would-be young artists—eager to gate-crash the creative life—falling for McLuhan's easy-do esthetic of media-manipulation instead of reading their Tolstoy or Shaw. And, in any case, it's always fun to pick apart pretensions, if only to see, for the record, how much in the way of intellectual murder you can get away with these days and still be treated seriously, indeed reverently, in cultural circles that should know better.

Let us, then, give a moment's attention to a few select elements in McLuhan's writing and see how they stand up to investigation. There is a very great deal more to criticize about McLuhan than what follows below. I restrict myself to only two of the many "media" McLuhan deals with. But the points I raise are central to his work and will serve our purpose here.

1. MEDIA ■ McLuhan's posture is that of a specialist in the field of "media." And in this respect his credentials are impressive: Director of Toronto University's Centre for Culture and Technology and former Chairman of the Ford Foundation Seminar on Culture and Communication. One expects the specialty to involve some order of highly technical competence, and indeed McLuhan misses no opportunity to exploit that expectation. It is as a specialist that he prefers to be approached and respected. But what are "media" as McLuhan understands them? "Media" are the "extensions of man." And as it turns out, the extensions extend a long, long way. They include all means of communication and transportation, the written and spoken word in all its forms, technology in general, fun and games, art and music, housing, fashions, weapons, social and economic systems. . . . Indeed, what do they *not* include? McLuhan's province of knowledge, quite simply, is universal. It allows him to speak, as he would have it, to everything and anything that comes his way. Last year, when he was in San Francisco, the local papers carried stories

259

of McLuhan pontificating on the subject of topless waitresses. (But perhaps this comes under the category of the extensions of women.)

Now I think it is admirable to aspire to broad-gauged intellectuality. I have no brief to make for technical specialization. But if one is a generalist, one must be prepared to say so—and to run the risks. It is really dirty pool to retire defensively, as McLuhan does under pressure, behind the barricades of a presumed specialization, when, in fact, one's "specialty" is everything under the sun. To begin with, then, one must insist that McLuhan is no sort of specialist at all. Nothing he has to say is based on esoteric knowledge or technical competence. He is best approached as a sort of social critic or perhaps a dilettante conversationalist—and his ideas stand or fall on the basis of their internal consistency or whatever evidence McLuhan can present for them. It is the plight of the generalist that he cannot expect anyone to defer to his authority on the subject at hand.

To yield to McLuhan as an "expert" on "media" is like yielding to Herman Kahn as an "expert" on "strategy." In both cases one is giving way to men whose "expertise" involves sweeping and most often profoundly ignorant opinions about the whole of human and social behavior.

2. "THE MEDIUM IS THE MESSAGE" ■ There is a deal of misunderstanding about this well known catchphrase. Many McLuhan devotees seem to think McLuhan, in assessing the effects of "media," is dealing with the impact technology directly has upon the social and economic environment. But if McLuhan had nothing more to tell us than that great inventions—the printing press, automobile, railroad, etc.—have vastly and unpredictably transformed society, he would be telling us nothing very new. But this isn't McLuhan's point. McLuhan's interest is in the perceptual and deep psychic impact of media. His claim is that the media "alter sense ratios or patterns of perception. . . ." And, by so doing, they radically alter the human agent. The environmental changes, then, follow from an initial transformation of the human psyche. Thus,

postwar America is what it is—socially, politically, economically, culturally—because of what electronic circuitry, TV in particular, has done to the psychology of Americans. Further, these psychic transformations have *absolutely nothing* to do with the content of the media. The media have their effects because of their inherent technical characteristics, regardless of what programming they carry. For McLuhan there is no significant distinction to be made between pure static and Archibald MacLeish's *Fall of the City*—both are simply "radio"; or between Tolstoy and Mickey Spillane—both are simply "typography." (One is reminded here of Jean Harlow's quip when asked what she wanted for her birthday: "Don't buy me a book; I gotta book." A perfectly sensible McLuhanite response.)

If TV had never gotten beyond broadcasting test patterns, its effect upon American society would, according to McLuhan, have been precisely the same and just as total—*if* you could have gotten the whole society to watch test patterns, which you couldn't. For McLuhan "content" is "the juicy piece of meat carried by a burglar to distract the watchdog of the mind." Only that and nothing more. (One should note, however, that McLuhan frequently loses his grip on this idea and—as in his treatment of photography—slides over into a discussion of content, crediting it with the significant influence. Such inconsistency at once suggests an untenable thesis.)

Now this is an extraordinary idea. And it is surely worth a few minutes' contemplation. But if we are to think any longer about it than that before rejecting it as absurd, McLuhan must offer us some evidence in support of the thesis. Alas, one searches in vain through *Understanding Media,* McLuhan's *magnum opus,* for evidence. It isn't there. McLuhan doesn't prove this thesis; he browbeats you with it. His contention is, if you don't believe me, you're hidebound, behind-the-times, bookish, square. And McLuhan delights in baiting the "conventionally literate."

It is perhaps the most remarkable aspect of McLuhan's career that so few of his critics (and of course none of his admirers) have ever asked him for proof of his central thesis. Perhaps because they are so readily intimidated? For to hear McLuhan hold forth, you would assume there is some large body of incontrovertible experimental evidence somewhere to support the assertion—and that everybody who is anybody knows all about it. *There isn't.* And yet, on the basis of this unexamined thesis, McLuhan is prepared to make extremely ambitious proposals. He tells us, for example, that the entire political character of a society can be determined by its "media mix." Thus, revolutionary discontent can be created by heavy exposure to radio and newspapers, and it can be assuaged by a hearty dosage of TV independently of anything these media say, mind!

McLuhan claims to have learned this deep truth about media from his study of post-impressionist painting. He is, of course, correct in observing that one of the directions in which Western painting has moved over the past century is toward the exploitation of paint—of its color and texture—as an autonomous medium independent of any content. The same may be said of music over a much longer period of time. Music has been, in a significant way, an autonomous sound medium, independent of any storytelling function, at least since the seventeenth century. But the fact that line, color and sound can be liberated from conceptual content does not mean that the language arts can move in a similar direction. Unlike music, which can direct itself at stimulating the auditory surface of the ear, or painting, which can direct itself at the visual surface of the eye, the written and spoken word are inseparable from what they have to say. The significant distinction to make with respect to the media is not McLuhan's distinction between "hot" and "cold"—which is largely senseless—but that between sensory media and conceptual media. A painting may only impinge on the eye, but the printed page strikes *through* the eye and into the mind. Similarly, the spoken word—whether part of a radio or television presentation—strikes *through* the ear and, again, into the mind. Such attempts as have been made to "liberate" the written or spoken word from conceptual content have always trailed off into marginal experiments that are more music or linear design than they are literature. Literature *says things*—base things or noble things, wise things or foolish things, exciting things or dull things. And in this lies its peculiar power over us, for good or ill. To the degree that any essentially literary art—poetry, the novel, the storytelling cinema, the drama—begins to manipulate itself as a "pure" medium and divests itself of having anything to say, it becomes trivial, and usually silly. The literary avant garde is littered with such misfortunate experiments, and they continue to take place. But their end is always the same: boredom and early death. In denying this fact about the nature of the word, McLuhan, himself a prodigious writer and talker, would seem to be involved in something like the paradox of Parmenides: he tells us in print that the content of print has no power over us. Thus, McLuhan's thesis and mine—which would seem to be logically contradictory—are nevertheless equivalent. For you, dear reader, are doing no more than sponging up typography, no matter which of us you read.

But in fact McLuhan's thesis is not simply unproven. It is false. There is no independent psychic effect that *any* mass medium has on an observer other than through its content. Indeed, no one witnesses a mass medium *except* for its content. In conjuring up the notion of a medium-in-itself, McLuhan is involved in a bit of metaphysics which is perhaps sensible to him as (I am given to understand) a devout Catholic, but not the least persuasive or even sensible to the skeptical mind. McLuhan's medium-in-itself is rather like the substance of the Catholic host and wine which supposedly underlies all the superficial accidents: a bladeless knife without a handle. But subtract the contents of the mass media and, like the Catholic host without its accidents, there's nothing there. Only a jabberwocky of printer's ink, static, and test patterns. To contend that these purely visual-auditory stimuli exert an independent and infinitely greater influence than any content they carry contradicts flatly the most fundamental of human experiences: that of human communication. McLuhan's thesis leads ultimately to the conclusion that human beings never communicate with one another (though I am not certain he would be willing to extend his argument to ordinary word-of-mouth communication). Mind is sealed off from mind and personality from personality. It is technology alone which intervenes between us: the printed page which conveys its own and invariable subliminal "message," the TV screen which imprints its own and always-identical psychic pattern. The reality of meaningful intercourse between people is thus abolished. Shakespeare has never spoken to us, nor Sophocles, nor Dante, but only the printing press, the radio wave, the electronic scanner.

To be sure, it *is* possible to create literature and drama and rhetoric which is empty of meaning and which does not communicate a thing: successions of words and images which baffle the understanding. Every second-rate political hack knows as much. And a great deal of contemporary theater, cinema, poetry, and prose specializes in such effects. Alas! *ad nauseam*. But not every movie is *Last Year at Marienbad*. Those of us who have been touched to the marrow by the power of an idea know better—and we ought not to let McLuhan tell us differently than our own living experience does. The thought of Socrates, of Thoreau, of Blake, of Freud has moved within our own; the trials and tragedies of Othello, of Anna Karenina, of Raskolnikov have participated significantly in our lives. (And I use the word "participate" here far more deeply than I suspect McLuhan would understand.) If McLuhan has never plumbed these depths of mind and feeling, that is indeed pathetic for one who purports to be an expert in "communication." But we *know* full well that we have been shaped by other human beings through this matrix of imagination and intellection called human culture and that in it lies all our hope of achieving wisdom. Who, then, is Marshall McLuhan that he should seek to talk us out of our richest experience with nothing more than a catchphrase? There is indeed a kind of ultimate barbarism about any conception of culture which allows itself to become obsessed with the physical artifacts of communication and ignores their profoundest personal meaning.

But perhaps the best way to demonstrate the falsehood of McLuhan's thesis is to review his handling of two significant mass media and see where it leads us.

RADIO ■ For McLuhan, radio is "the tribal drum." The hammering of radio waves at the ears during the Thirties had the effect of "retribalizing" Western society and thus producing the primitive aggressions of totalitarian mass movements. But, one observes, there were no significant totalitarian movements in Britain . . . or America . . . or, well, any number of other countries where radio was prominent in the Thirties. McLuhan has an answer. The Americans and the British were further along in industrialism and literacy than the "more earthy and less visual European cultures" and so they were "immune to radio." The Germans, we are to believe, had in the Thirties "only brief and superficial experience of literacy." As a matter of fact, America and Germany were at equivalent stages of industrialism and the Germans were probably far more literate—but never mind. Let's get back to those "more earthy Europeans." Unfortunately for the Germans, Hitler and the Nazis just happened to come along a generation too soon. "Had TV occurred on a larger scale during Hitler's reign, he would have vanished quickly. Had TV come first there would have been no Hitler at all."

So we are to believe that the triumph of Nazism is wholly explained by the impact of radio upon the peculiar psychology of the German people. And what was that psychology? "The tribal past," McLuhan tells us, "has never ceased to be a reality for the German psyche." Herr Goebbels, we learn, was right after all: the German people are children of the forest, possessed of a "preliterate vitality." Shall we say they "think with their blood?" Indeed, "their tribal mode gave them easy access to the new non-visual world of subatomic physics in which long-literate and long-industrialized societies are decidedly handicapped." (Apparently, the German Jews, who did so much of this work in physics, are to be assimilated to this Wagnerian *Schwärmerei*—despite their long tradition of advanced literacy.)

Thus we see where McLuhan's analysis leads us: straight back to Nazi anthropology. But how else to explain fascism in Germany once one has discarded the historical setting of post-World War I Europe with its peculiar social and economic stresses?

For McLuhan, once you have described radio as a "hot" medium, you have said all there is to say. History and social realities are banished and the German people are left to their tragic destiny. One cannot protest that Hitler's successful use of radio had everything to do with the Nazi monopolization of the medium (indeed, the Nazis exploited *all* the media successfully by virtue of censorship) for this is to introduce the factor of content. Censorship and control of media, remarkably enough, play no part in McLuhan's system. Nor can his system account for the (apparent) fact that in England the same medium, radio, could be masterfully used by Stanley Baldwin to soothe and calm, and, with equal mastery, by Churchill to excite and arouse the identical population. (The same observation holds true in the U.S. with respect to the differing use of radio by Father Coughlin and F.D.R.) Here, again, we're introducing variables that McLuhan rejects: social setting and content.

TELEVISION ■ McLuhan's analysis of TV leads him to his best-known and most heroic generalizations. For McLuhan, TV is the total explanation of why America is what it is today. TV is a "cool" medium, a "mosaic mesh" of electronic dots that invites "participation in depth." It produces a "unifying synesthetic force on the sense life" and leads to a "convulsive, sensuous participation that is profoundly kinetic and tactile." From this flows everything in sight: compact cars, the Kennedy Administration, scuba diving, the twist, a "do-it-yourself pattern of living," beehive hairdos and fishnet stockings. (Incidentally, McLuhan is a great one for fashion analysis. That the fashions on which he has founded his eternal truths change by the year doesn't seem to bother him.)

Now the fact is, McLuhan's knowledge of TV is very shoddy. For the major psychic effect of TV—and it comes through the content of the medium—is a narcotic disintegration of the sensibilities. It is the standard strategy of commercial TV to frustrate continuity of thought and to screen off depth of feeling. Take the TV news, for example. What is the effect of rapid cuts from stark tragedy to trivialized "human interest," from political complexity to breezy sportscasting? Or take children's programming, where the level of artistic and linguistic imagination is kept consistently higher in the exploitative commercials (which come every three minutes) than in the so-called entertainment. These fragmenting effects show up clearly in variety programming (the Ed Sullivan show, Merv Griffin show, etc.). In the standard TV situation comedy or melodrama they take the form of canned laughter and the emotional cliché.

Now what is the result of programming techniques that chop and cut the attention span, that keep the mentality turning over at the lowest level of efficiency, that screen the emotions from all originality? The result is a mushing up of the personality, a psychic anomie that neatly lowers the resistance to merchandising—which is what TV is all about in America. What McLuhan mistakes for "participation in depth" is actually malaise: the fixed stare, the mindless drift. (One exception to this has to do with young children, for whom solitary TV viewing serves as an opportunity for masturbation. They are "participating" and "doing it themselves," but not in any way McLuhan seems to be aware of.)

Of course, what McLuhan has to tell Madison Avenue and the TV moguls about themselves is exactly what they want to hear. McLuhan gets them off the hook with respect to any kind of social or cultural responsibility. While they peddle and exploit a degraded form of sensory distraction, he tells them they are single-handedly transforming American society, and especially the kids, into vital members of a participatory cultural community. One is reminded at this point of Andrew Ure telling the world, in the dark ages of industrialization, what marvelous things the cotton mills were doing for children: improving their manual dexterity, regularizing their habits, alerting their young minds. . . . The more sophisticated the technology, the more sophisticated the apologetics.

The boob tube replaces the dark satanic mill as a form of social discipline, and "participation in depth" replaces "the light play of the little elves' muscles."

But, in fact, the effect of TV has nothing to do with McLuhan's electronic dots, which at most invite a low-grade *Gestalt* response. And not very much of that, since the *Gestalts* the TV screen offers are banal and obvious. The major psychic effect of American TV has to do with the unrelenting insult it poses to human dignity by its insistent mass-marketing and its shallow, disjunctive programming.

Which is what we all knew in the first place. The country's most addicted TV viewers are not McLuhan's rebellious beatniks, but C. Wright Mills's "cheerful robots," for whom the narcosis of the electric screen has become an alienation from living experience. By cheapening thought and screening off the deeps of the human condition, TV contributes to the enervating deprivation of mind and sense which is *the* characteristic of contemporary American life—but not only because of the existence of television in our midst.

Of all the single-factor explanations of human and social behavior I have ever come across, McLuhan's exaltation of "media" is, I fear, the most inane. But to all the objections one can make against him, McLuhan has developed a standard defense. McLuhan's assertions are not, he would have us believe, propositions or hypotheses. They are "probes." But what is a "probe"? It is apparently any outrageous statement for which one has no evidence at all or which, indeed, flies in the face of obvious facts. This is, no doubt, the hip version of what Washington these days calls a "credibility gap" and what the squares of yesteryear used to call a falsehood.

"Probing" has served McLuhan well. It has allowed him to pose as a cultural lion while ingratiating himself with IBM and *Time* magazine. Of the latter, for example, he tells us: it is "neither narrative nor point of view nor explanation nor comment [surprise! surprise!]. It is a corporate image in depth of the community in action and invites maximal participation in the social process." In fact, *Time* magazine is pernicious crap.

But no one who says as much winds up with his face on the million-dollar cover. "Probing" has allowed McLuhan to go barnstorming the country as a Container Corporation of America lecturer and—so the London *Observer* reports—to pin down a hundred-thousand-dollar-a-year super-professorship at Fordham University. His most recent literary effort, *The Medium Is the Massage (sic.)*—a gimmicked-up non-book —is fetching $10.95 a copy in the hardbound edition. He should worry about intellectual respectability? About as much as Andrew Ure or Samuel Smiles, who long ago discovered the secret of becoming successful "fee-losophers" in an exploitative social order.

james w. carey*
harold adams innis
and marshall mcluhan

Commenting on the abstruse and controversial scholarship of
Harold Innis and Marshall McLuhan is a rather audacious
and perhaps impertinent undertaking. It is also a thankless
task. McLuhan has often argued that the attempt to analyze,
classify, and criticize scholarship—the intent of my paper—is
not only illegitimate; it also represents the dead hand of an
obsolete tradition of scholarship. I am sensitive to treading for-
bidden waters in this paper. But I am content to let history or
something else be the judge of what is the proper or only
method of scholarship, as I at least am uncomfortable pro-
nouncing on such weighty matters.

Despite the dangers in scrutinizing the work of Innis and
McLuhan, I think students of the history of mass communication must assume the risks of analysis. Innis and McLuhan,
alone among students of human society, make the history of

* JAMES W. CAREY is an Assistant Professor of Journalism and also a Research Assistant Professor in the Institute of Communications Research at
the University of Illinois. His research and writing concern propaganda,
television, and popular culture.

the mass media central to the history of civilization at large. Both see the media not merely as technical appurtenances to society but as crucial determinants of the social fabric. For them the history of the mass media is not just another avenue of historical research; rather it is another way of writing the history of Western civilization. Innis and McLuhan do not so much describe history as present a theory of history or, less grandiloquently, a theory of social change in the West. It is a theory that anchors social change in the transformations in the media of communication on which this civilization has been progressively dependent. Therefore, an assessment of the meaning and reasonableness of the positions they represent seems to me to be a principal task for students of the history of mass communication.

In this paper, I would like to suggest an interpretation of Innis and McLuhan and to compare the kinds of arguments they offer on the role of the mass media in social change. Second, I want to offer a critical commentary of their positions, principally directed at the relative merits of their arguments in organizing the historical material in question. Finally, I want to recommend a direction for future research on the role of the media in social change and to offer some reflections on the social meaning of the scholarship of Harold Innis and Marshall McLuhan.

Harold Adams Innis was a Canadian economist and historian who devoted most of his scholarly life to producing marvelously detailed studies of Canadian industries—the fur trading industry, the cod fisheries, the Canadian Pacific Railway, for example. During the last decade of his life (Innis died in 1952), he undertook an extensive analysis of all forms of human communication and produced two major works, *The Bias of Communication* and *Empire and Communications,* and two important collections of essays, *Changing Concepts of Time* and *Political Economy and the Modern State.* His interest in communications was not, however, independent of his concerns for economic history. Rather, the former grew out of the latter. In his studies of the economic history of Canada, Innis

271

was confronted by two important questions: (1) What are the underlying causes of change in social organization, defined broadly to include both culture and social institutions? (2) What are the conditions that promote stability in any society? Stability here is defined as both the capacity to adapt to changing realities in politics and the economy and also as the capacity to preserve the integrity of culture, the continuity of attitude, sentiment, and morality upon which civilization is based. Further, Innis wanted to answer those questions in a manner that would capture not only the major currents of history in the West but also the eddies and tributaries, streams and backwaters of social change.*

Innis felt that the answer to his first question—the question of the source of social change—was to be found in technological innovation. He was, like McLuhan, a technological determinist, though unlike McLuhan a rather soft determinist. Innis and McLuhan agree that while there are various kinds of technology—military, industrial, administrative—these technologies were not equal in their impact on society or in their ontological status. For Innis the technology of communication was central to all other technology. He does not make at all clear why this should be so. However, let me make this suggestion. There are presumably two reasons for the centrality of communications technology—one logical, one historical.

* The literary style adopted by Innis to convey the complexity of social change is a principal barrier to any adequate understanding of his work. He amasses on each page such an enormous body of fact, fact rarely summarized or generalized, that one becomes quickly lost in the thicket of data. Further, Innis disdains the conventions of written book scholarship; indeed, he attempts to break out of what he takes to be these limiting conventions by presenting an apparently disconnected kaleidoscope of fact and observation. He avoids arguing in a precise, serial order and instead, like the proprietor of a psychedelic delicatessen, flashes onto the page historic events widely separated in space and time. With such a method, he attempts to capture both the complexities of social existence and its multidimensional change. Nowhere does he present an orderly, systematic argument (except perhaps in the first and last chapters of *Empire and Communications*) depending rather on the reader to impose order, to capture not merely the fact of history but a vision of the dynamics of historic change.

Innis assumes that man stands in a unique, symbiotic relationship to his technology. In McLuhan's phrase, technology is literally an extension of man, as the axe is an extension of the hand, the wheel of the foot. Most instruments are attempts to extend man's physical capacity, a capacity shared with other animals. Communications technology, on the other hand, is an extension of thought, of consciousness, of man's unique perceptual capacities. Thus communications media, broadly used to include all modes of symbolic representation, are literally extensions of mind.

Innis also suggests that historically fundamental breakthroughs in technology are first applied to the process of communication. The age of mechanics was ushered in by the printing press, the age of electronics by the telegraph. The explanation for this historical fact Innis derived from a conception of society based upon a model of competition appropriated from economics and extended to all social institutions. And in this competitive model, competition for new means of communication was a principal axis of the competitive struggle. Innis argued that the available media of communication influence very strongly the forms of social organization that are possible. The media thus influence the kinds of human associations that can develop in any period. Because these patterns of association are not independent of the knowledge men have of themselves and others—indeed, consciousness is built on these associations—control of communications implies control of both consciousness and social organization. Thus, whenever a medium of communication and the groups that control the media have a hegemony in society, Innis assumes that a principal axis of competition will be the search for competing media of communication. New media are designed to undercut existing centers of power and to facilitate the creation of new patterns of association and the articulation of new forms of knowledge. I will return to this point later. Let me note now only that Innis assumed that disenfranchised groups in society would lead the search for new forms of technology in seeking to compete for some form of social power.

The bulk of Innis' work was devoted to analyzing the kinds

of control inherent in communications media. He considered, as near as one can tell, all forms of communication, from speech through printing, including what he took to be the four dominant preprinting media—clay, papyrus, parchment, and paper. With each of these media he also considered the types of script employed and the kinds of writing instruments used. Innis argued that various stages of Western civilization could be characterized by the dominance of a particular medium of communication. The medium had a determinate influence on the form of social organization typical of the stage of society and on the character of the culture of that stage. Further, the succession of stages in Western civilization could be seen in terms of a competition for dominance between media of communication. The results of this competition among media progressively transformed the character of social institutions and the nature of culture.

I think it important to note Innis' emphasis on both culture and social organization. He was concerned not only with the ways in which culture and institutions were interrelated but also the sense in which they were *both* epiphenomena of communications technology. Usually the social history of the West takes either the route of August Comte, emphasizing the progressive transformation of culture from the theological to the metaphysical to the positivistic, or the route taken by Lewis Mumford, emphasizing the transformations in social organization from the tribe to the town to the city. Innis, however, attempts to marry these two traditions into a unified view of social change. Moreover, he attaches changes in both social organization and culture to changes in the technology of communication. The generality of Innis' argument is seldom recognized, I think, because of a failure to appreciate the meaning of the phrase "the bias of communication" and the dual sense in which he defines his two principal variables, space and time.

Innis argues that any given medium of communication is biased in terms of the control of time or space. Media that are durable and difficult to transport—parchment, clay, and stone —are time-binding, or time-biased. Media that are light and

274

less durable are space-binding or spatially biased. For example, paper and papyrus are space-binding, for they are light, easily transportable, can be moved across space with reasonable speed and great accuracy, and they thus favor administration over vast distance.

Any given medium will bias social organization, for it will favor the growth of certain kinds of interests and institutions at the expense of others and will also impose on these institutions a form of organization. Media that are space-binding facilitate and encourage the growth of empire, encourage a concern with expansion and with the present, and thus favor the hegemony of secular political authority. Space-binding media encourage the growth of the state, the military, and decentralized and expansionist institutions. Time-binding media foster concern with history and tradition, have little capacity for expansion of secular authority, and thus favor the growth of religion, of hierarchical organization, and of contractionist institutions. The hegemony of either religion or the state imposes a characteristic pattern on all secondary institutions, such as education, and also leads to a search for competing, alternative modes of communication to undercut this hegemony. Thus, the dynamic of social change resided in the search for alternative forms of communication alternately supporting the kingdom of God or man.

At the level of social structure, a time bias meant an emphasis upon religion, hierarchy, and contraction, whereas a space bias meant an emphasis upon the state, decentralization, and expansion. But the terms "time" and "space" also had a cultural meaning.

In cultural terms, time meant the sacred, the moral, the historical; space the present and the future, the technical and the secular. As media of communication favored the growth of certain kinds of institutions, it also assured the domination of the culture characteristic of those institutions. On the cultural level, his principal contrast was between the oral and written traditions. Let me try to develop the contrast.

Although speech is not only the only means of communication in traditional societies, it certainly is the principal means.

JAMES W. CAREY

Traditional societies are organized in terms of, or are at least severely constrained by, certain features of speech. For example, spoken language can traverse only relatively short distances without being altered and distorted, giving rise to dialects. Speech not only moves over short distances but travels slowly compared with other means of communication. Speech also has a low capacity for storage; there is no way of preserving information except by storing it in the memories of individuals or by symbolizing it in some material form. Life in traditional societies must be collective, communal, and celebrative as the medium of communication requires it to be.

Innis argues that speech encourages the development of a society with a strong temporal bias, a society that focuses on the past and emphasizes tradition, that attempts to conserve and preserve the existing stock of knowledge and values. Such societies are likely to have limited conceptions of space, conceptions restricted to the village or geographical area currently occupied by the tribe. Space beyond that is invested with magical qualities, frequently being the home of the gods; for example, cargo cults. While the mind of primitive man can traverse extraordinary reaches of time, it is radically limited in traversing space. The hegemony of speech is likely to also lead to magical beliefs in language. Words become icons, they do not represent things, they are themselves things. The care, nurture, and preservation of language is likely to occupy much collective energy of the society.

Oral cultures, then, are time-binding cultures. They have consequently a limited capacity for technical change. The imbalance toward time rooted in the available means of communication emphasizes the cohesion of people in the present by their "remembrances of things past." With media such as speech, Innis associated tradition, the sacred, and the institutionalization of magic and religion.

Speech as the dominant mode of communication gave rise to an oral tradition, a tradition that Innis not only described but admired. By an oral tradition Innis meant a "selection from the history of a people of a series of related events, culturally defined as significant, and their transmission from generation

276

to generation." The recitation of artistic works within the oral tradition was a social ceremony that linked audiences to the past and celebrated their social cohesion in the present. While individual performers would modify an oral tradition to make it more serviceable in present circumstances, they began with the tradition and thus became indissolubly linked to it.

Furthermore, the oral tradition was flexible and persistent. Linked as it was to the collective and communal life of a people, built into their linguistic habits and modes of symbolic expression, the oral tradition was difficult to destroy. Through endless repetition an oral tradition "created recognized standards and lasting moral and social institutions; it built up the soul of social organization and maintained their continuity. . . ."

Oral traditions and time-binding media led to the growth of a culture oriented toward a sacred tradition that built consensus on the sharing of mutually affirmed and celebrated attitudes and values, and placed morals and metaphysics at the center of civilization.

Written traditions, in general, led to quite different cultures. They were usually space-binding and favored the growth of political authority and secular institutions and a culture appropriate to them. Let me warn you that Innis did not admire oral cultures and derogate written ones. Some of his language could easily lead one to that conclusion, but, as I hope to show, that was decidedly not the case.

Written traditions and their appropriate culture grounded relations among men not in tradition but in attachment to secular authority. Rather than emphasizing the temporal relations among kinship, written tradition emphasizes spatial relations. Rather than emphasizing the past, it emphasizes the present and the future, particularly the future of empire. Rather than emphasizing knowledge grounded in moral order, it emphasizes the technical order and favors the growth of science and technical knowledge. Whereas the character of storage and reception of the oral tradition favor continuity over time, the written tradition favors discontinuity in time though continuity over space.

277

What Innis recognized was the hostility that seemed inevitably to develop between the written and the oral tradition. The innovation of writing would first lead to a recording of the oral tradition. It would thus freeze it and make it of interest to subsequent generations largely for antiquarian reasons. The written tradition, after its initial contact with the oral, would go its own way. It would favor change and innovation and progressive attenuation from the past as a residue of knowledge, values, and sentiment. The hostility between these traditions and between time-binding and space-binding media generally led to the creation of a monopoly of knowledge. He used the term monopoly in a straightforward economic sense. Very simply, Innis contended that the culture of the favored institution would infiltrate every aspect of social life and ultimately drive out, define as illegitimate, or radically transform competing traditions. Only knowledge that conformed to the concerns and cultural predispositions of the dominant medium would persist. In a written tradition, knowledge must be technical, secular, and future-oriented for it to be defined as legitimate or recognized as valid.

By now it should be obvious that Innis defined as the central problem of social science and social change the same problem which was the focus of Max Weber's work: the problem of authority. Innis wanted to know what, in general, determines the location of ultimate authority in a society and what will be recognized as authoritative knowledge. His answer was this: Media of communication, depending on their bias, confer monopolies of authority and knowledge on the state, the technical order, and civil law or on religion, the sacred order, and moral law.*

Innis believed that an overemphasis or monopoly of either

* Innis was interested in all forms of monopolies of knowledge. In his teaching he was interested in the tendency of social science research to become focused around one man—a Keynes, Marx, or Freud—or one narrow attitude of speculation. He himself preferred an open and vigorous competition of viewpoints and felt that the reliance of Western education on the book severely reduced the possibility of vigorous debate and discourse in education. See Donald Creighton, *Harold Adams Innis, Portrait of a Scholar* (Toronto: University of Toronto Press, 1957).

278

time or space, religion or the state, the moral or the technical, was the principal dynamic of the rise and fall of empire. Time and space were thus related as conjugant variables in which the progressive presence of one led to the progressive absence of the other. The bias toward time or space produced instability in society. A stable society was possible only with the development of mechanisms that preserved both temporal and spatial orientations, that preserved competition between religion and the state, and that preserved independence and tension between the moral and the technical. In *The Bias of Communication* Innis commented that

in western civilization a stable society is dependent on an appreciation of a proper balance between the concepts of space and time. We are concerned with control over vast areas of space but also over vast stretches of time. We must appraise civilization in relation to its territory and in relation to its duration. The character of the medium of communication tends to create a bias in civilization favorable to an overemphasis on the time concept or on the space concept and only at rare intervals are the biases offset by the influence of another medium and stability achieved.

Classical Greece was such a rare interval. The relative isolation of Greece from the older civilizations of Egypt and the Near East enabled her to develop an oral tradition. The written tradition was slowly introduced into Greece from these neighboring cultures, but it did not destroy the oral tradition. The tradition was committed to writing, but the oral tradition continued to flourish. For example, the dialogue remained the principal instrument of Greek culture, and an oral literature constituted the common moral consciousness. The written tradition with its spatial emphasis encouraged the growth of political authority and allowed Greece to deal with problems of administration. Eventually, writing triumphed over the oral tradition in the latter part of the fifth century B.C., and the spatial bias gave rise to a divisive individualism.

Generalizing from the experience of classical Greece, Innis argued that a healthy society requires competition not only in the marketplace but also in ideas, traditions, and institutions.

JAMES W. CAREY

Typically, media favor the development of cultural and institutional monopolies. Unless media favoring time and space exist as independent traditions offsetting and checking the biases of one another, the society will be dominated by a narrow monopoly. In such biased states, politics becomes sacralized or religion secularized; science destroys morality or morality emasculates science; tradition gives way to the notion of progress or chronic change obliterates tradition.

The history of the modern West, Innis argues, is the history of a bias of communication and a monopoly of knowledge founded on print. In one of his most quoted statements, Innis characterized modern Western history as beginning with temporal organization and ending with spatial organization. The introduction of printing attacked the temporal monopoly of the medieval church. Printing fostered the growth of nationalism and empire; it favored the extension of society in space. It encouraged the growth of bureaucracy and militarism, science and secular authority. Printing infiltrated all institutions, being the major force in creating what is currently celebrated as "the secular society." Not only did print destroy the oral tradition but it also drove underground the principal concerns of the oral tradition—morals, values, and metaphysics. While print did not destroy religion, it did, as Max Weber has argued, transform religion to meet the needs of the state and economy. Ultimately, the obsession with space, with the nation, with the moment, exposed the relativity of all values and led Western civilization, in Innis' eyes, to the brink of nihilism. The death of the oral tradition, the demise of concern with time, not only shifted the source of authority from the church to the state and of ultimate knowledge from religion to science; it also insisted on a transformation of religious concerns and language from the theological and sacred to the political and secular.

Innis viewed the rampaging nationalism of the twentieth century with anger and anguish, attitudes not untypical of contemporary intellectuals. But his emotion-charged writing should not obscure his central argument. The primary effect of changes in communication media is on the form of social

280

organization that can be supported. Social organization produces a characteristic culture which constitutes the predispositions of individuals. The centrality of communication media to both culture and social structure implies that the principal axis of change, of the rise and fall of empire, will be alternations in the technologies of communication upon which society is principally reliant.

There are many similarities between the thought of Innis and that of Marshall McLuhan. Although I do not intend to obscure those similarities, I would like to emphasize, at least in this paper, some significant points of difference. The question I am asking is this: What is absolutely central to Innis' argument and how does it compare with the central notion in McLuhan's work? Although McLuhan has occasionally characterized his work as an extension of Innis', I want to suggest that McLuhan has taken a relatively minor but recurring theme of Innis' work (perhaps only a suggestion) and made it central to his entire argument. Conversely, McLuhan has neglected or ignored the principal argument developed by Innis.

Both Innis and McLuhan agree that historically "the things on which words were written down count more than the words themselves"; that is, the medium is the message. Starting from this proposition, they engage in quite different kinds of intellectual bookkeeping, however, and are seized by quite different kinds of implications.

Both McLuhan and Innis assume the centrality of communication technology; where they differ is in the principal kinds of effects they see deriving from this technology. Whereas Innis sees communication technology principally affecting social organization and culture, McLuhan sees its principal effect on sensory organization and thought. McLuhan has much to say about perception and thought but little to say about institutions; Innis says much about institutions and little about perception and thought.

While McLuhan is intellectually linked to Innis, I think he can be more clearly and usefully tied to a line of speculation in sociolinguistics usually referred to as the Sapir-Whorf hypothesis.

The Sapir-Whorf hypothesis proposes that the language a speaker uses has a determining influence on the character of his thought. While it is a trusim that men think with and through language, Edward Sapir and Benjamin Lee Whorf proposed that the very structure of reality—if I may use that grandiose and overworked phrase—is presented to individuals through language. When a person acquires a language he not only acquires a way of talking but also a way of seeing, a way of organizing experience, a way of discriminating the real world. Language, so the argument goes, has built into its grammar and lexicon the very structure of perception. Individuals discriminate objects and events in terms of the vocabulary provided by language. Further, individuals derive their sense of time, their patterns of classifications, their categories for persons, their perception of action, in terms of the tenses, the genders, the pronouns, the pluralizations that are possible in their language. This argument, then, largely reduces the structure of perception and thought to the structure of language.

McLuhan adopts the form of argument provided by the Sapir-Whorf hypothesis with two important modifications. First, he adopts a quite unorthodox characterization of the grammar of a language. Second, he extends the "grammatical analysis" to modes of communication such as print and television which are normally not treated as types of languages.

McLuhan does not view the grammar of a medium in terms of the formal properties of language, the parts of speech or morphemes, normally utilized in such an analysis. Instead, he argues that the grammar of a medium derives from the particular mixture of the senses that an individual characteristically uses in the utilization of the medium. For example, language —or better, speech—is the first of the mass media. It is a device for externalizing thought and for fixing and sharing perceptions. As a means of communications, speech elicits a particular orchestration of the sense. While speech is an oral phenomenon and gives rise to "ear-oriented cultures" (cultures in which people more easily believe what they hear than what they see), oral communication synthesizes or brings into play other sensual faculties. For example, in conversation men are aware not only of the sound of words but also of the visual properties of the speaker and the setting of the tactile qualities of various elements of the setting, and even certain olfactory properties of the person and the situation. These various faculties constitute parallel and simultaneous modes of communication, and thus McLuhan concludes that oral cultures synthesize these various modalities, elicit them all or bring them all into play in a situation utilizing all the sensory apparatus of the person. Oral cultures, then, involve the simultaneous interplay of sight, sound, touch, and smell and thus produce, in McLuhan's view, a depth of involvement in life as the principal communications medium—oral speech—simultaneously activates all the sensory faculties through which men acquire knowledge and share feeling.

However, speech is not the only mass medium, nor must it necessarily be the dominant mass medium. In technologically advanced societies, print, broadcasting, and film can replace speech as the dominant mode through which knowledge and feeling are communicated. In such societies speech does not disappear, but it assumes the characteristics of the dominant medium. For example, in literate communities oral traditions disappear and the content of spoken communication is the written tradition. Speech no longer follows its own laws. Rather it is governed by the laws of the written tradition. This means not only that the "content" of speech is what has previously been written but that the cadence and imagery of everyday speech is the cadence and imagery of writing. In literate communities, men have difficulty believing that the rich, muscular, graphic, almost multidimensional speech of Oscar Lewis' illiterate Mexican peasants was produced by such "culturally deprived" persons. But for McLuhan speech as an oral tradition, simultaneously utilizing many modes of communication, is almost exclusively the province of the illiterate.

McLuhan starts from the biological availability of parallel modes for the production and reception of messages. These modes—sight, touch, sound, and smell—do not exist independently but are interdependent with one another. Thus, to alter the capacity of one of the modes changes the total relations among the senses and thus alters the way in which individuals organize experience and fix perception. All this is clear enough. To remove one sense from a person leads frequently to the strengthening of the discriminatory powers of the other senses and thus to a rearrangement of not only the senses but of the kind of experience a person has. Blindness leads to an increasing reliance on and increasing power of smell and touch as well as hearing as modes of awareness. Loss of hearing particularly increases one's reliance on sight. But, McLuhan argues, the ratios between the senses and the power of the senses is affected by more than physical impairment or, to use his term, amputation. Media of communication also lead to the amputation of the senses. Media of communication also encourage the overreliance on one sense faculty to the impairment or disuse of others. And thus, media of communication impart to persons a particular way of organizing experience and a particular way of knowing and understanding the world in which they travel.

Modes of communication, including speech, are, then, devices for fixing perception and organizing experience. Print, by its technological nature, has built into it a grammar for organizing experience, and its grammar is found in the particular ratio of sensory qualities it elicts in its users. All communications media are, therefore, extensions of man, or, better, are extensions of some mix of the sensory capacities of man. Speech is such an extension and thus the first mass medium. As an extension of man, it casts individuals in a unique, symbiotic relation to the dominant mode of communication in a culture. This symbiosis is not restricted to speech but extends to whatever medium of communication dominates a culture. This extension is by way of projecting certain sensory capacities of the individual. As I have mentioned, speech involves an extension and development of all the senses. Other media, however, are more partial in their appeal to the senses. The exploitation of a particular communications technology fixes particular sensory relations in members of society. By fixing such a relation, it determines a society's world view; that is, it stipulates a characteristic way of organizing experience. It thus determines the forms of knowledge, the structure of perception, and the sensory equipment attuned to absorb reality.

Media of communication, consequently, are vast social metaphors that not only transmit information but determine what is knowledge; that not only orient us to the world but tell us what kind of world exists; that not only excite and delight our sense but, by altering the ratio of sensory equipment that we use, actually change our character.

This is, I think, the core of McLuhan's argument. It can be most conveniently viewed as an attempt, albeit a creative and imaginative attempt, to extend the Sapir-Whorf hypothesis to include all forms of social communication.

Let me attempt to illustrate this abstruse argument with Mc-Luhan's analysis of print. Print, the dominant means of communication in the West, depends on phonetic writing. Phonetic writing translated the oral into the visual; that is, it took sounds and translated them into visual symbols. Printing enormously extended and speeded up this process of translation, turning societies historically dependent upon the ear as the principal source of knowledge into societies dependent upon the eye. Print cultures are cultures in which seeing is believing, in which oral traditions are translated into written form, in which men have difficulty believing or remembering oral speech—names, stories, legends—unless they first see it written. In short, in print cultures knowledge is acquired and experience is confirmed by sight: as they say, by seeing it in writing. Men confirm their impressions of Saturday's football game by reading about it in Sunday morning's paper.

Besides making us dependent on the eye, printing imposes a particular logic on the organization of visual experience. Print organizes reality into discrete, uniform, harmonious, causal relations. The visual arrangement of the printed page becomes a perceptual model by which all reality is organized. The mental set of print—the desire to break things down into elementary units (words), the tendency to see reality in discrete units, to find causal relations and linear serial order (left to right arrangement of the page), to find orderly structure in nature (the orderly geometry of the printed page)—is transferred to all other social activities. Thus, science and government, art and architecture, work and education become organized in terms of the implicit assumption built into the dominant medium of communication.

Moreover, print encourages individualism and specialization. To live in an oral culture, one acquires knowledge only in contact with other people, in terms of communal activities. Printing, however, allows individuals to withdraw, to contemplate and meditate outside of communal activities. Print thus encourages privatization, the lonely scholar, and the development of private, individual points of view.

McLuhan thus concludes that printing detribalizes man. It removes him from the necessity of participating in a tightly knit oral culture. In a notion apparently taken from T. S. Eliot, McLuhan contends that print disassociates the senses, separating sight from sound; encourages a private and withdrawn existence; and supports the growth of specialization.

Above all, print leads to nationalism, for it allows for the visual apprehension of the mother tongue and, through maps, a visual apprehension of the nation. Printing allows the vernacular to be standardized and the mother tongue to be universalized through education.

While the book ushered in the age of print, developments such as newspapers and magazines have only intensified the implications of print: extreme visual nationalism, specialist technology and occupations, individualism and private points of view.

By such argument McLuhan insists that the meaning and effect of any communications innovation is to be found in the way it structures thought and perception. The excitement that currently surrounds McLuhan derives from his extension of this argument to the newer media of communication, particularly television, and the effect these newer media have on the venerated tradition of print and on the mental life of contemporary man.

For McLuhan the civilization based on print is dead. A science based on its assumptions, which searches for causal relations, encourages orderly, non-contradictory argument, fosters the specialization and compartmentalization of knowledge, is obsolete. Education that relies on the book and the lecture—itself merely reading from written script—and the traditional modes of sciences is likewise obsolete.

Print culture was doomed, so McLuhan argues, by the innovation of telegraphy, the first of the electronic media. Radio further undercut the hegemony of print, but the triumph of electronic communication over print awaited the permeation of the entire society by television. We are now observing, McLuhan concludes, the first generation weaned on television for whom the book and printing are secondary, remote, and ephemeral kinds of media. It is not only that television, as Storm Jameson has recently argued, leads to a devaluation of the written word. Television is not only another means for transmitting information; it is also a radically new way of organizing experience. Unlike print, television is not merely an eye medium but utilizes a much broader range of sensory equipment. That television marries sight and sound is obvious; but McLuhan also argues that television is a tactile medium as well. Television, as a result of the scanning system on which it operates, is capable of conveying or eliciting a sense of touch. Thus, in the apprehension of television not only the eye but the ear and the hand are brought into play. Television reorchestrates the senses; it engages, if you will, the whole man, *these are catered to, not engaged* the entire range of sensory qualities of the person.

Moreover, television is, in one of McLuhan's inimitable phrases, a "cool" medium. By this McLuhan means only that television, like the cartoon and line drawing, is low in information. You don't merely watch a television screen. You engage it; you are forced to add information to complete the message. The capacity of the screen to transmit information is determined by the number of lines in the scanning system. In American television the scanning system is particularly low, 525 lines, and thus the medium is low in information relative to, say, movies. Thus the viewer must get involved; he must fill in auditory, visual, and tactile cues for the message on the screen to be completed. Because television appeals to all the senses, because it is a cool or active participational medium in front of which a viewer cannot remain passive, a culture in which television is the dominant medium will produce a person characteristically different than will a culture based on print.

McLuhan observes we are now witnessing in maturity the first generation who were suckled on television, who acquired the conventions of television long before it acquired traditional print literacy. The generational gap we now observe by contrasting the withdrawn, private, specializing student of the fifties with the active, involved, generalist student of the sixties McLuhan rests at the door of television. For the characteristic differences in these generations are paralleled by the differences between print and television as devices of communication. The desire of students for involvement and participation, for talking rather than reading, for seminars rather than lectures, for action rather than reflection, in short for participation and involvement rather than withdrawal and observation he ascribes to the reorchestration of the senses provoked by television.

The conflict between generations of which we are now so acutely aware is ultimately a conflict between a generation bred on the book and a generation bred on the tube and related forms of electronic communication. The generational gap involves much more than politics and education, of course. In every area of life McLuhan observes youth asserting forms of behavior and demanding kinds of experience that engage the total self. Dance and dress, music and hair styles must not only have a "look"; they must also have a "sound" and above all a "touch." They must appeal to all the senses simultaneously. It is not only that youth wants experience; it wants experience that unifies rather than dissociates the senses. Moreover, in the new styles of literature, which destroy all the conventions of print, in the new argots, which destroy all the conventions of traditional grammar, in the new styles of political action, which demean the traditionally radical forms of ideology and organization, in the demands for change in education, in music, in art, in dance, in dress, McLuhan sees the retribalization of man restoring him to the integrated condition of the oral culture in which the sensual capacities of men are again made whole.

This retribalization presumably involves the extension in space of the entire nervous system. Sight, hearing, and tactility derive from a nervous system originally contained within the skin. Each of the media has in turn extended these mechanisms, these aspects of the nervous system, beyond the skin. They have externalized them. The book and camera extend the eye, radio and the listening device extend the ear, television extends not only the eye and the ear but also the hand. Electric circuitry in general represents an extension of the entire nervous system. Think, for example, of the imagery of the computer with its network of wires and nodes linked to a television system. This is the sense in which communications media are extensions of man—extending with the aid of the computer the entire sensory and neurological system of the person in space, heightening the capacity of the organism to receive and digest information, literally turning the person now extended by his technology into an information processing system.

It is through such an analysis that McLuhan arrives at or expresses his central point: every medium of communication possesses a logic or grammar that constitutes a set of devices for organizing experience. The logic or grammar of each medium that dominates an age impresses itself on the users of the medium, thus dictating what is defined as truth and knowledge. Communications media, then, determine not only what one thinks about but literally how one thinks.

In the exposition of this notion McLuhan, of course, treats more than print and television. These are merely the end-points in an exposition that includes commentary on films, radio, cartoons, light bulbs, political candidates, and virtually every other technique and folly of man. But in each case he attempts to determine the grammar inherent in the technology of the medium. While McLuhan normally defines the grammar of a medium in terms of the sense ratios it elicits, he frequently resorts to the more simplified method of designating media as "hot" or "cold." A hot medium is one that presents a lot of information in one sense; it bombards the receiver with information or, in another favorite phrase, is in high definition. A cool medium, or one in low definition, is a medium that presents relatively little information; the receiver must complete the image, must add values to what is presented to him, and is thus more involving or participational. The halftone photo in four colors is visually hot; the cartoon is visually cool. Print is a hot medium, television a cool medium. The quality of having temperature applies also to persons and cultures, dance and dress, autos and sports. Temperature, then, is another way of designating grammar. However, it is the least satisfactory of all McLuhan's concepts and arguments. This is unfortunate, because for most critics it is the terms "hot" and "cool" that are taken to be McLuhan's principal contribution to the study of media, and a lot of unanswerable critical fire can be heaped on McLuhan at this point. The terms "hot" and "cool" are applied in very haphazard ways. Media that are hot one minute seem to be cool another. It is impossible to tell if temperature is an absolute property of a medium or whether a medium is hot or cool relative only to some other medium. And the classification of media into these categories seems to be always quite arbitrary.

McLuhan's argument does not, however, stand or fall on the usage of the terms "hot" and "cool." One can simply agree that while media do possess an inherent grammar, the exact structure and logic of this grammar has not, as yet, been particularly well worked out. Some latitude should be allowed McLuhan at this point anyway. He obviously is doing a good deal of experimenting with the classification of media. There is little resemblance between the classification one finds in the "first edition" of *Understanding Media* (a report to the United States Office of Education, 1960) and that in the McGraw-Hill edition currently in circulation. His argument must, I think, be assessed in terms of its most general point: men stand in a symbiotic relation to all media, and consequently the dominant mode of communication dictates the character of perception and through perception the structure of mind.

At this point I would like to make some critical notes on the arguments that have been presented. My only reluctance in doing so is that Innis and McLuhan present rather convenient targets for criticism if only because their arguments are so unconventional. Also, criticism, let us be reminded, is easy. It is still harder to write novels than to write reviews. Further, not only the structure of McLuhan's argument but also his current popularity stand as an incautious invitation to criticism and thus most critical fire that I might muster would inevitably be aimed at McLuhan. Marshall McLuhan is, after all, not only a social analyst; he is also a prophet, a phenomenon, a happening, a social movement. His work has given rise to an ideology —*mcluhanisme*—and a mass movement producing seminars, clubs, art exhibits, and conferences in his name.

Besides, I'm convinced that a technical critique of McLuhan is a rather useless undertaking. If Robert Merton cannot dent his armor by pointing out inconsistencies in his argument and lacunae in his observations, I'm quite sure that my own lesser intellectual luminosity shall have little effect on McLuhan or his devotees. I am thinking here of such inconsistencies as the fact that while he is a serious critic of traditional logic and rationality, his argument is mechanistic, built upon linear causality, and illustrative of all the deficiencies of this type of analysis. His terminology is ill-defined and inconsistently used and maddeningly obtuse. More seriously, he has a view of mind, directly adopted from the *tabula rasa* of John Locke, that is not only simple-minded but contradicted by much of the work currently being done in linguistics, psychology, and psychotherapy. But I sense that such criticism is analogous to criticizing Christianity by pointing out contradictions in the Bible.

McLuhan is beyond criticism not only because he defines such activity as illegitimate but also because his work does not lend itself to critical commentary. It is a mixture of whimsy, pun, and innuendo. These things are all right in themselves, but unfortunately one cannot tell what he is serious about and what is mere whimsy. His sentences are not observations or assertions but, in his own language, "probes." Unfortunately, a probe is a neutral instrument about which one can say nothing

291

but congratulate its inquisitiveness. One may resist his probes or yield to their delights, but to quarrel with them is rather beside the point.

Despite these disclaimers, a manageable enterprise remains. I would like to judge McLuhan's argument not in absolute or universal terms but only in relation to the work of Innis. If we can for the moment grant the central assumption on the role of communications technology in social change, who has presented us with the more powerful and useful argument? This is a question both manageable and germane to the paper. Less germane but at least of importance to me is the concluding question I would like to raise: What is it that makes McLuhan an acceptable prophet of our times? I think the answer to this question will also shed some important light on the argument of Innis.

I have suggested that Innis argued that the most visible and important effects of media technology were on social organization and through social organization on culture. Radio and television, I assume Innis would argue, are light media that quickly and easily transmit large amounts of information. Moreover, electronic signals, while highly perishable, are difficult to control. Unlike print, electronic media do not recognize national boundaries, as the Canadians have discovered. Thus, the effect of the electronic media is to extend the spatial bias of print, to make new forms of human association possible, and to foreshorten one's sense of time. As spatially biased media, radio and television, even when used by religious institutions, contribute to the growing hegemony of secular authority and to the extension of political influence in space. Further, they have contributed to the weakening of tradition and to the secularization of religion. Or so Innis might have it.

McLuhan treats quite a different effect of the media—the effect of the media not on social organization but on sensory organization. As I have previously mentioned, Innis and McLuhan do treat both kinds of effects. The effect of the media on sensory organization is a minor but persistent theme in Innis' writings.* McLuhan also treats the effects of media on

* Here are some examples culled at random from Innis' writings: "Schol-

social organization, as the previous discussion of nationalism, specialization, science, and education illustrated. However, the major direction and thus the implication of the two arguments is quite different. Moreover, McLuhan, deliberately or otherwise, confuses these two quite different effects of media technology. Much of his evidence is not directed at nor does it support his analysis of the sensory bias of media. Rather it supports Innis' claim for the institutional or organizational bias of media. For example, xerography, a process which very much interests McLuhan, is an important innovation in communication. While the innovation is based upon discoveries in electronic technology, its usual product nonetheless is the orderly, linear type of the printed page. The effect of xerography is not on sensory organization. However, by increasing the rate of speed at which information can be transmitted and reproduced, by allowing for the rapid recombination of printed materials, xerography does encourage the creation of novel vehicles of communication and novel groups of readers. That is, xerography encourages or at least permits certain structural reorganizations of social groups. Developments in offset printing have a similar effect.

My argument is simply that the most visible effects of communications technology are on social organization and not on sensory organization. Much of McLuhan's evidence can be more plausibly, directly, and productively used in support of the form of argument offered by Innis. I will subsequently return to this point. Here I much want to suggest that Innis provides a more plausible accounting of the principal phe-

---

ars were concerned with letters rather than sounds and linguistic instruction emphasized eye philology rather than ear philology" (*Empire and Communications*, p. 159). "The discovery of printing in the middle of the 15th century implied the beginning of a return to a type of civilization dominated by the eye rather than the ear" (*The Bias of Communication*, p. 138). "Introduction of the alphabet meant a concern with sound rather than with sight or with the ear rather than the eye" (*ibid.*, pp. 40–41). "In oral intercourse the eye, ear and brain acted together in busy co-operation and rivalry each eliciting, stimulating and supplementing the other" (*ibid.*, p. 106). "The ear and the concern with time began to have its influence on the arts concerned with eye and space" (*ibid.*, p. 110).

nomena in question and is of greater usefulness to students of the history of mass communication. My preferences for Innis are partly esthetic; they stem partly from a simple aversion to much of what McLuhan represents. In addition I feel that Innis' argument will be ultimately productive of more significant scholarship. Finally, I feel that McLuhan's position awaits the same fate as the Sapir-Whorf hypothesis to which it is so closely tied. The Sapir-Whorf hypothesis, while it is a perfectly plausible notion, has never turned out to be productive of much insight or research or to have particularly advanced the study of language and perception.

The same fate awaits McLuhan, I fear, and stems from an argumentative similarity between the positions. For McLuhan states his case on very general grounds and defends it on very narrow grounds. Because he views the effect of the media as principally acting on the senses, his entire argument ultimately rests on the narrow grounds of the psychology of perception. This is, I think, a very weak foundation to support such a vast superstructure. This is not only because many of his comments on the psychology of perception are highly questionable, but also because given what we know about the complexity of behavior, it is hard to understand how such a vast range of social phenomena are to be so simply explained. When McLuhan is writing about the oral tradition and about print, areas in which he is backed by the extensive scholarship of Innis, his work has a cogency and integration and is sensitive to the complexity of the problems at hand (for example, in large portions of *The Gutenberg Galaxy*). When he probes beyond these shores into the world of television and the computer, the water gets very muddy indeed, for here he attempts to explain every twitch in contemporary society on the basis of the sensory reorganization brought about by the media. I do not have the time, nor the knowledge, to examine McLuhan's theory of perception. However, a couple of problems should be pointed out.* The phenomenon of sensory closure upon which McLuhan's theory is built is a very primitive perceptual mechanism. It is found in all experiments on perception, though not al-

* Here I am indebted to Sidney Robinovitch of the University of Illinois.

ways in predictable ways. Moreover, the *Gestalt* movement in psychology was based upon the operation of this mechanism, though it was largely limited to the study of visual closure. An obvious strength of McLuhan's argument is his isolation of this primitive and important perceptual phenomenon and his generalization of the phenomenon beyond visual closure to include the relations among all the senses. However, the assumption that the pattern of sensory closure is dictated by the structure of the media seems to be an unnecessary and unwarranted oversimplification.

For example, McLuhan severely overestimates the inflexibility of media of communication. While any given medium confronts an artist with certain inherent constraints, media still allow wide latitude for innovation and artistic manipulation. McLuhan does not consider, for example, that any medium can be used, in any historical period, either discursively or presentationally. Speech and writing, while they have a bias toward discursive presentation, can also be used presentationally. It is difficult to imagine why McLuhan does not utilize the distinction between presentational and discursive forms, a distinction of some importance in modern esthetic theory.* Elements in a presentational form have no individuated meaning but take on meaning only in relation to the whole. Elements in a discursive form have individuated meaning, and the elements can be combined by formal rules. Ordinary language is highly discursive, but it can be used presentationally. And "this is the distinguishing mark of poetry. The significance of a poetic symbol can be appreciated only in the context of the entire poem."

The same can be said of other forms. A given medium of communication may favor discursive presentation or the presentation of perceptual *Gestalts,* but they can be and are manipulated in either genre. These media are, of course, constraining forces: they limit and control to some degree the expressive capacities of men. But the history of these forms is the history of attempts to overcome the deficiencies seemingly

* Susanne K. Langer, *Philosophy in a New Key* (Cambridge, Mass.: Harvard University Press, 1957).

inherent in media of communication, to make the media bend to thought and imagination rather than allowing thought and imagination to be imprisoned by them. Thus, metaphor and simile, incongruity and hyperbole, personification and irony, are all devices, imaginative and productive devices, for overcoming the formal constraints of speech and writing. Similarly, while print, radio and television, and movies have inherent technological constraints, artists within these media have constantly struggled to overcome the limitations of the form through invention of new modes of symbolic representation. Think only of the history of film editing.

While McLuhan frequently excludes artists from the laws of perceptual determinism, he does not exclude audiences. However, I want to suggest that devices such as metaphor, simile, and personification are used not only by artists but are part of the linguistic repertoire of every five-year-old child. They are devices through which all of us attempt to overcome the inherent constraints of speech. There is, I suspect, much more freedom in perception and invention in everyday communication than McLuhan is willing to admit. To propose the audience as an empty vessel, a black box, that has no significant autonomous existence but is, instead, filled or wired up by sources exclusively external to the self is not only to deny an enormous amount of everyday evidence but also casually to dismiss a significant amount of reasonably sound scientific evidence. The empty organism view of the self is, I think, not only pernicious but also unsupportable from the evidence at hand on perception.

But the most important criticism to make of McLuhan is that much of the argument he wants to make and most of the contemporary phenomena he wants to explain—particularly the conflict between generations—can be more effectively handled within the framework provided by Innis. Furthermore, the utilization of the perspective of Innis opens up, I think, a number of important and researchable questions and puts the argument once more in a historical context.

In this final section let me tentatively attempt to bring Innis' argument up to date; that is, to extend it from the early

1950s, where he left it, into the 1960s. You will remember that Innis argued that Western history began with temporal bias and was ending with spatial bias. I want to suggest that contemporary developments in the electronic media have intensified this spatial bias. Electronic media, particularly with the innovation of satellite broadcasting, increasingly transcend all national boundaries, thereby weakening nationalism or at least tending to undercut the parochial limitations of national identifications. Further, such media are a potent force in generating a more universal, worldwide culture which is urban, secular, and, in Innis' terms, unstable.

Let me put it this way. Among primitive societies and in earlier stages of Western history relatively small discontinuities in space led to vast differences in culture and social organization. Tribal societies separated by a hundred miles could have entirely different forms of economic, political, and religious life and grossly dissimilar systems of expressive symbolism, myth, and ritual. However, within these societies there was a great continuity of culture and social structure over generations. Forms of life changed slowly, of course, and the attitudes, hopes, fears, and aspirations of a boy of fourteen and a man of sixty were remarkably similar. This does not mean there were no conflicts between age groups in such societies. Such conflicts are probably inevitable if only because of biological changes accompanying aging. However, the conflict occurred within a system of shared attitudes and values and within a system of mutual dependencies across age groups. Such societies were based on an oral tradition with a strong temporal bias. The continuity of culture was maintained by a shared, collective system of ritual and by the continuity of passage rites marking off the entrance of individuals into various stages of the life cycle. In such a world, then, there were vast differences between societies but relatively little variation between generations within a given society. In Innis' terms, temporal media produce vast continuity in time and great discontinuity in space.

The spatial bias of modern media, initiated by print but radically extended by film and the electronic media, has re-

297

versed the relations between time and space. Space in the modern world progressively disappears as a differentiating factor. As space becomes more continuous, regional variations in culture and social structure become ground down. Further, as I have already suggested and as other modern writers have persuasively argued, the rise of a worldwide urban civilization built upon the speed and extensiveness of travel and electronic media have progressively diminished—though they have come nowhere near eliminating—spatial, transnational variation in culture and social structure. It is this fact which has led Claude Lévi-Strauss to re-echo the traditional keen of the anthropologist that primitive societies must be intensively studied now because they are rapidly disappearing.

If in fact the spatial bias of contemporary media does lead to a progressive reduction of regional variation within nations and transnational variation between nations, one must not assume that differences between groups are being obliterated as some mass society theorists characterize the process of homogenization. As Lévi-Strauss has argued, there may be a principle of diversity built into the species or, from our standpoint, built into the organization of man's communication. I am suggesting that the axis of diversity shifts from a spatial or structural dimension to a temporal or generational dimension. If in primitive societies time is continuous and space discontinuous, in modern societies as space becomes continuous, time becomes discontinuous. In what seems like an ironic twist of language, spatially biased media obliterate space while temporally biased media obliterate time. The spatial bias of modern media, which have eliminated many spatial variations in culture and social structure, have simultaneously intensified the differences between generations within the same society. The differences in modern society between a boy of fourteen and a man of sixty—differences in language and values, symbols and meanings—are enormous. It is modern societies that face the problem of generations. It is not only that conflict across age groups continues but there are gross discontinuities between generations in culture and symbols, perhaps best symbolized by the phrase, "Don't trust anyone over thirty." * This inversion in the relation of time and space in contemporary society seems to me a logical extension of Innis' argument. The inversion depends on the observation that spatially biased media obliterate space and lead men to live in a non-spatial world. Simultaneously, such media fragment time and make it progressively discontinuous. Temporal media, on the other hand, obliterate time, lead men to live in a non-temporal world, but fragment space.

I think it is important to remember that Innis argued that media possessed a bias or a predisposition toward time or space. He was not arguing for some simple monocausality. Thus, if generations have become an increasingly important axis of diversity, in modern society, the causes include factors other than the media but to which the media are linked in a syndrome. I cannot, of course, attempt to trace out all such factors here, but a couple should be mentioned if only for their suggestive value. The importance of generations and the phenomena of generational discontinuity is linked most directly to the rate of technical change. In traditional societies, societies that change very slowly, the old are likely to be venerated as the repositories of the oral tradition and, consequently, as the storage banks of tribal wisdom. In societies such as ours, where knowledge and technique change very rapidly, the old are not likely to be so venerated. It is the young, the bearers of the new techniques and knowledge, that are likely to have both the power and the prestige. As the transmission of this knowledge is in the educational system, it is in this institution that generational discontinuities are likely to become most apparent. Also, because rapidly changing technical knowledge is difficult

* Of course, generational discontinuity is a universal of history. Normally, these discontinuities are explained by the periodic and random shocks to a system caused by relatively unsystematic variables such as wars, depressions, famines, etc. I am suggesting that generational discontinuity no longer depends on these random shocks to the system but that generational discontinuities are now endogenous factors, built into the normal operation of the system and very much "caused" by the bias of contemporary communication.

JAMES W. CAREY

to acquire beyond school, the old are likely to be continually threatened by competition from the young and to be subject to fairly early obsolescence, and conflicts between generations bearing different knowledge and different values are likely to become a fact of life in all institutions.

This conflict is muted and disguised somewhat by the reorganization of the age composition of society. Some 40 per cent of the population is now under twenty, and within the year 50 per cent of the population will be under twenty-five. With the rapid expansion of the economy and institutions such as education, the young overwhelm older generations merely by numbers, and thus the intensity of the conflict is frequently masked by the ease of the political solutions. One thus must not discount the sheer fact of larger numbers in younger generations in heightening our awareness of generational discontinuity. The proportion of youth in the total population is also intensified by the progressive lengthening of adolescence; that is, one is young much longer today than in previous centuries.

Finally, the weakening of tradition caused not only by the media but also by the pace of technical change and progressive dominance of the educational system in the socialization process intensifies, I think, generational discontinuity. I am led to this argument by the belief that structural elements in the society are less able to provide useful and stable identity patterns to youth. Religious, ethnic, regional, and class identifications are weakening, and they are identifications that are *not* temporal in character. As religious and ethnic traditions weaken generational identity becomes more important as a means of placing oneself and organizing one's own self-conception. This is true not only in the society at large but also in all subordinate institutions. The importance of generational identity is enhanced by the decline of ritual and passage rites which formerly served as devices for confirming and symbolizing structural identity. In addition, these structural identities simply come into conflict with one another, they counterpoint, and the young are frequently led to reject all past identities and seize upon membership in a generation as the key to understanding what is happening to them. This is a phenomenon

300

Erik Erikson has usefully analyzed under the label the "total-ism" of youth.

I am suggesting that generations are becoming more important sources of solidarity than other social groups in spite of Harold Rosenberg's observation that being a member of an age group is the lowest form of solidarity. The spread of a worldwide urban civilization built upon rapid and ephemeral means of communication ultimately means that individuals of the same age in Warsaw, Moscow, Tokyo, and New York sense a membership in a common age group and feel they have more in common with one another than with individuals older and younger within their own societies. This is a phenomenon Innis did not anticipate. When Innis spoke of competition to establish a monopoly of knowledge, he normally was thinking of competition coming from institutions or structural groups: competition from the clergy, politicians, or the middle classes. Similarly, when other scholars have spoken of the role of groups in social change, they have normally thought of structural groups such as the burghers, the aristocracy, or the Jews. The implication of my suggestion is that the bearers of social change are increasingly age groups or generations rather than structural groups. Instead of groups representing individuals of all ages bound together by a common structural characteristic such as religion, race, or occupation, the most important groups of the future will be those of a common age who are structurally variegated. A generational group finds its solidarity in a common age even though some of its members are Catholic, some Jewish, some Protestant, some Northerners, some Southerners, some middle-class, some working-class. If this is correct, then political conflict, to choose just one example, which we have normally thought of in structural terms as conflict between regions, classes, and religions, becomes focused instead around generations. If I correctly interpret the behavior of Robert Kennedy, he is aware of the phenomenon.

Now, unfortunately, things are neither as neat, as simple, or as true as I have painted them in these pages. There are still strong differences within generations. One must speak of generations of musicians and novelists, physicists and sociologists,

JAMES W. CAREY

Northerners and Southerners, Catholics and Jews. Obviously, one has to pay attention to the intersection of structural variables such as class and generational variables or the entire analysis quickly slides into a tautology. But I do think that in modern society generations become more important in all spheres of life. There is a competition to name generations, to symbolize them, to characterize the meaning of a generation. There is a competition within and between generations to choose the culture by which the generation shall be known. Further, there is competition to impose the culture of a generation on the entire society. And this, of course, is what Innis meant by a monopoly of knowledge. It was only a few years ago that David Riesman was suggesting that the media, particularly television, were devices for imposing the culture of the middle class on the entire society. Let me merely suggest that the media, particularly television, are devices by which the culture of youth is imposed on the entire society. In the competition to determine whose culture shall be the official culture and whose values the official norms, the axis of conflict is between generations.

These perhaps overlong notes on the sociology of generations illustrate, I hope, Innis' central point: the principal effect of media technology is on social organization. The capacity of Innis to deal with such phenomena in a reasonably direct and clear way leads me to prefer his characterization of media effects to that of McLuhan. However, this does not mean that Innis will ever have the social impact or perhaps even the intellectual impact of McLuhan, for McLuhan's appeal and his meaning reside not in the technical quality of his argument but in his capacity to be an acceptable prophet of our times. It is with an analysis of the basis of McLuhan's social appeal that I wish to close this paper.

Perhaps the most interesting thing about McLuhan is the degree of success he has enjoyed. Criticism of his position usually starts out, as does this paper, with the admission by the critic that he may represent an obsolete tradition, that McLuhan may be right in claiming that most scholars are merely "prisoners of print." Criticism, such as it is, usually gives away

302

the game before the players are out of the dugout. No useful criticism can be made of McLuhan, I am now convinced, on technical grounds. There is no way of applying standards of verisimilitude and verification to his analysis. The only criticism of McLuhan that can hope to be effective is one that admits the possibility of a system of values and meanings preferable to those implicit in McLuhan's work.

It is unfortunate, I think, that some of the daring and exquisite insights McLuhan has into the communication process are largely vitiated by his style of presentation, his manner, and his method. The meaning of McLuhan is not in his message, his sentences, but in his *persona* as a social actor, in himself as a vessel of social meaning. The meaning of McLuhan is, I want to argue, mythical and utopian. Consequently, one cannot ask whether he is correct about the effects of communication technology, for this is a question irrelevant to his message. One can only determine how one feels about the attitudes toward life implicit in his utopian projections.

Unlike the traditional scholar, McLuhan deals with reality not by trying to understand it but by prescribing an attitude to take toward it. McLuhan is a poet of technology. His work represents a secular prayer to technology, a magical incantation of the gods, designed to quell one's fears that, after all, the machines may be taking over. Like any prayer, it is designed to sharpen up the pointless and to blunt the too sharply pointed.* It is designed to sharpen up the mindless and mundane world of popular culture which consumes so much of our lives and to blunt down the influence of modern technology on our personal existence. The social function of prayer is, I suppose, to numb us to certain gross realities of existence, realities too painful to contemplate, too complex to resolve. Ultimately, McLuhan himself is a medium and that is his message. As a medium, he tells us we need no longer ask the imperishable questions about existence or face the imperishable truths about the human condition. The fundamental problems of existence are to be solved automatically and irreversibly by the

* Kenneth Burke, *A Grammar of Motives* (New York: Prentice-Hall, 1945), p. 393.

subliminal operation of the machines on our psychic life. McLuhan represents an apocalyptic vision, an eschatological prediction about the future that can quell our frequently ambivalent feelings about ourselves and our inventions. He represents in this guise the ultimate triumph of the technical over the moral, for he tells us that concerns for morals and values and meanings in the age of electric circuitry are unnecessary.

Harold Innis wanted to preserve the oral tradition and its characteristic concern for values and meaning in the face of a rampaging technology favoring the demands of space. The oral tradition and moral order were important *even if* contemporary media did not support such concerns. For McLuhan, on the other hand, modern technology obviates the necessity of raising moral problems and of struggling with moral dilemmas. When asked if one can make moral judgments about technology, McLuhan answers: "Does one ask a surgeon in the middle of an operation if surgery is ultimately good or bad?" I suppose not. But there are days on which the propriety of surgery must be questioned. If we had raised these questions some time ago we might have avoided a generation of frontal lobotomies.

Let me be clear on the utopian and mythical aspects of McLuhan. While McLuhan insists that he is not attacking print and he is not an enemy of books, his public meaning is unmistakably as follows: printing gave rise to the Age of Reason, to scientific logic, and to the liberal tradition. The liberal tradition argued that human freedom is solely the result of man's rationality. McLuhan contends, however, that the overemphasis on reason in the liberal tradition has resulted in man's alienation from himself, from other men, and from nature itself. This is an important point, of course. It is a theme common to many critics of our civilization, is central to the argument of Innis, and is expressed much more cogently and persuasively in Norman O. Brown's *Life Against Death*.

McLuhan's relevance stems from the fact that he goes beyond this critique and argues that the reunification of man, the end of his alienation, the restoration of the "whole man" will result from autonomous developments in communications technology. All individuals have to do to be put back in touch with their essential nature is to detach themselves from tradition and submit to the sensory powers of the electronic media.

We are being saved again! This time, however, the salvation does not entail a determined act of will, the endurance of suffering, the selflessness of sacrifice, the torment of anxiety, but only the automatic operation of technology. I won't bore you by piling up quotations in which McLuhan argues that the effect of the media on sensory organization is automatic, without resistance, subliminal. Its operation is independent of the will and the wish of men. McLuhan thus represents a species of a secularized, religious determinism, a modern Calvinism that says, "Everything is gonna be all right, baby."

But is it? And should we take it seriously? The only thing of which we can all be sure is that even in the age of electric circuitry men are born alone and individually attached to nature and to society by an umbilical cord that all too quickly withers away. The fact of the terrible loneliness and isolation of existence is what has motivated much of the great art produced in any period of history. We should not need Eugene O'Neill to remind us in the face of McLuhan's onslaughts that "man is born broken; he lives by mending; the grace of God is glue."

Human communication, by language and every other technique, is the fragile means by which men attempt to overcome the isolation of existence and wed themselves to other men. Under the best of circumstances, communication is rarely successful, is always halting, is always tentative and tenuous. "Stammering *is* the native eloquence of we fog people." But the act of communication, as O'Neill and Camus among other modern artists remind us, is the only source of joy and tragedy humans have. One can all too easily forget that the word "communication" shares its root with "communion" and "community," and it is the attempt to establish this communion that theories of communication, vulgar as they are in present form, attempt to capture.

McLuhan's relevance and meaning resides in our attempts to deal with the dilemma of communion. In an age when men are more than ever divided from the basis of an authentic communion with one another, when men's relations with machines and technology seem more durable and important than their relation to one another, McLuhan finds man's salvation in the technology itself. For McLuhan (and I must admit for Innis also), the vision of the oral tradition and the tribal society is a substitute Eden, a romantic but unsupportable vision of the past. What McLuhan is constructing, then, is a modern myth, and like all myths it attempts to adjust us to the uncomfortable realities of existence. The Iceman cometh again but this time in the cloak of the scientist. But even this shouldn't surprise one, for science is the only legitimate source of myths in the modern world. Science is, of course, the unquestioned source of authoritative knowledge in the modern world. Scientific myths enjoy the claim of being factually true even if they are in no way demonstrable, even if they must be taken on faith, even if they attempt to answer what are, after all, unanswerable questions. Scientific myths have the great advantage in this self-conscious society of not appearing as myths at all but as truths, verified by or capable of being verified by the inscrutable methods of the scientist.

McLuhan's parable on the restorative powers of the media in expanding the consciousness of man is one more myth, one more illusion by which men can organize their lives. Unlike most of the utopias of the modern world—*1984, Brave New World, The Rise of the Meritocracy,* and even B. F. Skinner's *Walden Two*—it celebrates not the evils of technology, but its glories, not its inhumanity but its terrible humanity; it celebrates Eros and not Thanatos. In a world in which electric technology is, like it or not, a reality of existence that shall not pass away, it attempts to offer a justification of optimism. McLuhan's vision quite closely parallels the specification of modern myths that Emerson offered in 1848. For modern myths to be effective they will have to be mechanical, scientific, democratic, and communal (socialistic).

What finally is one to think about this myth, this New Jerusalem the media are creating? One cannot help being overwhelmed by its awful vulgarity, by its disconnection from whatever sources of joy, happiness, and tragedy remain in this world. Scott Fitzgerald was right: Modern men would invent gods suitable only to seventeen-year-old Jay Gatsbys and then would be about their Father's business: "the service of a vast, vulgar, and meretricious beauty."

One need not be against myths. Men live by illusions; only gods and devils are without them, and it is our illusions ultimately that make us human. But it is the quality of moral imagination contained in McLuhan's myth that is disquieting; it is as if it were offered as a scientific footnote to Yeats's "The Second Coming."

Finally, let me note that McLuhan himself is the ultimate verification of the more prophetic aspects of Innis' work. For central to Harold Innis' vision was the certainty that the spatial bias of communication and the monopoly of knowledge forged in its name would lead to the triumph of the secular over the sacred. The divorce of the written from the oral tradition is now complete; the hegemony of science over religion, of technical authority over moral authority, has been accomplished. If McLuhan is the prophet of the collapse of all tradition, it is fitting, I suppose, that it should be evidenced by a concern with the media of communication. It is also ironic that it should come from a student of literature who views art as a vehicle of communication. For as Allen Tate has reminded us, the very concept of literature as communication represents an unexamined victory of modern secularism over the human spirit. "Our unexamined theory of literature as communication," he says in *The Forlorn Demon*, "could not have appeared in an age in which communion was still possible for any appreciable majority of persons. The word communication presupposes the victory of the secularized society, of means without ends."

McLuhan, then, is no more revolutionary than I am. The death of values he represents is not some twentieth-century revolution. It is the end point of a positivistic revolution against meaning and metaphysics. And thus it is no surprise that his utopianism should be based on the sanctity of science and the fact.

But let me remind you that it was precisely this revolution that Harold Innis tried to resist; it was precisely this revolution that he saw as ending the possibility of a stable civilization in the West. For Innis, the oral tradition representative of man's concern with history and metaphysics, morals and meanings had to be preserved if we were not to fall victim to a sacred politics and a sanctified science. It is an irony and an uncomfortable fact that the prophecy is borne out by one who has identified himself as a disciple. But such is the frequent result of discipleship.